Advance Praise for
Hope Is Not a Method

"Gordon Sullivan is one of the Army's most visionary leaders. His insights into leadership and human behavior are truly profound. His experience transforming the Army is a powerful story—one from which leaders in all walks of life can learn."

—COLIN L. POWELL

"The challenge we now face is to make change an essential element of our corporate culture. *Hope Is Not a Method* will be an important tool in achieving that objective."

—JAMES R. MELLOR,
chairman and CEO, General Dynamics Corporation

"Former U.S. Army Chief of Staff Gordon Sullivan is an extraordinary leader: part visionary, part historian; part strategist, part cheerleader; part soldier, part servant. The story he and Colonel Harper tell of how the Army has succeeded where so many large, established organizations have failed carries a simple yet profound message: Tapping an organization's capacity for deep change starts with seeing the soul of your people."

—PETER SENGE,
author of *The Fifth Discipline*

"*Hope Is Not a Method* offers an enormously useful approach, based on practical experience, to the process of thinking, planning, and acting strategically. It will benefit anyone facing changing realities in business."

—WOLFGANG R. SCHMITT,
chairman of the board and CEO, Rubbermaid

"In *Hope Is Not a Method*, Sullivan and Harper present a clear, compelling, and detailed map for leadership. Only those who heed their message will successfully lead us into the future."

—MARGARET WHEATLEY,
author of *Leadership and the New Science*

"General Gordon R. Sullivan, a distinguished soldier and forward-looking manager, shepherded the U.S. Army through its recent changes with minimum fanfare but exceptional effectiveness. *Hope Is Not a Method* divulges some of the techniques he used, techniques that should be of great value to leaders in organizations of all kinds."

—JOHN S.D. EISENHOWER,
former U.S. ambassador to Belgium

"Students of organizational change regard the transformation of the U.S. Army as among the most remarkable shifts in both culture and capability of the past twenty years. Their book enriched by examples from military history and contemporary corporate situations, the authors trace the Army's journey and offer new tools that are readily applicable to business problems. All in all, a fresh, readable, and informative book on leadership and the architecture of transformational change."

—RICHARD PASCALE,
author of *Managing on the Edge*

"Business leaders should be grateful for Gordon Sullivan's *Hope Is Not a Method,* which is both a study and a meditation on the challenges of directing complex institutions as the world reshapes itself for the years ahead. This book can be an important tool for the twenty-first-century executive."

—ROGER J. SPILLER,
George C. Marshall Professor of Military History,
U.S. Army Command and General Staff College

"When it comes to transforming an organization, Sullivan and Harper know what they are talking about—they did it. The U.S. Army has learned to lead in the flexible, dynamic, fast-paced environment we all face. *Hope Is Not a Method* shows us how."

—LLOYD S. BAIRD,
director, Boston University CEO Leadership Forum

9 DEC 96
Boston

Bob Lacog —

With respect and admiration — Thanks for your selfless & loyal service

[signature]

HOPE IS NOT A METHOD

HOPE
IS NOT A METHOD

★ ★ ★ ★

WHAT BUSINESS LEADERS
CAN LEARN FROM
AMERICA'S ARMY

GORDON R. SULLIVAN
MICHAEL V. HARPER

TIMES BUSINESS

RANDOM HOUSE

ISBN 0-8129-2787-7

Random House website address:
http://www.randomhouse.com/

Book design by Maura Fadden Rosenthal

Illustrations by Robert Scudellari

Printed in the United States of America on acid-free
paper
98765432

To the men and women of America's Army

FOREWORD

★ ★ ★ ★

Much of the way American management works was learned from the World War II practices of the U.S. military. That "command and control" model of management is structurally hierarchical, top-down driven, and precise in its statistical controls. It was taken by American industry from the Pentagon in the late 1940s and early 1950s. Many civilian and senior military officials joined industry following the war and helped install the new management systems. So long as U.S. firms competed primarily with one another in the first quarter century following World War II, that management system was effective.

However, the two oil crises of the 1970s altered the competitive playing field for all time. America faced new competition from abroad, particularly from Japan and Germany. Those countries, which had been reconstructed following the devastation of the war, had become major industrial powers. They offered high-quality goods produced efficiently, and, in the case of the Japanese, at lower cost. Since then, countries such as Korea, Taiwan, Singapore, Malaysia, India, and now China have entered the game. These burgeoning industrial countries have their own non-American management styles and approaches.

Over the past fifteen years, it has become increasingly clear that America's "command and control" management is not sufficiently agile; in fact, it is an obstacle to world-class efficiency.

Every management team today faces the imperatives of improving reaction time, increasing quality, achieving the lowest real cost, and accelerating product and service innovations—all in an effort to remain competitive in a world growing smaller. To cope with this rapidly changing environment, executives are focusing on the need for a clear organizational vision and mission, on the empowerment of the workforce, on effective teaming, on organizational learning, on process (versus functional) orientation, and on measurements that capture the true "systemwide" effects of decisions. This new management challenge confronts not only businesses but health care organizations, nonprofit institutions, and government agencies—all of which are trying to reduce costs and improve operating effectiveness.

It is remarkable, I think, that the American organization that has arguably reinvented both its management system and its leadership culture most dramatically is the United States Army, the very organization from which industry learned the original management approach it is now trying to change. In fact, the Army is once again leading industry in the creation of new approaches to management challenges.

My respect for the management innovations of the U.S. Army was heightened when I participated in the Army's CEO Conference at the Army War College at Carlisle Barracks in the spring of 1994. Like most Americans, I had seen television coverage of Desert Storm, and I was curious as to how the Army had made such a transformation since Vietnam. I was at best only vaguely aware of other things the Army was doing. Several of our professors at Boston University's School of Management had written very favorably about the Army's approach to organizational learning and information technology transfer; it was partly at their urging that I accepted the invitation to the gathering at Carlisle. I was, however, largely unaware of the revolution that had gone on in America's Army since the Vietnam War and how the U.S. Army had become one of the most advanced organizations in the world, with a truly contemporary management approach.

Our conference brought in senior generals and experienced CEOs, a small group, in a seminar format, to learn from one another. I was the lone "academic" participant. The format was unique: we were there to learn and to teach each other, a method, I soon found out, that is typical of the way today's Army does business. One by one, each of the participants contributed. These were not speeches

written by public relations departments but rather frank and open
discussions about the real problems we all faced as leaders of major
institutions. About half of the time was reserved for discussion—
serious discussion about how we lead our organizations. We finished
with a visit to the Gettysburg Battlefield National Military Park,
where, in the company of an accomplished historian, we spent an afternoon examining our own views of leadership in the context of the
decisions made there in July 1863. It was a powerful way of being reminded of the importance of values, responsibility, and the moral
courage it takes to be a leader—on the battlefield, in business, or
anywhere else. In my twenty-seven years at Ford Motor Company
(ten as a corporate officer) and in my experience as dean of a major
business school, I had never seen such an impressive display of organizational learning by such senior people. It was clear that something
powerful had happened to America's Army—something about which
most of us had no idea.

Today, the kind of learning environment I saw at Carlisle pervades
America's Army from top to bottom. It is an organization that has
downsized by 600,000 people since the Berlin Wall came down, yet it
has focused on the future and sees itself as growing to become something different from what it was during the Cold War—growing, in
my terms, to meet the demands of totally new markets and with totally new and different technologies. Perhaps more important, at a
time when people are questioning loyalty and organizational values,
America's Army has strengthened its values, and its people appear as
dedicated and loyal as at any time in its history.

Today, the Army is creating new, flexible organizational concepts.
The Army is teaching us the role of values in a large organization.
And the Army has transformed itself into a learning organization—
maybe the foremost learning organization in the United States.

Hope Is Not a Method is what the authors call an After Action Review. It is their personal assessment of this new Army, how it came
into being, and how it is managing itself today. Gordon Sullivan is the
most recent Chief of Staff of the Army. Mike Harper was one of his
principal planners. Both lived this transformation every day from before the Berlin Wall came down until the summer of 1995. Their story
is the story of what happened to America's Army in that six years.

But it is more than that. In this book, these two exceptional leaders have distilled their own lessons learned in a way that leaders from all walks of life can understand. As we think about the difficult issues of strategy, the role of vision, how we build teams, how we develop leaders, and all of the many other strategic issues that face us daily, their experiences form a lens through which all of us can see and understand our own organizations better.

Hope Is Not a Method is a book for leaders and for those who would lead. It is not just a book for CEOs and others at the top; it is a book for all who participate in institutional leadership and who aspire to lead their organizations to greatness.

Louis E. Lataif
Dean, Boston University School of Management
Boston, Massachusetts
March 1996

CONTENTS

★ ★ ★ ★

Minutes: Organizing Around Information ★ Transformation as Human Drama

INTRODUCTION

★ ★ ★ ★

In 1995, after serving sixty-two years between us, we retired from the United States Army. Both of us were and are soldiers. We were trained and educated in the Army school system and universities, one as a political scientist and historian, the other as an MBA. But we were and are soldiers. Which raises the question "What do two soldiers have to say to America's leaders?"

The answer lies in understanding and appreciating what the Army has accomplished in recent years and in our belief that that experience is much less unique than it might seem at first glance. Despite dramatic budget and manpower reductions, the Army has succeeded in retooling for new missions, upgrading the skills of its people, developing new ways to assimilate and exploit technology, and achieving a higher degree of effectiveness than at any time in its recent history. By some measures, in fact, the Army has become America's most respected institution. We're proud to have been part of the Army during this historic organizational transformation.

Recently, we have found more and more business leaders seeking out the Army, looking for leadership ideas and learning. The business leaders we meet want to know: Can the management methods we applied to the Army work for them? Can today's businesses and non-profit organizations be transformed following the same philosophy we used with the Army?

We're convinced that the answer is "Yes." That's why we've written this book: to let leaders from business and other walks of life look over our shoulders and learn what they can from the Army's continuing transformation. Your experiences will not mirror ours completely, but if the comments and reactions of our friends in the business world are any indication, almost all of our experiences can suggest ideas that are directly applicable to the challenges every organization faces today.

What are some of the challenges we faced when we were asked to assume leadership roles in the post–Cold War Army? How do these challenges compare with those faced by businesses today?

1. The competitive environment is changing rapidly. For the Army, change has been driven by the ending of the Cold War and the resultant reshuffling of the structure of international power. For business, changes are coming from a variety of sources: new foreign competitors, new methods of marketing products and services, new demands and expectations from customers. In both cases, strategies that worked in the relatively stable postwar decades have become all but irrelevant in the wake of the upheavals of recent years.

2. Emerging technology poses new opportunities and difficulties. The last decade has seen the birth of the information-based enterprise. Digital systems for gathering, interpreting, and communicating information have made these processes much more efficient than in the past, but we've discovered that the change demanded of us is not just about making old ways more efficient. The rethinking demanded is far more profound and difficult than we once imagined, and far too important to be left to computer experts.

3. The technical skills and teamwork abilities of our people must be continually upgraded. Today's Army, like any business, is constantly searching for high-quality people and striving to more effectively train, motivate, and retain them. Yesterday's knowledge base just won't suffice in tomorrow's world; our job now is to figure out what we'll need to know in the twenty-first century and find ways to disseminate that knowledge throughout our workforce.

4. Our increasingly demanding stakeholders are assigning us unexpected new tasks. The Army answers to our national leadership in the White House and in Congress and, ultimately, to the American people. Today, the Army needs to be flexible enough to succeed not only in traditional warfare but in new missions such as peacekeeping, providing humanitarian aid and disaster relief, and building democracy, both at home and abroad. Today's rapidly evolving world has forced many businesses to redefine themselves similarly: for example, manufacturing firms are building service and financial operations that in many cases are growing faster and generating more profit than the parent businesses. Taking on new tasks without losing sight of the traditional strengths and values of an organization is a difficult challenge.

5. Financial pressures are forcing massive cost cutting and downsizing. A lean cost structure is no longer a competitive advantage; today, it is the price of admission to the game. In the Army's case, the demand for a post–Cold War "peace dividend" forced budget and manpower cuts of up to 40 percent—with no reduction in readiness or effectiveness. Businesses are facing the same pressure to do more with less. How can the necessary downsizing be handled without losing vital human skills or demoralizing the workers who remain?

We discovered that not only must we change, we must *change the way we change*. We think our experience tackling problems like these on behalf of the Army can shed some light on the similar problems business leaders face. Think of it this way: if the Army were a private enterprise, it would be a U.S.-based multinational corporation with nearly 1.5 million employees, annual revenues of $63 billion, branch offices in more than one hundred countries, and strategic alliances in virtually all the major nations of the world, under intense pressure to perform more effectively every day. The problems we faced as military leaders have much in common with those faced by the leaders of IBM, General Motors, McDonald's, Wal-Mart, and Microsoft—and vice versa.

Despite these similarities we occasionally encounter skeptics who question the relevance of our Army experience to the problems of business. Their skepticism generally arises from three widely believed myths. Here's how we respond to these myths.

MYTH NUMBER 1: "IN THE MILITARY, GETTING RESULTS IS AS EASY AS GIVING ORDERS. IT'S NOT SO SIMPLE IN CIVILIAN LIFE."

We would say that getting results is as easy (or as difficult) as giving the *right* orders, whether in the military or in business. Making the right decision and building a team to execute the decision is a challenge for any leader. Military leaders do have some tools business leaders do not have and vice versa—their environments are obviously not the same. But in both spheres, the leader must act through people.

Making a lasting leadership impact requires the formulation of a viable, foresighted long-term strategy; clear, persuasive communication of the leader's vision; and intelligent, flexible balancing of the conflicting interests and demands of many constituencies, both inside and outside the organization. A military leader, like a business leader, must be a master of details as well as of the big picture; must be a superb motivator and influencer; must understand human beings and what makes them tick; and must know his organization inside and out. Dwight D. Eisenhower's ability in all these areas made him a great general—*and* an effective president whose leadership talents are gaining increasing respect from historians.

Myth Number 2: "As a businessperson, I have to make a profit. In the military, you don't face that pressure."

It is true that we in the military do not face the same kind of bottom-line pressure that business faces. But in the final analysis, the pressure that all of our organizations face is pressure to perform, to succeed, and to win.

The Army doesn't face precisely the same kind of financial pressure a business in the private sector faces; there's no price per share in the newpaper each morning, no Wall Street community demanding improved quarterly performance. However, in today's world, with political demands for accountability and efficiency reaching deep into every area of government, including the military, the Army has been forced to reduce its costs and improve its productivity as surely as any private enterprise—and under just as much scrutiny.

Today, the military operates in a fishbowl of public scrutiny that's as unrelenting as anything experienced in the private sector. Everything we do—every base closing, policy change, troop deployment—is widely reported and subject to criticism by politicians, the media, interest groups, and concerned citizens. And facing Senate or House committees can be just as demanding as facing directors or stockholders.

Myth Number 3: "In business, I have to struggle to get and keep customers, but the military is a public institution—you don't have to go out and find customers."

Certainly, it is true that in the sense that America's citizens are our customers, we are in no danger of losing them. The danger is in failing them on the battlefield. In that sense, competition is at the core of the Army's being.

Our competitors aren't businesses trying to steal away our market; they are, potentially, the armed forces of any nation hostile to American interests, as well as terrorists and paramilitary groups anywhere in the world who may attack American soldiers or civilians for any reason, at any time. When a business operates at less than full efficiency, chances are it will lose market share and eventually go out of business. If America's Army becomes ineffective, the nation will pay a price on some future battlefield.

For the Army, this threat is constant and real, not hypothetical, as can be seen by a mere glance at the list of operations the Army has been involved in during just the last few years: Panama, Desert Storm, Haiti, Bosnia . . . the idea of "competition" takes on a new intensity when bullets, mines, and bombs are involved.

The business world, in fact, pays tribute to the military by borrowing its language: we speak of marketing "campaigns," an advertising "blitz," "offensive" and "defensive" business strategies, and so on. Even the word "strategy" is from the Greek word for "generalship"; the original strategic planner was a Homeric warrior.

More to the point, we believe that it was by applying many of our ideas from the battlefield that we were able to effect such a successful transformation. Obviously, there are differences between what we did in the Army and what the leaders of other organizations, whether in the for-profit or nonprofit sphere, must do, just as there are differences among industries and companies. But we believe that the similarities, in the end, are more significant. In any organization, the leadership challenge is creating the future. Thus, many of the same abilities that made leaders like Ulysses S. Grant, George C. Marshall, and Eisenhower effective are shared by executives like Jack Welch of General Electric, Bob Galvin of Motorola, Roberto Goizueta of Coca-Cola, and others. Our experience led us to reshape our thoughts about leadership—*strategic leadership*, that is, directing and controlling rational and deliberate change in the organization—what we call "creating the future."

It *is* possible to create your own future—to break down outmoded structures and create organizations that can thrive in tomorrow's uncertainty. It is a process grounded in values, shaped by vision, guided by a strategy that is rooted in the critical processes of an organization, focused by deliberate action, and matured through structured learning. We think of it as being like a military campaign. Some facts are known, many unknown—yet we have to go forward. The key to success is the resoluteness of the leader and how he or she can integrate and synchronize the available means, moving from objective to objective, leveraging, learning, and growing.

The challenge for the leader is not to get "it" exactly right, because there is no "it." The challenge is to become "good enough": good enough to seize and exploit developing opportunities, good enough to deploy your forces more rapidly than competitors, good enough to get it "about right" in execution.

This kind of leadership is not passive or accommodating. It is a roll-up-your-sleeves kind of leadership, short on buzzwords and wishful thinking, in which transformation starts at the top with a deep and uncompromising commitment to the values and purpose of the organization, both today and tomorrow. Neither is this kind of leadership shoot-from-the-hip stuff. It is built on a foundation of quality management and an enduring commitment to the strength of people and teams. We say "Hope is not a method" to help leaders understand that the future is created by positive action—not by slogans, not by fad surfing, not by more perfect planning, but by action.

This book is about the actions the Army took to create the force that is active around the world today and to lay the foundations of tomorrow's force. It is about what we learned in one relatively short phase of the Army's long history. It tells the story of how the Army's leadership team addressed and accomplished its responsibility to the American people. Finally, this book is about the power of people to move, shape, and grow an organization.

This book is for leaders—not just CEOs, but leaders at every level. The measure of a leader is seldom what he or she appears to accomplish as reported in the daily press or an annual report. It is, rather, the enduring character of his or her organization and the success of those who follow. It does not matter whether an organization is the largest corporation in America or the smallest volunteer group, for profit or not for profit, government or private. The measure is the same: Did you create a future or merely contend with the present? How well did you prepare those who will follow you? Were you a builder or merely a maintainer?

This is a book for those who aspire to build.

Gordon R. Sullivan   Michael V. Harper

HOPE IS NOT A METHOD

Remaking America's Army

THE COLD WAR ARMY

As we watched the crowds pull down the Berlin Wall on November 9, 1989, we knew that the world was changing in profound and unpredictable ways. There was no Cold War symbol more powerful than the Wall, which for a generation had been the physical manifestation of the imprisonment of the people of Eastern Europe. Most of us in the Army had spent years in Germany. Many of us had personally patrolled the German border and watched the East German guards in their towers. That the Wall would come down at the hands of the German people while a helpless Red Army looked on was almost impossible for us to comprehend.

Much has happened since that day in 1989, but it is not hard to remember what we felt at the time. It was momentous. It was as if we were IBM contemplating the first Apple computer, or General Motors the first Volkswagen or Toyota. The collapse of the Iron Curtain represented a fundamental change in the world in which we operated, a shift so basic that it was hard to understand. The fact that

CNN brought it to us live and in color merely underscored its almost surreal quality.

America's Army was the best army in the world—a fact demonstrated in Panama less than six weeks later and in the Persian Gulf War less than a year and a half later. But we faced enormous uncertainty that day—the future was cloudy, dangerous and ambiguous. The Army that showed such competence and flexibility on the battlefield had been perfected for a world that suddenly no longer existed.

In the aftermath of these events, the challenge was to displace a sense of satisfaction with the Cold War, Panama, and the Persian Gulf and imbed a passion for growth.

The challenge was to keep the Army ready to fight while we were demobilizing 600,000 people—something we had never done successfully in more than two hundred years of history.

The challenge was to bring the alacrity and learning we had demonstrated on the battlefield into the bureaucracy.

The challenge was to transform the Army, creating a future of service to America.

After Vietnam, the Army had turned inward and rebuilt itself. The regular army had been exhausted in Vietnam. The noncommissioned officer corps had been decimated; officers had little sense of training and operations beyond that demanded by the Southeast Asian battlefields; modernization of the armored force had fallen a generation behind; the Army was demobilizing far too rapidly to maintain any semblance of readiness; the reserve forces were largely untrained; lack of discipline was a chronic problem in some units; and many in and out of uniform questioned the very values of the institution. With the stroke of a pen, the nation ended the draft, forcing the Army to recruit a force six times larger than it had ever maintained in peacetime without a draft. The years right after Vietnam were a very difficult time.

The long journey from Saigon to Kuwait City and beyond was difficult and sometimes painful. In that process, the Army began to chip away at old ways and to understand quality, operational flexibility, and organizational learning. By 1989, the Army did not look particularly different from the outside; but inside it had already made one major transformation. What came out of that first transformation was an unprecedented degree of operational flexibility. You could see it in men such as General John Shalikashvili, who led the successful operation to resettle the Kurds after the Persian Gulf War: nothing like that, on that scale, had ever been done before. Those of us inside the Army could see it in a thousand ways. At the operational level, the Army had become a high-quality, flexible, learning organization.

In other respects, the United States Army at the end of the Cold War looked frustratingly as it had at the end of World War II. The World War II Army had been built on the same kinds of ideas about structure and decision making that the great industrialists had used to build American industry. Over the intervening years, it had become more and more layered with expensive, time-consuming bureaucracy that had added enormous cost, slowed down innovation, and made it harder and harder to respond effectively to change. Our ideas about structure and process were very fixed. The Army was good—very good—at gradual change, but it was poorly prepared to handle the avalanche of change thrust upon it as the Cold War came to a close.

The necessity to reduce the Cold War–era overhead was never in question. To grow into the future, to change the Army, we had to make it smaller while keeping it ready to fight. But maintaining readiness while shrinking by more than one third—by more than 600,000—was a challenge that had never before been successfully met. What was needed was a *transformation* at the strategic level. Our task was to transform a successful organization, to take the best army in the world and make it the best army in a different world—a world of Somalias and Haitis and Bosnias—a world moving into the Information Age. How would we focus on a quick-changing, uncertain future?

Panama and the Persian Gulf: Triumph and Reality

As it turned out, the world was impatiently awaiting our answers. In December 1989, the world saw the first battle of the new age unfold in Panama.[1] U.S. forces, in a superb partnership of land, air, and naval forces, projected overwhelming power from the United States and forward bases to overwhelm Panama in one simultaneous sweep. On December 20, 1989, our forces hit twenty-seven objectives between midnight and daybreak, ensuring the safety of the Panama Canal while neutralizing Manuel Noriega's government and its means of resisting.[2] There were remarkably few casualties on either side and little damage to property. The teamwork demonstrated by the U.S. forces provided a measure of just how good they were.

Less than a year later, we were in the Persian Gulf. The Gulf War was fought on a much larger scale than Panama, and it was much farther from our bases and our supporting infrastructure. The Army moved soldiers in from all over the world, including large formations out of central Europe, conducting the most successful mobilization of reserve forces in our history. Desert Storm provided a further reaffirmation of the quality of America's Army as well as a basis for the Army to reevaluate itself and its role in the world. It had taken more than a generation to build the Desert Storm Army,[3] and our faith in quality soldiers, good training, and the best equipment American industry could provide was vindicated beyond our expectations.

But we also could see that in many respects the Gulf War was the last conflict of the passing age. We found that:

- Logistics systems based on huge depots and large inventories had become badly outmoded.

- Our ability to deploy forces quickly to the world's trouble spots was inadequate.

- Planning processes little changed since World War II made airpower unresponsive to forces on the ground.

• Intelligence, though better than ever, was not getting to the people who needed it.

•Our early-deploying forces lacked sufficient punch and staying power.

We shipped roughly forty thousand containers to the Gulf, but without a modern tracking and inventory system, many lost their identification and on arrival had to be opened just to see what was inside. We transmitted high-priority requisitions to the United States over satellite links, only to lose track of them when they arrived on the ground. CNN gathered data about the air defense battle as fast as the Pentagon did. And we were shooting the most modern Patriot missiles, in critically short supply to begin with, faster than industry could replace them.

NEW MISSIONS, NEW TOOLS

For some, success in Panama and the Persian Gulf tended to reinforce the Cold War model of the Army. But a more critical consideration of the events of 1989 and 1990–1991 provided the catalyst for us to face change in two fundamental directions: new missions and new technologies. Both created challenges and opportunities.

As an institution, the Army was beginning to appreciate that its missions were changing. We were being asked to do things that were largely unfamiliar to the generation of soldiers accustomed to facing the Soviet Union and the Warsaw Pact. Worse yet, these new missions were also unfamiliar to a generation of defense analysts, who insisted that the Army explain its purpose. But we knew why the nation needed an army. In the years after the Berlin Wall came down, the Army's operational commitments tripled. These operations went far beyond Panama and the Persian Gulf. They included humanitarian assistance in Somalia and Rwanda; disaster relief after Hurricanes Hugo, Andrew, and Iniki; peacekeeping in Macedonia and the

Sinai; deterrence in Korea and Kuwait; riot control in Los Angeles; refugee operations in Turkey, Cuba, Panama, and elsewhere; support for the United Nations; fighting forest fires and environmental disasters; and a host of other national and multinational operations. In the first six years after the Berlin Wall came down, the Army made more than seven hundred awards of the Purple Heart, the nation's medal for wounds received in action. New missions brought a greater need for power projection, the ability to move forces quickly to virtually any region of the globe. The crises we would face would not permit the luxury of large-scale buildup and mobilization. We needed to be able to move very quickly and with great versatility, and to reach very selectively into the reserve components. Those were very different capabilities than we had envisioned needing during the Cold War.

We were also beginning to understand that the tools of war were changing rapidly and dramatically. Information was becoming the critical component of our weapons; sensing, communicating, and data-handling technologies were rapidly reaching the point that we could truly make the battlefield transparent and focus our capability as never before. These technological advances were leading to fundamental changes in how we put the Army together, but we could not, nor can we yet, fully understand what harnessing the information engine means to the full range of land warfare and other military operations.

As we sought to handle new missions and assimilate new technologies, we had to shape and develop the appropriate skills in the force. The men and women who will serve as general officers and sergeants major in 2020 will be drawn from the lieutenants recruited in 1995. We had to begin to ask ourselves what these men and women would need to know and how to develop them. Thinking about this human aspect of the organization helped us keep our expectations within realistic bounds.

Knowing that we were facing a world of enormous uncertainty, we needed to accommodate a wide range of possible futures. Our strategic thrust would have to be to create a more flexible, versatile force, one capable of learning and adapting even while conducting operations.

Finally, throughout this transformation, we knew we would have to keep the Army ready, to break the pattern of unreadiness that has always accompanied demobilization. The key to that was continuing to train. Training was the glue that would keep the Army ready as it changed.

Thus began a purposeful journey of change, beginning with the hard front-end work of thinking about where we were and where we were going.

FRONT-END WORK

As had been the case after Vietnam, we went back to values. The Army is a values-based institution, and emphasizing our values—our people, our sense of commitment to one another, our sense of service to one nation—helped our people understand what was *not* going to change, what we were going to take with us into the future.

Our vision then provided a direction for change; by articulating a clear sense of purpose, it enabled us to define the Army today *and* tomorrow. Together, values and vision gave us a lever for change; they created a basis for fostering innovation and growth by giving people boundaries within which they could make bold moves, learn, and grow. The vision was crafted as an expression of the Army's most basic competency—service to nation—but in a broad, yet meaningful context.

AMERICA'S ARMY
Trained and Ready to Fight,
Serving the Nation at Home and Abroad,
A Strategic Force, Capable of Decisive Victory—
into the 21st Century.[4]

As we talked about the vision, we emphasized that hope is not a method: talking about what we stand for and what we could become would not be enough. The Army's transformation would have to be grounded in action—positive, aggressive action guided by the vision and consistent with our values, action that people could see and understand. Leaders would have to think and act purposefully, to make good things happen, and to keep bad things from happening. We would have to demonstrate the future so that people would understand it and stick with us as we helped them build it.

Doctrine as the Engine of Change

The critical next step was the decision to write new doctrine, to redefine the Army's culture of warfare so that it would include a broader range of operations and open the door to the power of the Information Age.

Doctrine is the Army's collective understanding of how it will fight and conduct other operations. As such, it guides how the Army organizes, trains, and modernizes. The concept is best explained by an example. At the battle of Crécy in 1346, employment of the longbow helped the English under Edward III defeat a larger French force. This battle is sometimes cited as an example of how technology can revolutionize warfare. That explanation, however, is inadequate, because the longbow had been in use for approximately two centuries prior to Crécy. What proved decisive at Crécy was the use of longbows en masse, at long range, with the archers protected by simple field fortifications. In essence, it took an employment concept for the new weapon—in other words, new doctrine—to realize the potential of a weapon whose characteristics had been understood for years. This new doctrine influenced the outcome of English battles on the Continent for the next century.

In the formal development of doctrine, missions and technologies come together with employment concepts to define how armies will fight. For the military professional, doctrine is not *what* to think but *how* to think. And by the summer of 1991, it was very clear to some of us that the changes that were taking place in our environment were so profound that simply adjusting our old thoughts and processes at the margin would be inadequate. We needed to expand our thinking about military operations as a guide to transforming the Army.

Consequently, in September 1991, before the Army had completed its redeployment from the Persian Gulf, the senior generals[5] met in council to consider whether it was time to rewrite Army doctrine for contingency operations, peacekeeping, power projection, and other aspects of the Army's rapidly evolving missions. The new commander of the Training and Doctrine Command was General Fred Franks, only recently returned from the Gulf, where he had commanded VII Corps. By chance, he was the most junior four-star general in the room. Freddie had the job of throwing the proposal onto the table, and there were a few who opposed him, arguing for change only at the margin. Others took equally strong positions for major change. At the end of the day, Freddie had sufficient sanction to go ahead; over the next year, the skeptics came on board one by one as we, as a group, thought our way through what was going on in the world.

The end result was a complete revision of the Army's basic concepts about operations.[6] The new doctrine provided the front-end work for more specific action planning. By personally participating in this process, the senior generals not only legitimized the process of change but also signaled their best judgments about the Army's new operational realities. The process of writing new doctrine was the engine that drove the Army's transformation in its largest sense.

Army doctrine has no precise analogue in business terms. We see some of it in the formulation of strategy and policy, some in the development of procedures and concepts—but in many respects it may be a level of thinking that is lacking in the business world. The power of doctrine for us is that it forces us to constantly reevaluate how the Army operates, which in turn opens doors to questions about how we should build and sustain the Army. It is an important concept, one to which we will return.

Integrating Change: The Louisiana Maneuvers

An army exists in one of three states: at war, preparing for war, or demobilizing.[7] Since the mid-1970s, we had been preparing for war; increasingly, we had been fighting little wars. With the Cold War's end, it was important that we keep that focus—that we not be seen or see ourselves as demobilizing. That is why it was so important to keep the Army training. An organization must look to the future, not to the past; it must see itself as growing, not as declining. To achieve that we needed to demonstrate the future, to show people what could be.

Demonstrating change on that level involved a series of linked experiments supported by a campaign to communicate the new themes throughout the Army and among its external constituents. Integrating all this required the establishment of a focal point designed to bring together and nurture new ideas. Our solution was an ad hoc staff organization that we called "the Louisiana Maneuvers," after the large-scale field exercises George Marshall had used to change the Army fifty years before. The name was a historical metaphor. Our task force neither was a maneuver nor had anything special to do with Louisiana, but using the name signaled our intention of making major changes; at the same time, association with Marshall's exercises appealed to our sense of history and seemed to make new processes less threatening.

The Louisiana Maneuvers Task Force was set up squarely under the direction of the Chief of Staff of the Army but was responsive to *all* the senior generals. It was kept separate from the headquarters staff and from the major commands to give it a degree of independence from the tyranny of existing processes and vested bureaucratic interests. This independence created real tensions between the task force and the bureaucracy that some found unpleasant, but the sponsorship by the Chief's office gave the Task Force a degree of protection. People who were interested in real change eventually found ways of participating constructively in the process.

The task force was kept small; its focus was on technological innovation and bringing together agencies for change. The direct responsibility for various projects remained in the traditional line and staff organizations. The Louisiana Maneuvers facilitated high-speed exchange of information, coordination, and access to knowledge and resources. By providing a relatively uninhibited flow of information to the most senior leadership, the Louisiana Maneuvers were especially useful in circumventing bureaucracy; facilitating technological breakthroughs such as the integration of virtual and constructive simulation; creating very-large-scale simulations across all the battle-field systems and all the services; and fast-tracking the development of digital communications on the battlefield. Ultimately, with the senior generals meeting regularly as a board of directors to review initiatives brought under the Louisiana Maneuvers umbrella, it was possible to introduce change much more rapidly across the Army than would otherwise have been possible.

With the senior generals involved, the process eventually drew in hundreds of others, the Army's best minds, in ways that combined and focused intellectual energy on growth. Effective change cannot take place if it is relegated to a staff or committee; it is the personal responsibility of leaders. Unless leaders are involved, it is impossible to work through the normal resistance fast enough to get out in front. With all of us at the top involved, the Army was able to "think out loud" about the future.

From Theory to Practice

While all this front-end work was going on, the Army was not standing still. In fiscal year 1992 (October 1991–September 1992), nearly 200,000 soldiers left the active force, and we recruited 80,000 new ones. The Army completed its recovery from the strain of the Persian Gulf War and redeployed nearly 100,000 soldiers and their families and equipment from Europe. And it kept to its pace of operations and training. All that activity—recovery from war, redeployment, training, downsizing—gave us the time we needed to do the intellectual work to create the future. There was no danger that the Army would lose its edge as a result of inactivity while we charted a course and worked to gain the consensus of the leadership.

But once we left the Cold War Army behind and created a more flexible power projection force, our challenge was to keep moving—to begin the process of creating the next Army, a true twenty-first-century force. It was hard to stand up and talk about growth in an organization that was releasing more than 600,000 people. It was necessary to subject the new ideas to legitimate and rigorous testing and experimentation, and to demonstrate a process of change that would not rupture the fabric of current operations or the Army's sense of itself. Doing that required multiple actions. Three important ones were learning how to apply emerging technologies, training for new missions and new partners, and developing leaders for the new force.

Benchmarking the Future: The Digital Task Force

Harnessing the microprocessor, the tiny computer in the hands of individual solders and imbedded in their equipment, represents the most important technological shift in land warfare in at least fifty years, maybe since the dawn of the Industrial Age. At first it was impossible for us to fully understand the implications of that, but our intuition told us that organizing around information, as opposed to battlefield functions (e.g., infantry, artillery, air defense), was the right course and that our existing modernization and force development processes were not keeping pace adequately with the changing information technologies.

The questions we faced, however, were not unlike those faced by business leaders: How do you benchmark the future? How do you determine best practices when you are stretching beyond today's limits? In some cases, especially in logistics processes, we found useful analogues. Civilian industry had long before solved the challenges of in-transit visibility of assets and just-in-time inventory techniques. In such cases, we were able to go out and examine the best industry practices to decide which to bring into the Army system and how to adapt them to our own unique requirements.

In other areas, especially our bread-and-butter war-fighting tasks, there were no easily recognizable benchmarks, so we needed to create a discovery process to learn about the future. We were tempted to do it by breaking things apart—by building an Information Age intelligence system one piece at a time, then wiring the pieces back together and stuffing them into the maneuver force with its tanks and howitzers and all the rest. The assumption would be that once we had completed that for every subsystem, down to the lowest level, we would have an Information Age macrosystem. That approach would have fit with the Army's existing development processes, but it would have been dead wrong. The Information Age has changed the relationship between the parts and the whole. The need to organize around information has created a different kind of synergy—one that we do not yet fully understand. We needed a discovery process that would give us a view of the organization as a whole—not just the "eaches."

We began with a series of small-scale experiments in sharing simple battlefield information horizontally among weapons (e.g., among tanks in a tank platoon) and then across systems (e.g., between the tanks and the artillery, without going "up" and "down" in the process). These simple, "crawl before you walk" experiments, begun at the Armor Center in 1992 and in the logistics and special operations communities at about the same time, gave us new ways of testing hypotheses with simple and flexible execution but with enough rigor to allow switching back and forth between simulation and live experimentation. In such complex systems there were many variables, and our sample size was always smaller than we would have liked. But we did not have the luxury of more precision. In the end, what we were able to accomplish proved to be sufficient.

This learning process brought together people who had been developing systems, or parts of systems, in separate organizational "stovepipes" optimized for the precision models of Cold War programming analysis. As people talked, walls came down and ideas flourished. The fact that the budget cuts hit the Army's research, development, and procurement hardest of all the forces' made all this very difficult, but the leadership held steadfast in its commitment to this investment in the future.

From these small-scale experiments, we went to the California desert in April 1994 to create the world's first "digital task force." We created an integrated task force of two companies of M1 tanks and two companies of infantry, plus artillery, aviation, and all the other combat systems that normally fight together. We then linked the support systems: intelligence on every level, including Air Force aircraft and satellites; medical; and supply and maintenance. Altogether, the task force and its direct support included about 1,100 soldiers and

150 major weapons and systems. It had taken forty-four different agencies to put it all together, many of which would never have had direct contact with one another from inside their organizational stovepipes. The task force was enmeshed in a digital network using a combination of military and commercial equipment to enable all the elements to exchange information horizontally. For the first time, a commander could create a common perception of the battlefield with all the available information in the hands of everyone who could use it.

The commitment to this experiment drove people to find solutions. People were making fixes right up to the kickoff date. In many respects it was, as they say, "not pretty." Some of the software was brought on board too late to properly train the soldiers in how to fully exploit some of the equipment, and some of the digital linkages were simply too awkward to use. The availability of information caused relationships to change, and some information became of little use because key people were not where the system designers had assumed they would be. All these things were important lessons learned, but there was no question about the overall outcome of the experiment.

In simulated combat with a first-class opposing force, the digital task force exceeded the benchmarks established by conventional task forces for many critical measures. By knowing more about both the enemy and his own force, the commander gained confidence and was able to move more rapidly. By most measures, the digital task force destroyed more of the enemy force and suffered fewer losses. More people were getting information they could use in time to apply it. Integration of the artillery and aviation assets supporting the task force seemed more effective. When it was all over, the water was muddy; we had seen lots of human error, and the prototype digital systems had not all lived up to their potential. But we had been able to demonstrate the power of the microprocessor on the battlefield: the fact that shared information can compress time and increase effectiveness, not by a little but by a lot. We had opened the door to the future, and, from that time forward, there was no looking back.

The digital task force was an important example of what we call a "thin thread," a mechanism for bridging the gap from today to tomorrow. Chapter 10 develops these ideas, along with other examples of ways in which leaders can demonstrate the future.

Building New Teams: Training for Future Battles

The other dimension of change—new missions—took us to our training centers. The most important thing an army does to prepare for war is to train in the most realistic environment possible. The most important training is unit training, learning how to bring together the complex and complementary elements of a military unit in a synergistic way. Large-scale training exercises, with structured feedback and careful learning processes built in, are expensive but extremely valuable. In the 1980s, the Army had invested in three unit-training centers: the Combat Maneuver Training Center at Hohenfels, Germany; the National Training Center at Fort Irwin, California; and the Joint Readiness Operations Training Center at Fort Polk, Louisiana. For larger units, the Army, participating with the other services, had developed a simulation capability that allowed divisions, corps, and interservice task forces to exercise without actually deploying.

These training centers had been built to give the Army a Soviet-style enemy that we called the "world-class opposing force." This force was actually made up of U.S. Army units, but they trained according to Soviet tactics, used equipment that looked like Soviet equipment, and wore a distinctive uniform. They were permanently assigned to the training centers, and they were good—very good; they helped the Army hone the edge that made it the best in the world. As part of the change process, we refocused these training centers and their resident experts to create new battlefields with the kinds of conditions we could expect in the future. Today, all major training exercises begin with an emergency deployment replicating as closely as possible the requirements of an operational deployment, and all the exercises include the most complex battlefield dynamics—multiple antagonists, and civilians, international agencies, and the media on the battlefield.

The most powerful dimension of this has been realized at the Joint Readiness Operations Training Center, to which the Army began inviting other governmental agencies, nongovernmental agencies, and the media to participate in major training exercises. In today's environment, wherever the Army goes, it goes into an environment populated with organizations such as the United Nations, the Red Cross, and the like. Training with these agencies has given the Army a new perspective on its new partners, and it has given our partners a better appreciation for what the Army brings to a crisis.

We believe that the issue of organizational learning is a critical issue for business today. We will return to that in Chapter 11, where we relate the Army's experience and some practical lessons learned.

Leveraging the Schoolhouse

Army officers and noncommissioned officers attend formal schools on a regular basis throughout their careers. These schools were generally designed to teach fairly specific skills and well-defined tasks. Teaching about the future—about the unknown—has been a new challenge, but this challenge is beginning to be met.

We went to the Command and General Staff College at Fort Leavenworth, Kansas, where officers with ten to twelve years' experience study in residence for about nine months. The college conducts an annual training exercise to bring together all that the students have learned. In this exercise, beginning in 1993, the Army has challenged both students and faculty to create a new kind of organization. Working with a prototype computer-based command system, they have developed an air-ground strike force able to move much faster and fight much more effectively than the conventional forces used in other parts of the exercise. Their organizational innovations, including new kinds of line and staff relationships and more networked structures, were startling. They found that increased access to information—a shared awareness of the battlefield—enabled their units to move faster, to strike over greater distances, to target enemy forces more effectively, and to survive better on the battlefield. Thanks to exercises like this, students are helping to discover the future, to answer questions about the twenty-first century. Perhaps even more important, these students are becoming change agents and advocates for new ideas. Every organization undertaking a massive change effort needs to be seeded with change leaders like these at every level.

DEFINING FORCE XXI

The future Army is called Force XXI. The name was first used in a March 1994 message to the Army that synthesized the many forces of change that had been unleashed in the previous five years. Force XXI is organized around information—shared operational awareness made possible by directly linked digital databases. Force XXI will mature as the lessons the Army is learning in its experiments and its current operations are incorporated in new organizational designs, tactics, and procedures. It will take a decade or more to grow Force XXI, to develop organizations and procedures that can best realize the potential of the new technology in the hands of motivated and trained soldiers. But the process is well under way.

FIVE YEARS LATER

At Fort Bragg, North Carolina, one Sunday night in September 1994, just shy of five years after the Berlin Wall had come down, paratroopers of the assault battalions of the 82d Airborne Division loaded for the long flight to Haiti. Formed into careful files, organized as they would be on the landing zones, with their combat equipment fastened to every conceivable part of their bodies, they made their way into the bellies of darkened aircraft parked wingtip to wingtip as far as the eye could see. Tired from days of preparation but pumped up on the adrenaline high that comes with the knowledge that "this is it," they took off into the growing darkness, prepared for what lay ahead.

Out at sea that same night, the men and women of the 10th

Mountain Division were embarked on the U.S.S. *Eisenhower*—a novel, effective marriage of Army helicopters and one of the world's largest aircraft carriers. On the U.S.S. *America*, the Rangers kept silent vigil in the closing hours of their preparation to go ashore. In little boats, the 7th Transportation Group worked its way across the Caribbean, bringing armored personnel carriers and tanks from the 24th Mechanized Division, as well as engineers, port handling equipment, and all the other gear necessary to open Port-au-Prince. Other helicopters flown in from across the United States waited in staging areas on nearby islands.

Newsman Sam Donaldson said it best: "There is something about sixty-two plane loads of paratroopers that focuses the mind." The deployment did its job. In the last minutes before H-Hour, former President Jimmy Carter and his team of negotiators persuaded Haitian strongman Raoul Cédras and his outlaw government to step aside, and a stop was put to the invasion.

Cédras blinked, President Clinton changed the mission, and the soldiers, sailors, airmen, marines, and coasties called an audible at the line. The invasion was off, and the mission changed to peacekeeping, to open the way for a return of the legitimate government of Jean-Bertrand Aristide. The planes turned around and flew back to North Carolina; the infantrymen from the 10th Mountain Division went ashore as peacekeepers and began sorting things out.

That same month, a brigade from the 24th Mechanized Division went to Kuwait to deter Saddam Hussein once again. Only a few weeks later, Patriot air defense missiles were on the way to Korea. Simultaneously, America's Army was all over the world: on a combined peacekeeping training exercise in Russia; in the Multinational Force and Observer mission in the Sinai; in refugee camps in Cuba; protecting Kurds in southern Turkey and northern Iraq; while still others were just getting home from humanitarian operations in central Africa.

The Army that existed on November 9, 1989, when the Berlin Wall came down, no longer exists. Today's Army has reaffirmed its values and sustained its readiness, but it is guided by a new and much broader vision. It has a new doctrine and a new approach to modernization, and it is developing and implementing new concepts for training and for developing leaders. In a very real sense, it is creating its future.

How did all this happen? What are the lessons that leaders of other organizations can take from our efforts? The chapters that follow are our answers to these questions.

CHAPTER 2

The Paradox of Action

★ ★ ★ ★

"Focus, Sully, Focus"

When I arrived in Washington in the summer of 1989 as the Army's operations deputy, it was my habit to run every morning before going down the hill from Fort Myer to the Pentagon. One morning when I was still very new to my job, the then Chief of Staff, General Carl E. Vuono, drove up behind me on his way to the gym. He rolled down the window of his car, and as I struggled with the heat of Washington in August he called out, "Faster, Sully, faster!"

Carl Vuono and I had grown up in different parts of the Army—he in the field artillery, I in tanks—but we had been friends ever since we had served together in the First Infantry Division in 1977–1978. As we worked together through the next two years, we often joked about that morning because it seemed as if the pace would never stop accelerating. During those two years, the Soviet Union crumbled and the Army fought in Panama and the Persian Gulf. Carl and I often found ourselves sharing coffee in the Army Operations Center in the wee hours of the morning as we waited for reports to come in from distant operations. At the same time, the inevitable pressure to reduce the Army was building. The nation wanted a peace dividend from the end of the Cold War, and the competition for the shrinking defense budget was intense. Those were hard days.

What I found, as we went through those days, was that Carl's advice to me that August morning had been slightly off the mark. His admonition should have been "Focus, Sully, focus." That was my real challenge, and I had to learn it the hard way—by living it. In retrospect, I believe it is the most important challenge for everyone who leads an organization of any size. As events pile up, you can become more and more consumed by your "in" box, worrying about the morning newspapers or the last person to wander through your office, all the while distracting yourself by making speeches and writing memos. But if your organization is to succeed, you must focus on what's important or you get eaten up going "faster, faster."

"Focus, Sully, focus!"

—GRS

★ ★ ★ ★

THE MANAGEMENT TREADMILL

Today, people are working harder than ever. People and organizations are reshaping. They are reengineering. They are reinventing. They are improving quality. They are reducing cycle time. But in a seeming paradox, their organizations are not maintaining a competitive edge. In many organizations, people are watching helplessly as traditional market leadership positions erode. Some become gripped in a death spiral of cost cutting in which real solutions are increasingly elusive and downsizing replaces strategy. The turnover in the ranks of the *Fortune* 500 companies continues to accelerate, standing today at one third every decade and rising.[1] The same pointless churning is found everywhere: in the private sector, in government, in not-for-profits. You cannot build a winning organization by simply adapting, trying to accommodate what is going on around you. To win, you have to get out in front.

Embracing speed, quality, or cost cutting as a strategy is tantamount to saying that you are going to run faster and faster, better and better, leaner and leaner—forever. And that is impossible. You cannot run faster and faster forever. You can fine-tune your engine, you can surge, you can stretch capacity—there are many ways of improving performance, but they all have limits. At some point, neither speed nor quality is a sustainable competitive advantage. Cost cutting as an end in itself is worst of all because it merely forces the old engine to labor harder and harder. To be effective, change must be substantive—it must add value and contribute to the long-run health of the organization. When unaccompanied by real change, cost cutting is all pain and little gain.

There are limits to performance in any system. Today, our organizations operate around the clock, seven days a week, without regard to weather or the seasons. Financial markets follow a never-setting sun; global transportation and distribution are realities; worldwide communication is nearly instantaneous; and any information available to one is quickly accessible by all. Stretching old ways to run faster, leaner, better, or cheaper is not what is needed.

The "Paradox of Action" is the fact that working harder and harder to do what you do better and better will not lead to success. Action, however intense, is pointless unless it is focused coherently on the future. Action without strategic direction merely drives an organization deeper into a hole. When a leader fails to understand this, the organization is doomed to an endless succession of seemingly random changes—surfing from management fad to management fad, trying to catch the wave of success. But without strategic underpinnings, fad surfing is a dead end, not the road to success. *Caught in the paradox of action, doing the wrong things better and better, an organization will fail.*

LEADERSHIP TRAPS

In today's rapidly changing environment, it is tempting to argue that the challenges leaders face are uniquely difficult, and in some respects that may be true. But it is useful to look at how some leaders and organizations have performed when confronted with the need to make strategic choices. It is possible to see some patterns. From the perspective of the Paradox of Action, we have identified three "leadership traps" into which it is particularly easy to fall. We call these traps "Doing Things Too Well," "Being in the Wrong Business," and "Making Yesterday Perfect." These traps are especially dangerous because they are difficult to see. When you become consumed with process, you can be working very hard, making difficult changes, yet not realize that you are in a trap, caught on a treadmill that keeps going faster and faster. To illustrate these traps, we provide two examples of each, one drawn from military history and one drawn from business.

Doing Things Too Well

The Doing Things Too Well trap may be the easiest trap into which you can fall because when you are doing well, it is hard to appreciate the need to change and harder still to instill a passion for change into an organization. By falling into this trap, leaders ignore or discount the implications of change in their environment; they lose touch with customers and other stakeholders and, ultimately, with the organization itself.

Tom Peters and Robert Waterman, in their classic 1982 book, *In Search of Excellence*, identified forty-three "excellent" companies on which they based their findings. A mere five years later, author Richard T. Pascale was able to show that only fourteen could still be considered "excellent" under Peters and Waterman's criteria, and, in fact, eight were genuinely troubled.[2] While there are stalwarts who manage to sustain above-average performance for years or even generations, most fall from excellence into this leadership trap. We can see the pattern in the Israeli Defense Forces (1973) and General Motors (1992).

The Israeli Defense Forces, 1973. After the 1967 Six-Day War, the Israeli Defense Forces—the Air Force and Army—were regarded by many as the best in the world. Their performance on the battlefield had been extraordinary; they had beaten much larger forces decisively and secured a much more defensible posture for Israel. The excellence of the IDF was all the more noteworthy because its superiority was clearly not in equipment or in staying power but in its people and in the way they could integrate intelligence, maneuver, and carry out the other very complex processes of modern battle. Its performance was a standard against which other armies, including the American Army, were judged. Its success was so complete, however, that it became complacent, blind to the capabilities of its enemies to innovate.[3]

Egypt and Syria, on the other hand, drew back after the 1967 war determined to avenge their humiliating defeat. They reorganized, rearmed, and undertook training programs to give them greater effectiveness in battle. Attacking during the Jewish High Holy Days in 1973, they caught the Israelis by surprise. Egyptian forces were able to force their way across the Suez Canal in a daring assault behind water cannon used to blast away Israeli fortifications and the huge sand berm that had been piled up along the canal. The jets of water quickly and unexpectedly turned the steep banks into assault boat landing sites. At the same time, an equally unexpected Syrian armored thrust regained much of the Golan Heights and threatened vital farming settlements in the north.

These setbacks for the IDF represented a failure of both intelligence and readiness. Resting on its laurels, it had become complacent, with too little respect for the ability of its competitors to innovate and grow. Neither the Army nor the Air Force had been in a position to defend when the attacks came. In the days following the initial Syrian and Egyptian successes, Israeli counterattacks were able to blunt the advances in both north and south and to regain much of the lost territory, but the cost was very high.[4]

General Motors, 1992. For more than half a century, General Motors was the symbol of mass production excellence. GM not only had perfected mass production in manufacturing but, by extending its ideas about specialization into the white-collar workforce, had created the model of twentieth-century industrial bureaucracy administered by professional managers compartmentalized by management disciplines or functional areas. With Chairman Alfred P. Sloan's simple but elegant marketing plan based around a five-model range of discrete products that ranged in price across the entire market, GM dominated the U.S. market and was the biggest player in the world market. With its complex array of engineering and management expertise, it was structured to roll on and on. GM was the best, most efficient organization of its kind in the world—so good, in fact, that it lived in its own world and was oblivious to what was going on in the manufacturing quality and design revolutions born in Europe and Asia.

By 1992, GM was awash in red ink. Its market share had eroded from about one half to about one third of the U.S. market; the traditional GM incremental product line was a blur, with models and prices badly overlapping from top to bottom. Serious people were suggesting that GM simply would not survive in a recognizable form. New CEO Jack Smith moved quickly to stop the bleeding. Through an aggressive program of cost cutting, strategic restructuring, and active leadership at every level in the organization, he stopped the decline and began to breathe new life into the organization, especially the troubled North American operation, which had been losing $500 million a month when he took over.[5]

Today, tensions in the Middle East are substantially relaxed compared to those of the 1970s, but the Israeli Defense Forces learned their lesson and restored their edge. GM is back from the brink and is transforming itself, but company leaders acknowledge that the process will take at least a decade. In Smith's words, we see the essence of the trap of Doing Things Too Well: "Size and success led to complacency, myopia, and, ultimately, decline. . . . We lost touch with the customer."[6] *Good leaders must understand that change in their strategic environment is a continuous process.* They must grow in the context of the changes going on around them—in the context of the future—not because their organizations are doing badly but precisely because they are doing well.

Being in the Wrong Business

The Being in the Wrong Business trap results from failing to understand the implications of change. This can be evidenced in many ways. Caught in this trap, a leader generally can see change happening but misinterprets its significance. The 1862 Battle of Antietam offers a superb example, as does the failure of Wang to leverage its dominance of word processing technologies in the 1980s.

Antietam, 1862. In September 1862, Confederate forces under General Robert E. Lee invaded Maryland. By engaging the Union Army in central Maryland, Lee threatened Washington. He believed a victory on northern soil would create conditions favorable to diplomatic recognition of the Confederate States by Britain and other European nations, and weaken Lincoln and his allies in the November congressional elections, possibly even leading to a negotiated settlement.

The Union commander was General George B. McClellan. Although he was newly in command of the Union forces, he was a seasoned, experienced commander, liked and respected in the Army. McClellan attacked Lee's positions near Sharpsburg, Maryland, on September 17 in a bloody day-long battle that historians regard as ending in a stalemate. On the second day, McClellan failed to renew the attack when a weakened Lee probably could have been pinned against the Potomac River. Lee then withdrew, but McClellan failed to pursue his weakened foe, citing a need to rest and refit his army. Prodded repeatedly by Lincoln, he eventually moved south, but too late to strike a decisive blow. As a result of his inaction, the popular

McClellan was relieved of command on November 5, the day after the congressional elections.

Although McClellan consistently overestimated the size of his opponent's force, throughout the battle on the seventeenth Lee was vastly outnumbered. Lee had his back to the Potomac River, and McClellan's larger force was better supplied and rested. Lee's single advantage lay in having a more cohesive, somewhat more experienced army. McClellan, however, was focused completely on his responsibility to prevent Lee from reaching Washington. Well aware that Union generals had failed so far to best Lee on the field of battle, and smarting from his own defeat at Lee's hands earlier in the summer, his strategic vision was *not to lose*. Consequently, his battle plan was neither imaginative nor well executed. The blows of his attack landed in an uncoordinated fashion, and he failed to press the advantage of his superior numbers. He withheld two veteran corps, a quarter of his force. Had he committed his reserve, it should easily have sufficed to break the tactical stalemate. Twice he was offered a plan to commit those reserves: once early in the fight, when he was near success, and again in the afternoon of the seventeenth, when he threatened Lee's flank. On the second occasion, the commander of the reserve corps, Major General Fitz John Porter, admonished, "Remember, General, I command the last reserve of the last army of the republic."[7] That was enough to discourage the timid McClellan, and he did not press his advantage.

In his concern for his own position, and by narrowly interpreting his responsibility to defend Washington, McClellan lost sight of the facts that only Lee lay between him and the Confederate capital at Richmond and that Lee was by far more vulnerable than he. Seeing only his own vulnerability, he was blind to the possibilities open to him if he took the initiative. He was in the business of defending Washington, a view he defended in his dispatches and memoirs. President Abraham Lincoln would go through several more generals before he found one who was in the business of winning—of beating the Confederacy.

Wang, 1982. In the early 1980s, Wang represented the preeminent office automation capability in the world—so much so that in many offices the name "Wang" had become a synonym for "office automa-tion," the same way "Xerox" was used to mean "photocopier." Wang dominated every step of the process, from research and development through manufacturing and sales to customer service and the after-market. Wang's Office Power software suite enabled the concept of shared office databases and was the state-of-the-art solution for word-crunching bureaucracies hungry to process more and more paper. With a reputation for quality and with proprietary hardware and software that guaranteed the uniqueness of its product, Wang had built a market position that seemed unassailable.

Yet in less than a decade, Wang faded to near obscurity, contract-ing dramatically and surviving only by transforming itself to leverage its software and engineering strengths in completely different ways. In place of Wang's proprietary, closed systems, versatile, capable per-sonal computers linked together in networks became the dominant office appliance. With their open architecture, interchangeable soft-ware, and integrated communications, personal computers first transformed the market for office automation networks and then obliterated the old market.

Wang saw itself as a specialized kind of computer company pro-viding service via a central processor with distributed workstations. Its excellence and leadership in innovation were highly respected, and it was important to Wang *not to lose* that position. That view led it to stick to its business until it was too late. It never saw the oppor-tunity presented by the personal computer and the potential to net-work smaller, distributed computers. The PC explosion took word processing out of the secretarial pool and put it onto everyone's desk, where it would become but one tool in an integrated system that could greatly enhance human productivity in all directions. Eventually, Wang did attempt to move into personal computers as a basis of integrated office systems, but by this time the company's op-portunity to move forward by leveraging its strengths was gone. There were too many other, already established hardware manufac-turers; Wang's proprietary software had become a liability; the new industry had become dominated by strong alliances of hardware, software, and marketing firms; and customers had already begun to associate Wang with old ways of doing business. The market no longer wanted or needed a more automated bureaucracy; instead, it was seeking innovation in organizational design and information systems. Wang had been badly outflanked and was left with no market.

Assessing this kind of failure—Being in the Wrong Business—is difficult, because the leaders involved seldom leave us their thoughts or explain their judgments. Sometimes leaders stumble into this trap by *waiting to see what develops*, trading time for the prospect of more information and less uncertainty. Sometimes the delay is to *gather more resources*, and sometimes the leader is simply so *averse to losing* that he or she is incapable of the bold action required for success, preferring instead a more conventional route, no matter how unlikely it is to succeed. Sometimes leaders simply commit the organization *too far in the wrong direction*, getting into the wrong business by mistake. There is no reason to suspect that either McClellan or Wang fully saw the trap, even after they had been forced from their positions. But in each case the leader was operating with limited vision and came out a loser as a result.

Making Yesterday Perfect

Making Yesterday Perfect is still another form of inability to cope effectively with external change. The Making Yesterday Perfect leader is often zealous in making change, even demonstrating great "progress," but always in terms of the old paradigm. Such a leader is a great "fixer" and often has elaborate inspection and control systems to measure processes and performance against precise standards. Making Yesterday Perfect is a particularly treacherous type of resistance to change within an organization because it is so easy to appear to be engaged in making changes and "modernization"; there can be a very high level of activity; and specific actions, usually incremental, are generally easy to defend because the context is stable and therefore risk invariably appears to be low.

France, 1940. Few military defeats in history were as stunning as the defeat of the French and Allied forces in northeastern France in May

1940. Unlike the British, who were unprepared for war, France had been preparing for renewed war with Germany for two decades and had executed a major modernization program during the 1930s. In addition to its fortified borders, France fielded a large, mobile armored force with approximately as many tanks as Germany had, including ample artillery, infantry, and other arms and services. The French Army had had eight months to mobilize and to train reservists; it was in position; it had good equipment; and it had a coherent, disciplined approach to war. Yet when the Germans attacked on May 10, they advanced to the English Channel in only ten days. Failing to destroy the British Army as it evacuated Dunkirk, the German Army turned on Paris, which fell on June 14, and a week later France surrendered.

The French were prepared. The problem was that they "had formulated a doctrine, organized and equipped . . . units, and trained . . . for the wrong type of war."[8] It is not that they were prepared to refight World War I; one need only look at the extensive modernization program of the 1930s to see that that was not the case. The issue is more subtle: they had built an army they thought could win decisively in a World War I–type struggle. If, in 1940, the German Army had attacked *the same way it had in 1914*, it is very likely that the French defense would have been successful. The French based their army on a belief in the strength of a relatively static defense, the destructiveness of firepower, and what they called the "methodical battle." The French Army in 1940 was an army created for precisely the kind of war the Germans did not want to fight.

Both Germany and France had looked back at World War I. In the technology of the second stage of the Industrial Revolution, France saw a means of perfecting the past; but Germany saw a means of leaping beyond it. Consequently, when the Germans attacked, in formations optimized for mobility and offensive action, they were able to pierce the French defenses with such force and speed that the integrity of the great French Army crumbled.

General Electric, 1981. By 1981, after a major post–World War II reorganization and modernization that had fueled great success well into the 1960s, GE, one of the oldest and most respected companies in the world, was in a slump. Real earnings had taken twenty-three years to double, and innovation was at an all-time low. GE's core businesses, with few exceptions, represented traditional technologies and heavy manufacturing. The company had failed to make successful inroads into computers, it had lost its strong positions in mobile communications and consumer electronics, and its housewares division was stagnant. There were bright spots, such as aircraft engines, plastics, and medical diagnostics, but invariably they were successful because of unique circumstances and leadership—in spite of, not because of, corporate policy. In the words of one former executive, GE "was a dull, unexciting company. We were an organization in decline—and that was not recognized."[9]

The GE of 1981 had perfected the management model of the 1950s. Following World War II, its huge, semiautonomous manufacturing works had been broken up, and a rigid system of centralized control was introduced to manage the company. The already large corporate staff was expanded, ultimately reaching a depth of nine management layers in many areas. To manage this complexity, GE pioneered management by objectives, decentralized profit centers, and numerous other management practices designed to eliminate the idiosyncrasies attributable to human behavior and lock in predictable performance. The corporation was governed by a system of financial management and policed by auditors. (Pascale reports that "Finance's total headcount exceeded 12,000 professionals and constituted 8 percent of GE's total employment."[10])

In this kind of climate, major innovations, such as mobile communications, robotics and factory automation, microelectronics, and computers languished because long-term, risk-taking managerial behavior was nearly impossible. In stable, mature areas, the bureaucracy simply siphoned off dollars; in more dynamic business areas, it was like an anchor that made GE's entries untimely and uncompetitive. It was an environment structured for the 1950s that was inadequate for the world as it had become.

GE avoided failure by beginning a transformation while it was still perceived as being on top. The absence of a clearly defined crisis made change controversial at the time, but that it has been effective is undeniable. Under the leadership of Jack Welch, GE has successfully divested its marginal segments, strengthened its core, flattened its bureaucracy, and focused intensely on markets where it has been able to use its financial and research strengths, speed, and quality to advantage. Today, GE, by every measure, is healthier and better postured for the future than at any other time in its history.

The recovery of the French Army was more difficult; it took a generation after World War II to regain its stature as one of the preeminent land forces in the world. The lesson of both stories is very clear: *The past can be very beguiling.* When we "modernize" without challenging our underlying assumptions, we run the risk of failing to come to grips with structural changes in our environment that make yesterday's basic concepts irrelevant or, worse, fatal.

These traps are simple characterizations, and the stories we have offered as examples can be understood from different perspectives. But they all have a common thread: on battlefields and in boardrooms, leaders failed to create the right future because they were blind to the real implications of their circumstances.

FALSE STARTS . . . STILL ON THE TREADMILL

As business grappled with increasing instability throughout the 1960s and 1970s, questions began to be raised about the basic assumptions of the science of management. A plethora of tools and techniques for solving the problems facing large American institutions in general, and American industry in particular, began to surface. In his 1994 book *Fast, Focused, and Flexible*, Gerald Sentell identified sixty-six distinct such tools (or at least sixty-six different buzzwords) from this period.[11] Richard Pascale's more critical list stops at twenty-seven, but he was able to show that the emergence of fads correlates well with strategic uncertainty. Pascale goes so far as to suggest, perhaps with tongue in cheek, that "an indicator of managerial panic is the consumption rate and shelf life of business fads." [12] If the growth of business-book publishing is a similar mirror, we are surely bordering on epidemic panic today as Industrial Age models increasingly fail to measure up to the needs of the new century.

Faced with that kind of environment, the natural reaction of most organizations is to focus inward, concentrating on adapting and trying to stay ahead of the next unexpected turn of events. Organizations are working harder to make the old models work, to achieve a greater degree of efficiency and more output per unit of input by implementing programs to improve existing processes—automation, teaming, process improvement, whatever—in what can be an endless "fad *du jour*" cycle. Of course, realization of the need for change is almost inevitably associated with shrinking profit margins. Thus, regardless of the declared policy, the "fad *du jour*" tends to take on a strong bias for short-term financial performance—hence cost cutting, often with all the finesse of a chain-saw massacre. Minimizing costs in both up and down cycles is essential to the health of any organization. But cost cutting is not a viable end unto itself. Infatuation with technique, be it cost cutting or whatever, can become a substitute for real strategy, but there is little to suggest that this "fad surfing" [13] leads to real and enduring improvement.

Quality is another tool that has been misunderstood by some as a strategy for growth. Total Quality Management, or TQM, has provided a valuable set of tools and is an effective way of beginning to empower people in an organization. But TQM, at its heart, is not necessarily about growing as much as about improving existing processes. If not imbedded in a strategy for the future, TQM can be little more than Making Yesterday Perfect.

Reengineering is another good example of how good-sounding ideas can be dysfunctional when decoupled from real strategic thinking. Its basic premises are compelling. Michael Hammer and James Champy subtitled their best-selling book on reengineering "A Manifesto for Business Revolution," and they made a very compelling case for "nothing less than a radical reinvention of how [American corporations] do their work." [14] Yet the discipline to do the front-end work is too often not part of the mind-set. Reengineering gurus acknowledge that changing business processes can lead full circle to changes in values and beliefs, but by seeing change as an internal process, reengineering prescriptions assume that the organizational strategic view is fixed. Reengineering focuses on issues with high potential to reduce cost, increase quality, or shorten cycle time and only then follows the unwinding ball of string to see where it leads. If you are doing the wrong things, reengineering will help you do them more efficiently; but so what?

Accompanied by an "all-or-nothing" battle cry for radical change, downsizing, TQM, and reengineering can compound the problem of the lack of strategic direction by completely undermining an organization's cultural and human dimensions. Gary Hamel and C. K. Prahalad call this process "denominator management" because it increases returns by decreasing investment or the costs associated with investment, as opposed to creating new or expanding markets—creating a future.[15]

Of course, there is value in improving efficiency and overthrowing outmoded Industrial Age bureaucracy. But where the driving force for these initiatives is simple cost cutting, where programs are driven by fiscal objectives and with little or no front-end work to establish meaningful strategic objectives, the results have been and will continue to be disappointing.[16] What is needed are new approaches, new processes, new ways of doing business. To realize that, what is needed is a new perspective.

ESCAPING THE TREADMILL

In 1991, when we assessed the Army, all three of the leadership traps were open to us. It would have been easy to make yesterday perfect, perfecting the Cold War systems on the basis of Persian Gulf War lessons learned. It would have been easy to glide along in the wrong business, continuing to focus on a hypothetical World War III fought by large armored formations in central Europe or someplace like it, but we would have been preparing for a war that was less likely to occur with each passing day. And it would have been easy to rest on our laurels, doing things well. We were, after all, the best army in the world—we had proved it in the Gulf War—and relying on the post-

Vietnam renaissance to perpetuate itself would have been logical. We could easily and comfortably have fallen into any of the traps.

We could also have embraced any of the fads. We had proven that quality makes a difference, and we could easily have leveraged our ideas about quality to convince ourselves that a smaller Cold War–style force would be better. But we knew that smaller is not necessarily better; better, in our case, meant becoming something different—not a smaller version of the Cold War Army but an army that could respond to expanding requirements. We did accept the 40 percent decline in budgets as a battle cry to reengineer, but we did it knowing that better processes were at best a step on the journey to new processes. Our greatest fear was that we would fall prey to embracing downsizing, making it our goal and taking satisfaction from the briefing charts showing how well we were doing it. But we knew that if downsizing became our focus, we would go into a death spiral, continuing to pay the bills by simply getting smaller and smaller and hoping for a turnaround in our fortunes until, like the Army of the 1920s, we became inept, burdened with hollow units, outmoded equipment, and unneeded bases, and unprepared for war.

It was clear that we were dealing with two kinds of change. We had to deal with change *as a permanent condition of our environment*, change in which there would be both new challenges and new opportunities. And we had to engage change *as a process*, growing a new army out of the victorious Cold War force, preparing to meet new operational challenges, and realizing the enormous power of the Information Age to transform warfare as we had known it. As we grappled with these facts, we knew we would have to lead the organization around the leadership traps and avoid fad surfing, to get off the treadmill of better, better; faster, faster.

The Army's transformation would require a journey of many steps over many years. It would require a reaffirmation of our values, a clear vision of the future, an effective strategy for real change, and an insatiable appetite for learning, because we were attempting to go where none of us had ever been. And we knew that words were not enough. We said "Hope is not a method" because we knew we had to *act*.

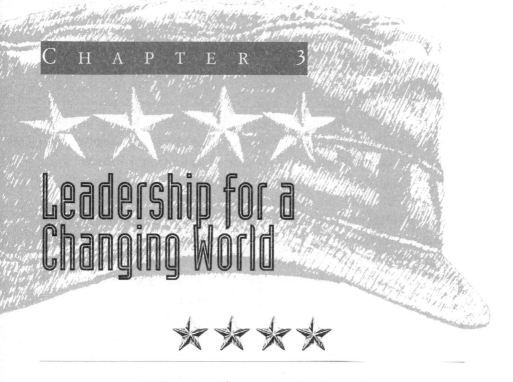

CHAPTER 3

Leadership for a Changing World

★ ★ ★ ★

"When in Charge, Be in Charge"

Olympic archer Ed Eliason tells of a Buddhist monk who
advised him, "When you wash dishes, wash dishes."[1] At
first the monk's Zen-like thought seemed obvious to me, of
no particular value, but upon reflection it began to make
more sense. Eventually, I translated it into a phrase that
had significance for me: "When in charge, be in charge," a
frequent admonition from General Max Thurman, commander of the 1989 Panama invasion. Being in charge of
any organization puts a burden on the shoulders of the
leader. Being in charge means that you must create the future.

My mind, like that of most leaders, was usually focused
on today's issues, oscillating between today and tomorrow
but always returning to the pressure of today. It was hard
to focus on the future. To handle that tension, I had to find
ways to act in today's world while at the same time focus-

ing on the future. I understood Creighton Abrams' and William DuPuy's lessons about values and the role of doctrine; Shy Meyer had taught the Army the importance of quality people and had highlighted to the American people the danger of hollow units; and Carl Vuono and others had taught me the importance of keeping the Army training, especially during times of turbulence and uncertainty.* Those were touchstones I could not walk away from. But I had to translate them into the future even as I was forming new ones. Our long-range planning processes had not been designed for the kind of world we were facing, with its uncertainty, ambiguity, and rapid change. Our planning processes had been designed for a stable planning environment and for incremental changes—for marginal resource adjustments and evolutionary technology.

The Army's long-range planning system was dominated by the programmatics of the Future Years Defense Plan (FYDP), a budget estimate that described in fiscal terms how the Department of the Army would generate and sustain ready forces for the next six years. The stability of the Cold War had enabled us to create a planning and budgeting environment in which we had estimated the Soviet threat, modeled a hypothetical war with the Soviets, and made investment decisions at the margin based on that analysis. This tedious process, rooted in the Robert McNamara years, had yielded increasingly precise point estimates of the future. By 1989, investment decisions were being driven by a single war plan to defeat a hypothetical global Soviet attack. But by 1990, that methodology was moving us toward a future that no longer existed. Yet

---

* General Creighton W. Abrams, Jr., Army Chief of Staff from October 1972 to September 1974; General William E. DuPuy, Commanding General, U.S. Army Training and Doctrine Command, from July 1973 to June 1977; General Edward C. Meyer, Army Chief of Staff from June 1979 to June 1983; General Carl E. Vuono, Army Chief of Staff from June 1987 to June 1991.

the machinery of the planning and budget process continued to grind on, attempting to accommodate change in an
unending process of marginal adjustments, bureaucratic
decisions, and ever-shorter planning cycles. The process itself did not really change much, even though dollars dried
up and missions expanded and changed.

It was clear that, inside the Army, we needed a more robust way to think about an unclear, ever-changing future.
On the one hand, we had to accept the limitations of the
FYDP and its process because that was our planning reality—that was where the money came from. On the other
hand, we had to transform ourselves into a new force that
could not be reflected very well in the formal planning
process, because the process demanded consensus and
precision six or more years into the future—both of which
were now impossible. We had to get out in front intellectu-
ally, learn about the future, and create it. Only then could
we reach back and connect to the programming process in
a coherent way. What's more, we had to do so in a way that
would be as transparent as possible to our soldiers so that
we would add as little turmoil and uncertainty to their lives
as possible. It was very difficult to think about all that.

Our approach was to leverage the learning culture others had created to train the Army and thereby create a
learning-based planning process. We postulated that the
nation needed a versatile force that, although smaller,
would be effective in a broad range of missions. Information would be the new source of power, not only in combat
but in all of our operations, with a shared situational
awareness creating an environment in which our units
could operate much faster and much more effectively than
any adversary. We called this future Army Force XXI. The
essence of Force XXI is not managing the complexity of
the Industrial Age battlefield more efficiently but raising
the conduct of all kinds of military operations to a new
level. Fleshing out the concept of Force XXI will be the
kind of shift not seen since agrarian warfare began to yield

to Industrial Age warfare in the nineteenth century. Setting out to create Force XXI was a way of breaking the tyranny of the Cold War planning processes and deliberately creating the future.

By disassociating Force XXI from existing processes, it was possible to begin the journey. But we still faced the challenge of creating the future while running the organization in the present. In other words, we could not ignore the force development and programming systems just because they had been perfected for a world that no longer existed. But our belief was that by a process of experimentation and discovery learning, it would be possible to feed the future back into the more formal planning processes. It remains to be seen how effective this will be. In some respects it is like joining two engines to a single transmission while both engines are running. But we have seen some early success in the revamping of the Army's modernization strategy to emphasize a range of capabilities that extend horizontally across the force, as opposed to the traditional vertical approach along functional lines.

Force XXI was our way of taking the initiative. To create purposeful forward momentum, you as a leader must take the initiative. You cannot be passive. When your people look into your eyes, they are asking whether you have what it takes to get them through today's crisis and whether you will be there for them when it is over. To be successful, you must lead to win in today's context and have a powerful drive to succeed in the long run. If you are not attacking, you are defending; while there can sometimes be good reasons to defend, in the end you will win only by seizing the initiative and attacking.

—GRS

★ ★ ★ ★

THE FERTILE VERGE

We are at the end of an era. There may be some seminal event that historians will point to as the turn of the century. Perhaps it will be the fall of the Berlin Wall; perhaps the development of ENIAC, the world's first electronic computer; perhaps the commercialization of the microprocessor; perhaps . . . whatever; finding the most appropriate tombstone for that which is passing is unimportant. What is important is to realize that we are in what the Pulitzer Prize–winning historian Daniel Boorstin called a "fertile verge . . . a place of encounter between something and something else."[2] We stand between a bureaucratic industrial society and an information society. The skills we have used all our lives are falling short of helping us face the new world; it is a time of great opportunity but also of ambiguity and uncertainty. In times like this, management is not enough. Ours is a time for leadership.

WHAT IS LEADERSHIP?

There is a useful and important distinction between leadership and management. Management has to do with an organization's *processes*—performing them correctly and efficiently; leadership has to do with an organization's *purposes*.

Today, management science enables executives to deal with complexity. Think about the traditional management disciplines: human resources, information systems, operations, finance, marketing, communications, organizational behavior, accounting, and the like. Each is very focused. Each is compartmented. Management has at its heart the notion that, as the organizational design consultant and author Margaret Wheatley comments, "we really believed that we could study the parts, no matter how many of them there were, to arrive at knowledge of the whole."[3] Wheatley and other scholars are beginning to create an understanding of the role of leadership and learning, as distinct from management and controlling. We are coming to understand that leadership and learning are the tools we now need to develop high-performing organizations.[4] The wisdom of these new approaches to organizational theory can be seen in the irony of the examples we used to illustrate the leadership traps. All six organizations were being *managed* very well—even McClellan was performing up to the expectations of his profession—but none was well *led*.

Leadership goes beyond creating the future and managing complexity. The leader must also build teams. A team is a permanent or ad hoc grouping of people to accomplish a task, and our organizations are teams of teams. Through teams, a leader influences and directs the course of the organization. From this perspective, leading is acting on an interpersonal level with small groups or individuals. It is communicating and aligning to influence behavior and performance. It is how we put creating the future and managing the present in context to move the organization, as a coherent body, from one state to the next.

Thus, "leading" has three dimensions, and we use the term "strategic leadership" to embrace this gestalt: managing, creating the future, and team building. Strategic leadership is directing and controlling rational and deliberate action that applies to an organization in its most fundamental sense: purpose, culture, strategy, core competencies, and critical processes. Strategic leadership includes not only operating successfully today but also guiding deep and abiding change—transformation—into the essence of an organization. If we picture the leadership dimensions as a Venn diagram (see Figure 3-1), it becomes clear that effective leadership depends on being able to operate with all three sets of skills. In terms of the diagram, strategic leadership is operating at the center.

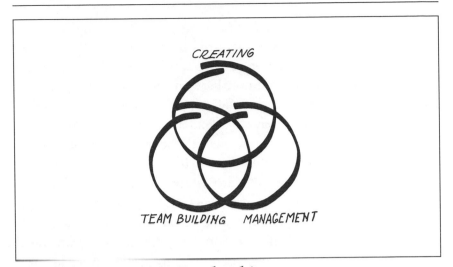

Figure 3-1—Strategic Leadership

This model does not denigrate managerial skills, nor does it overly exalt the "soft stuff" of team building and other interpersonal aspects of leadership. Rather, it shows that all three kinds of skills are necessary for success: good management, working effectively with people, and creating the future.

THE POWER OF REFLECTION

One paradox of this new age is that information, by itself, does not represent knowledge, and therefore merely having more information is not in itself an advantage. It is difficult for leaders to internalize and act on the constant stream of information they are exposed to every day. In fact, trying to react to constant bombardment by "information" may be dysfunctional. In the seventeenth century, it took the better part of two years to turn around a message concerning European interests in India or the Far East. European managers on the scene were "empowered" far beyond our late-twentieth-century imaginings! Or think about World War II, when Franklin D. Roo-

sevelt and Winston Churchill had time to meet in the middle of the
North Atlantic, both blacked out from being able to influence day-
to-day operations, to reflect on the war at its strategic level and nego-
tiate how it would be carried out. How many leaders today are able
to step back and reflect strategically on what they are trying to accomplish? Yet that is precisely what leaders must do.

One of our favorite illustrations of leadership in action comes
from a battle in Vietnam.[5] By 1965, the North Vietnamese had
moved large regular army units into South Vietnam to reinforce the
Viet Cong guerrillas. In response, the United States deployed conventional units. In the first major clash of the two armies, Lieutenant
Colonel Hal Moore led the 1st Battalion, 7th Cavalry, into the Ia
Drang Valley of the central highlands, into a clearing called "LZ
X-Ray." We now know that the North Vietnamese were seeking a
major engagement to learn how the Americans would fight. Moore's
assault went into an area that had long been a Communist stronghold, and he and his men were quickly surrounded and fighting for
their lives, outnumbered by four or five to one or more. The tough,
bloody fighting went on for four days. When it was over, half the
troopers from Moore's understrength battalion were dead, as were
hundreds of North Vietnamese. Moore's command had distinguished itself against an enemy that was far superior in numbers and
that had held the initiative throughout much of the battle. Ultimately, both sides would claim victory, but the tenacity of the 7th
Cavalry and its indomitable spirit are a monument to effective leadership.

During the fight, Moore established his command post in the center of the primary landing zone, partially protected by a large termite
hill. With his radio operators, forward observers, and others he
worked the artillery, air support, and resupply while he led the battalion in the fight. From time to time he was observed to withdraw, appearing to those around him to be shutting down and blocking them
out for brief periods of time. When the battle was over, Moore and
his men were debriefed extensively to learn as much as possible
about the North Vietnamese regular forces and how they had fought.
When asked about his periods of seeming withdrawal, Moore said
that he had been reflecting, asking himself three questions: "What is

happening? What is not happening? How can I influence the action?"

The Leader's Reconnaissance

- What is happening?

- What is not happening?

- What can I do to influence the action?

Moore's behavior captured the essence of strategic leadership. Moore was scanning his environment, thinking about his situation, then determining his best course. The future was winning the battle, not simply parrying each thrust. The genius in Moore's approach lies in his second question. *By reflecting on what was not happening, he was able to open his mind to broader opportunities, to see the full range of his options.* He was better able to anticipate what might or might not happen next and to plan his moves to best advantage. When asking "How can I influence the action?" he could thus envision a far greater range of responses than if he had simply been thinking in terms of action and counteraction.

Few are presented with the challenge of leading soldiers in battle, but our leadership reflexes and intuitions must be similar. At Antietam, McClellan got the management right. At LZ X-Ray, Moore got the leadership right.

It is in Moore's second question that opportunity lurks. Think of Eli Whitney: he "invented" interchangeable machine parts because of the shortage of gunsmiths in late-eighteenth-century America.[6] Whitney saw opportunity by asking himself "What is not happening?" and answering "The traditional system is not meeting the demands of the market." Henry Ford was not the first to make an automobile, nor was his the best. But he asked himself "What is not happening?" and concluded that the craft-based automobile manufacturers had assumed away the mass market. Steve Wozniak and Steve Jobs asked themselves "What is not happening?" and concluded that IBM and the others had failed to grasp the power of computers in the hands of real people. Their Apple changed the lives of all of us.

THE COMPRESSION OF TIME

The dynamic that makes all of this so vital is the speed of change. Things are happening so fast that a move in the wrong direction can quickly become overwhelming; for most of us the downside risk associated with our decisions is greater than ever before. Shortly after we had published an article about the future of the U.S. Army, a colleague wrote us, "You make it sound as if the Army is rushing headlong into the twenty-first century." In his view, we were recklessly threatening proven ways of doing business, processes carefully built up over a generation or more. We wrote back, "The twenty-first century is rushing headlong into the Army." From that inside-out perspective came this insight: The defining characteristic of the Information Age is not speed, it is the compression of time. If we think in terms of speed, we are back on the treadmill. But realizing we have less time suggests new limits to old ways; and we can open up a broader perspective and range of action, one more ominous in its implications but more challenging in its opportunities.

The leader seemingly no longer has time to digest the nuances of rapid and widespread change. It would be unfair and supremely arrogant to suggest that leading today is any more difficult than a generation ago or a hundred years ago, but it does seem fair to argue that change (whatever we take that to mean) is taking place much faster than ever before. Dee Hock, the creative genius who "invented" Visa International, coined the term "change float" to describe this phenomenon. He noted, "You may not recall the days when a check might take a couple of weeks to find its way through the banking system. It was called 'float.' Today, we are all aware of the speed and volatility with which money moves through the economy and the profound effect it has on commerce. However, we ignore vastly more important reductions in float, such as the disappearance of information float." Events that once took months or years to become known and accepted can now be known virtually instantaneously. Hock concluded, "This endless compression . . . can be described as the disappearance of . . . the time between what was and what is to be, between past and future."[7]

We can see the compression of time in the great campaigns of military history. The campaigns that Napoleon took seasons or years to accomplish could be accomplished in months by the dawn of the Industrial Age a hundred and fifty years ago and in weeks or even days today. The trend is equally unmistakable in the world of commerce. In the automobile industry, we see a proliferation of models and faster and faster cycle times. In telecommunications, we see unrestrained competition as more and more products and services are introduced daily. In retailing, we see traditional annual and semiannual product cycles reduced to monthly or even weekly just-in-time cycles. We see it in software development, in health care—in fact, in virtually every sector of economic activity. The game has quickened so that players have less and less time to play each hand. We live in a world in which the useful life of assets is unpredictable, workforce skills require continual renewal, and markets can disappear overnight, a world in which versatility and flexibility are far more valuable than specialization.

THE LEADERSHIP ACTION CYCLE

With less time to act, what you do to create the future becomes vitally important. Reflection is critical, but it must be connected to deliberate, structured action in an iterative, constantly adjusted leadership process.

The way a tank commander uses his tank follows a simple four-step model—observe, orient, decide, act—nicknamed the "OODA Loop."[8] First, the tank commander observes his environment, using all his on-board sensors, his human faculties, and whatever information is being broadcast into his tank. Upon observing a threat he orients on it, intensifying his data collection and information processing. Trading time for information, he gathers information about what the rest of his unit is doing, what supporting actions are under way, and the extent of the enemy resistance. Quickly, he decides what to do, and then he completes the cycle by acting. Today, all that happens very fast, at ranges of up to two miles, day or night. Feedback is immediate, and the cycle begins anew.

The challenge for the executive is much the same as it is for the tank commander. Integrating learning and feedback, more formally, he follows a five-step model we call the "Leadership Action Cycle"[9] (see Figure 3-2).

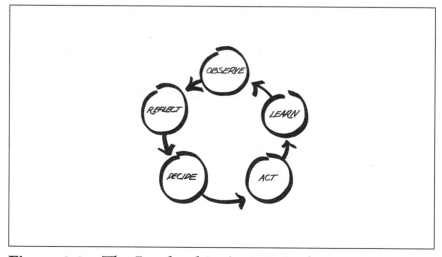

Figure 3-2—The Leadership Action Cycle

Observe. The Leadership Action Cycle begins with observation. In this phase the leader is asking "What is happening?" and "What is not happening?" This is not only a process of looking outside the organization; it is also a process of looking inside and assessing strengths and weaknesses, basic competencies, cultural tendencies, and needs. It must include all of the organization's constituencies, including customers, shareholders, employees, competitors, analysts, regulators, and whoever else has an influence on the ability of the organization to function.

Reflect. Reflection is the thinking phase: "What can I do to influence the action?" The leader interprets the information gathered by observation, deducing both threats and opportunities and formulating courses of action, options, and alternatives. In this phase, the leader establishes objectives. An important dimension of the thinking phase is determining what in the environment is subject to change and what must be accepted as a given. It is a process of segregating uncertainties from relative certainties and of identifying and testing assumptions. It is also a process of assessing and mitigating risk.

Decide. Next, the leader determines how best to go forward to realize the objective. This involves identifying tasks, including specific roles for the key participants, and setting constraints, limits, and measurable standards for success.

Act. The organization then begins to execute the leader's decisions, often beginning with specific pilot projects so that learning can begin immediately. The leader must be personally involved, especially early in the change process. The leader's sponsorship and involvement demonstrate the importance of change and reinforce participation by other leaders.

Learn. This most important step in the Leadership Action Cycle closes the loop by relating the outcomes of decision and action to the environment *and to future action*. In the learning phase, the leader and the organization modify their behavior to become more effective. They adjust decisions and refocus objectives as necessary, asking "If we had known then what we know now, what would we have done differently?"

Not only is more information available than ever before, but the compression of time means the leader has less time in which to digest and apply it. The leader can use assistants to help in this process—to dialogue about the situation, the alternatives, the risks, and the difficulties. Having an effective leadership team can greatly enhance the leader's ability in each phase of the cycle, but a team may also tend to constrain the leader along conventional paths and make it more difficult to think "out of the box." In the end it all comes back to the leader: "When you wash dishes, wash dishes."

SOMALI ROAD

When Army forces went into Somalia in December 1992, their commanders quickly began to refine their estimates and plans using the Leadership Action Cycle. Their initial objectives were to work with international relief agencies to stem the starvation and dying. These goals were fairly quickly met, but longer-term solutions were initially elusive. As the commanders took stock of the situation, what they observed was that the food crisis had been created by the destruction of the national infrastructure, which in turn had forced people out of the countryside and into small towns and villages that could not support them. Thus, longer-term resolution of the crisis required the reestablishment of sufficient infrastructure to sustain the rural economy in the interior of the country. The key to that was the badly deteriorated road network.

The decision to act came quickly. The Army deployed engineer units to reopen the most critical road links. The project, nicknamed "Somali Road," reopened more than 1,000 miles of road, opening the interior to relief agencies and truck convoys of food and matériel. Opening the roads prompted refugees to return to their homes from neighboring Kenya as well as from temporary camps in the interior.

The fighting that broke out in the fall of 1993, specifically the events of October 3 and 4, when Army forces engaged in bitter fighting in and around Mogadishu, makes it difficult even now to fully assess what we learned from our experience in Somalia. But the lessons of Somali Road were clear. An important step in this kind of disaster relief is fostering the reestablishment of the sinews of civil society, in this case the most basic elements of the economic infrastructure. The Army was later able to apply this lesson in Rwanda, where fostering conditions for the international relief agencies to reestablish themselves led to success, and in Haiti, where fostering conditions that enabled others to begin to restore the basic economy led to success.

RULE ONE: CHANGE IS HARD WORK

Leading change means doing two jobs at once—getting the organization through today and getting the organization into tomorrow. Most people will be slow to understand the need for change, preferring the future to look like today, thus displacing their lives and sense of reality as little as possible. Transformational leadership requires a personal and very hands-on approach, taking and directing action, building the confidence necessary for people to let go of today's paradigm and move into the future.

Transforming an organization is hard work because the leader and his or her leadership team must do it. Change will not spring full blown from the work of a committee or a consultant. Not everybody will agree that you are doing the right thing. You will have to spend a lot of time communicating, clarifying, generating enthusiasm, and listening (including listening to negative feedback, resistance, and genuine disagreement). You will have to spend a lot of time away from your desk and get out where the critical processes of the organization are happening. You will have to personally work the organization's external constituencies, including media that may not fully understand or appreciate what you are doing. You will have to think a lot about the future and make others do the same.

Leading change is hard work because it requires action. Your cal-

endar and diary are the most telling evidence of your commitment.
Are you spending your time with the traditional or the innovative
parts of your organization? Are you fostering experimentation and
learning? Have you delegated control within a wide range of behavior that people understand? Are you promoting the risk takers or
those who represent business as usual? Are you pictured as reinforcing the status quo or championing change in in-house magazines,
newspapers, and videos? Is your investment budget oriented to the
past or the future? Does the organization filter what it tells you? In
short, are you part of the "new" or the "old"? Words are important.
What you say is important. But people look to your actions to vali-
date your words; their behavior will reflect yours.

★ ★ ★ ★

Time to Reflect

It is easy to say that leaders must reflect; it is also hard to
do. There seem to be two ingredients: time and context.
Both are difficult to find, although time may be the easier
of the two. I took time to reflect in the study of history,
more often than not in the context of our Civil War Battlefield Parks.

On one such occasion, the Saturday after Thanksgiving
in 1994, I went to Chancellorsville, the site of an interesting battle best remembered for the tragic fratricide resulting in the death of "Stonewall" Jackson but more
interesting to me as a contrast in the timid generalship of
Union General Joseph Hooker and the risk-taking style of
Lee and Jackson in their last battle together. In November
1994, we were facing one of our seemingly endless budget
battles, we had troops in Haiti and the Persian Gulf, things
were a bit uneasy in Korea, and Bosnia was threatening. It
was not an easy time. In my notes from that day, subsequently transcribed into one of my periodic letters to the
Army's general officers, I wrote this: "As is often the case

for me when I go on a staff ride, my mind moves from then—1863—to now, and I find myself thinking more clearly about a contemporary challenge. . . . We are now not unlike commanders on a battlefield—a bit overextended in our lines. It is now time to consolidate our lines while at the same time maintaining momentum, movement, initiative." [10] My notes go on to describe how, on that crisp fall afternoon, I saw our situation in 1994, as well as my intent, my assumptions, my fears. Taking time to reflect that day helped me clarify our strategic situation.

I also read a lot of biography. The ghosts speak to me. I told this anecdote to a group at West Point one evening:

"Here's what one brigade commander, relating his first contact, said to me about that learning experience. 'As we approached the brow of the hill from which it was expected we could see the enemy's camp and possibly find his men ready formed to meet us, my heart kept getting higher and higher until it felt to me as though it was in my throat. I would have given anything to be back in Illinois, but I had not the moral courage to halt and consider what to do; I kept right on. . . . The place where the enemy had been encamped a few days before was still there . . . but the troops were gone. My heart resumed its place. It occurred to me that the enemy had been as much afraid of me as I had been of him. . . . From that event to the close of the war, I never experienced trepidation upon confronting an enemy. . . . I never forgot that he has as much reason to fear my forces as I had his. The lesson was valuable.'

"That brigade commander wasn't out at the National Training Center. He wasn't in Panama or Germany. He was Ulysses S. Grant, then colonel of the 21st Illinois Regiment of volunteers. He spoke to me, through his memoirs. Telling me to persevere." [11]

History does not repeat itself. Going to battlefields and reading biography does not prepare one to solve tomorrow's problems. Human nature and the human condition, though, do replicate themselves. Standing on battlefields asking "Why?" gave me insights into how other leaders have handled difficult and ambiguous challenges. Understanding Grant's fears gave me counsel of my own. History gave me context.

Your context will be different. Some people tell me the most valuable part of their day is getting outdoors in the early morning, taking time to be alone with their thoughts, perhaps running or walking, stretching themselves physically. Some find their context during sojourns to new places. Some find it in a sport or hobby that forces their mind to switch gears and lock itself into a different world. What worked for me will not necessarily work for you and vice versa.

But you can make the time. And you can find your best context. You just have to do it.

As you reflect, you must ask the same three questions that Hal Moore asked himself in the Ia Drang Valley: "What is happening? What is not happening? What can I do to influence the action?" When all is said and done, being a leader is about standing up, making judgments, accepting responsibility, and taking action. Twenty years from now, people won't ask how you did last quarter; they will ask whether or not you created a future.

—GRS

★ ★ ★ ★

Values: The Leverage of Change

Touchstones

One of the most important lessons we learned during the rebuilding of the Army after Vietnam was the importance of values—a commitment by all soldiers to something larger than themselves. Army officers, noncommissioned officers, and soldiers alike were adrift in the late 1960s and early 1970s. Knowing that, the Army's first post-Vietnam chief of staff, General Creighton Abrams, chartered a small group of midcareer officers to look at the Army's officer corps with particular focus on the moral and ethical foundation of the officer corps.

Abrams was a legend in the Army. West Point class of 1936, he had risen rapidly in rank during World War II, commanding the first tank battalion into Bastogne to re-

lieve the 101st Airborne Division in the tough fighting of
the Battle of the Bulge.[1] His last job before becoming Army
chief was as commander in Vietnam. He knew firsthand
the difficulties facing the Army, and he knew how to begin
the long job of turning things around. General Abrams
knew that the Army needed to reinvest in its deep sense of
values by emphasizing people, and commitment to a strong
ethical foundation.

The results of the study Abrams chartered were unset-
tling. It revealed deep-seated cynicism, a perception of
widespread dishonesty in determining readiness, incompe-
tence to handle the demands of peacetime, and excessive
favoritism and self-serving behavior on the part of many officers. Many would have preferred to avoid the unpleasant-
ness of confronting the problem. But ultimately, this study
and similar efforts gave Abrams and those who followed
him the basis for tackling this difficult issue. Ultimately, it
led to much stronger individual and institutional values.

There are many concrete examples of the resulting
shift in emphasis, of leaders taking units back to values.
The Army's core values of courage, candor, commitment,
and competence were given a place in both the doctrinal
literature and Army Regulations. More important, senior
officers were sharing their personal values with their subordinates, in writing and in seminars, to help provide junior leaders with a moral foundation for their actions. That
work was carried on in our schools, in our units, and in our
literature. Efficiency reports—our periodic performance
appraisals—began to emphasize the assessment of such
professional ethics as integrity, selflessness, and moral
courage. These changes did not create a perfect institution,
but they did help to create an institution in which human
frailty is not overlooked and values count.

Shared values are the foundation of today's Army. People and units know what to expect and that they can count
on one another. Each soldier can see him- or herself not
only as individually important and responsible but also as

part of a much greater whole. It is shared values that in October 1993 prompted Master Sergeant Gary I. Gordon and Sergeant First Class Randall D. Shughart to give their lives trying to save a downed aircrew in Mogadishu, Somalia, in an action for which they were posthumously awarded the Medal of Honor.

In the turmoil of downsizing, it was critical that we not lose this strong identification with values. The year 1992 was especially traumatic for America's Army. The euphoria over our victory in the Persian Gulf quickly gave way to turbulence and hard work. Redeployment involved moving half a million men and women home from the Gulf; at the same time, their equipment was in transit or out of service for refurbishment for months. More than 100,000 Desert Storm troopers had come from garrisons in Europe that were scheduled to be closed; most returned to Europe only long enough to link up with their families and move back to the United States. In the year after the Gulf War we released 213,000 soldiers from active duty and recruited 80,000 for a net loss of 133,000.[2] All of that was in addition to demobilizing 147,000 National Guard and Army Reserve troops called up for the Gulf War. Those are enormous numbers. Faced with that kind of turbulence, we knew the Army could change its character at the grass roots very quickly and could easily become disoriented, losing its sense of values and purpose. In 1989 and 1990, Carl Vuono had stressed pace and continuity, warning that rapid demobilization would have a negative impact on readiness and morale. My challenge now was to deal with the acceleration he had warned against.

Our soldiers did not need to be told about change; they were being overwhelmed by it. As the leader, I realized that I needed to emphasize continuity: to help soldiers and their families understand what would not change. I wanted them to understand that the Army might be asking them to do different things and to endure unexpected hardships but that the Army's essence would not change. Knowing that our roots give us a sense of identity, I knew I could draw on the Army's history to find symbols of its enduring values.

Thus, I began to use my speeches, articles, and other communications to emphasize normative themes, using symbols to capture the essence of our shared values: the soldier (and by extension his or her family), our sense of commitment, and our sense of duty and service to nation. I did not deny what I called "physical change," the tough business of getting smaller and relocating, of seeing proud colors retired; and I continued to emphasize growth, the process of becoming something different, to help people gain confidence in the future. But above all else, I wanted to emphasize that in our journey we would not leave our essence behind. I began this in my annual address to the Association of the United States Army in October 1991, when I asked my audience to "take a trip with me." In our minds we visited Lexington Common, where it had all begun; Antietam with its towering monument: "NOT FOR THEMSELVES, BUT FOR THEIR COUNTRY"; then Fort Leaven-worth, the dowager queen of frontier posts and today the crossroads of the Army. Next we went to Normandy and the cemetery overlooking Omaha Beach; then to today's united Berlin; and finally to the Vietnam Memorial, to which Americans go, day and night, to honor soldiers. I told them, "This is the essence of America's Army. Compe-tence, character, sacrifice—Duty, Honor, Country; linked inextricably with this nation; achieving victory; protecting the Republic." I concluded, "I am confident that these val-ues will persevere—today they are our roots, and tomorrow they will be our legacy. There is strength for us in our Army's history. The values imbedded in our history are the foundation on which change must be based."[3]

In later speeches, I shifted my emphasis from past achievement to talk about the men and women who exem-plify those symbols around the world today. I talked not only about men like Gordon and Shughart, but also about ordinary soldiers, men and women performing their duties selflessly in the Sinai, Macedonia, Rwanda, Cuba—around the world. One of the most powerful moments in my tour of duty as chief of staff resulted in one such example that I repeated over and over. In December 1993, I went to Fort Drum in upstate New York to participate in a welcome-home ceremony for a battalion returning from Somalia. That's where I met Chris Reid.

Because of the bitterly cold weather, the ceremony was held in a field house. Family members, friends, and fellow soldiers filled the huge hall. Flags and banners covering the walls welcomed the soldiers home from their difficult campaign in Mogadishu and the surrounding countryside. Their tour of duty had been unusually long, and they had seen and participated in some tough fighting.

As I stood on the small reviewing stand, I noted a soldier with a cane walking with difficulty to take his place in the ranks. I watched him stand proudly with his comrades during the brief ceremony. As the troops were dismissed into the waiting arms of their friends and families, I walked down to see if I could find the soldier with the cane. I did, and I shall never forget him. He was Sergeant Christopher Reid, 3d Platoon, Charlie Company, 14th Infantry, 10th Mountain Division.

Sergeant Reid had been wounded in action on September 25, when fighting had erupted in Mogadishu. He told me his squad and members of his platoon had fought through three city blocks to reach a downed U.S. Army helicopter. The last thing he remembered was the heat of the helicopter burning and everything turning red. When he woke up, he was in a hospital, missing a leg and part of an arm. Chris told me his story in a strong, unwavering voice. He did not have to be there that cold, winter morning, but he wanted to be with his squad, with his friends, one more time. He then looked into my eyes and with great determination said, "You know, sir, knowing what I know now, I would do it again."

Chris Reid is not alone in my memory. There are many others. In my mind's eye, I can see their faces. I can recite their names, ordinary men and women somehow raised to greatness. They exemplify what we are trying to achieve: selfless service to their nation and to one another. Invariably, they accomplished more than we in Washington could ever imagine. They are the evidence that a generation of hard work to reinstall values in our Army paid off.

The strength of our values was a theme that I returned to over and over. In a very difficult time, I believe that going back to our values, our essence, gave us the strength and direction we needed. Some may have thought I was too strident or too optimistic, but I think that, if anything, I was not strident enough when I was talking about values. I think a frequent failing of people in leadership positions is that they are likely to be too reticent, too timid about extolling virtue. We have a tendency to want to talk about the "substantive" things, the numbers or whatever. But our people also need to hear us talk about the normative things. Those are the real substance. As the leader, you must create a moral context for what you are trying to accomplish. No matter what your organization does or hopes to do, it revolves around people, and inside each individual there is an ideal person that you must draw out. You have to keep going back to values.

—GRS

Values give an organization a self-ordering quality, a kind of organizational ballast, which provides direction and stability in periods of turmoil, stress, and change. They give both leaders and followers a basis for looking more confidently beyond the issues of the day.

As our organizations come to grips with the need to transform, a well-articulated and widely held set of beliefs about substance enables people to understand that what they do can evolve over time. This is important not just to shareholders, not just to employees, not just to portfolio managers and analysts, and certainly not just to the evening news commentators and other pundits, but also to an organization in its largest sense. Effective leaders understand that core values rooted deeply within the people who make up an organization are the essence of its organizational culture and an enormous source of strength.

UNDERSTANDING THE ESSENCE OF YOUR ORGANIZATION

In a discussion with the leaders of one of America's leading companies recently, we were chided, "Remember, we're in business to make money for the stockholders," as if to suggest that as soldiers we did not understand the importance of financial results. We discussed that idea for a few minutes and posed the question "If we could persuade you that the return on your assets would be greater if you were in software, would you get out of the business you are in and go into software?" The answer came back quickly: "Of course not, we're not a software company." This company, like many others, in public statements and in private conversation, states a belief that profitability—responsibility to stockholders—drives what they do in a strategic sense. But in fact, that is only one element in a complex mosaic of organizational values.

Think of America's great corporations: Motorola, with its genuine focus on people and organizational learning; Nordstrom, with its legendary focus on customer service; Coca-Cola, with its exceptional focus on quality and value; Harley-Davidson, which rebuilt itself on the basis of quality and its legendary trademark; L. L. Bean, which has grown from a simple Maine outfitter to a national market leader by sticking to customer service and never compromising on quality; Johnson & Johnson, with its deep sense of contribution to society; Hewlett-Packard and its uncompromising integrity. The list could go on; every reader has candidates. The point is that the common attribute of those companies is not longevity or even profitability but a strong sense of values that represents something much more important than what they "do." In their book *Built to Last*, James Collins and Jerry Porras write, "we did not find 'maximizing shareholder wealth' or 'profit maximization' as the dominant driving force or primary objective through the history of most of the visionary companies."[4] *The reality is that companies with a strong sense of values are the most successful over time.*

In winning organizations, the corporate sense of identity is more important than short-term performance because it creates the strategic context within which an organization can accommodate today's events and fulfill its responsibilities to all its constituents. A weak sense of identity dissipates energy and focus, contributing to dysfunctional short-term behavior or even failure; a strong sense of identity provides a much better basis for successful action. Make no mistake, you have to achieve, on a consistent basis, recognizable success, be it trained and ready divisions, as in the case of the Army, return on assets, earnings per share, or whatever. It would be wrong to pretend otherwise. "The numbers" are an important measure of success, and people look at them every day. But long-term success derives from a sense of purpose and shared values, which, when all is said and done, is much more substantive than "the numbers."

RULE TWO: LEADERSHIP BEGINS WITH VALUES

Shared values express the essence of an organization. They bind expectations, provide alignment, and establish a foundation for transformation and growth. By emphasizing values, the leader signals what will not change, providing an anchor for people drifting in a sea of uncertainty and a strategic context for decisions and actions that will grow the organization. Leadership begins with values.

Capturing the Essence: Motorola

Motorola is one of America's most remarkable and most successful corporations. One basis of that success is a strong sense of shared values, a common corporate ethic that provides a foundation for individual responsibility. Every "Motorolan" carries a card in his or her pocket or clipped to his or her security badge. It summarizes Motorola's fundamental objective, key beliefs, key goals, and key initiatives—all on a card the size of your driver's license. The company's key beliefs are "A constant respect for people" and "Uncompromising integrity"—not many words, but powerful ideas.

Out of this process of values clarification has come an even more powerful manifestation of values called "Individual Dignity Entitlement" and subtitled "Renewing Our People Values." Individual Dignity Entitlement is a six-point creed, phrased as questions for the employee and his or her immediate superior:

- Do you have a substantive, meaningful job that contributes to the success of Motorola?

- Do you know the on-the-job behaviors and have the knowledge base to be successful?

- Has the training been identified and made available to continuously upgrade your skills?

- Do you have a personal career plan and is it exciting, achievable, and being acted upon?

- Do you receive candid, positive or negative, feedback at least once every 30 days which is helpful in improving your personal performance or achieving your personal career plan?

- Is there appropriate sensitivity to your personal circumstances, gender, and/or cultural heritage so that such issues do not detract from your success?

Our friends at Motorola tell us that Individual Dignity Entitlement is a hard standard to meet but that, in striving to meet it, they have made progress not simply in strengthening their shared "people values" but in building a climate of shared responsibility.

Some suggest that this kind of manifestation of shared values is window dressing, but the evidence is quite to the contrary. Motorolans strive to live by these beliefs, and together they have built one of the greatest corporations in the world.

Identifying Organizational Values

One logical place to look for evidence of organizational values is in the published statements an organization makes about itself. An even more important place to look, however, is in the organization's actions. The official value set—shown by the posters on the walls—may be at odds with actual practice. So the best way to think about organizational values may be empirically, by asking the question "What do you mean when you say . . . ?" For example, if you say your organization values its people, ask yourself how that value is manifested. Ask your people how it is perceived. The declared policy may be quite different from the real one.

Dissonance between stated values and actual values is commonplace. Dissonance tends to be driven by the clock or by the calendar. Investing in values is a long-term undertaking, and in the short term it is almost impossible to measure the bottom-line contribution from programs that develop values. Looking at today's "in" box, it often appears to be easier to "fix" a problem—any problem—than to try to build a future in which different behaviors will prevent it from occurring. For just that reason, investing in the right values takes real moral courage on the part of the occupants of the executive suite. Thus the question is not whether or not an organization is values-based; every organization is values-based. The question is, what are the values, and are they the ones that will help the organization prosper in the long run?

Core values evolve uniquely in every organization, but there are some common threads a leader can use to begin a process of value clarification and redefinition. Thinking about values as issues will not necessarily yield a poster for your wall, but it does provide a starting point from which you can begin to clarify your real values and think about how you may need to change them.

Purpose

People who belong to an organization with a strong sense of purpose can identify themselves with that purpose. Like the proverbial medieval stonemason, they can see themselves in a context far greater than their immediate roles—not just cutting stones but building cathedrals. We wanted every soldier to identify him- or herself not merely as a soldier, nor merely with a job or a unit or a base, but as a soldier in America's Army, something bigger and more important than any of us; something with such an enduring sense of purpose that each of us was enriched by our sense of belonging.

Continuity

Far too many organizations disregard their history. Often there is a sense, sometimes articulated, sometimes not, that what is done is done; you do not look back. Certainly, there is little to be gained in wringing our hands over yesterday's decisions; but to ignore our history is to deny ourselves a strength. The past is a reflection of our collective identity and enhances our sense of being. History can give us confidence in the knowledge that others have succeeded in the face of adversity—that we are not the first men and women to face enormous challenges. And it can give us the strength to go on where others have failed. In Chapter 3, we mentioned the 1965 battle at LZ X-Ray in Vietnam. The unit in that fight was the 7th U.S. Cavalry, the unit George Armstrong Custer led to annihilation at the Little Big Horn. Cut off and surrounded by a superior force, Moore remembered that history as he fought nearly a hundred years later. He and his troopers were determined that it would not happen again. The history of the unit's defeat nearly one hundred years before was a strength. Your organization must preserve its victories, its accomplishments, its heroes—not just because of what they once were but because of what they represent: engineering excellence, research and development excellence, best in class, customer excellence, moral courage, determination, creative genius, community service, whatever. Names are important, trademarks are important—not just because of market equities but because of what they represent to the people who stand behind them. Never underestimate the power of a winning tradition.

People

People and organization are inseparable; you cannot value your organization without valuing the people in it. You cannot expect your people to have a customer focus or a commitment to quality, or to seek greater responsibility, unless you value them as much as you value whatever it is that you produce. How we value people shows in how we hire and fire them, our commitment to training and development, equal opportunity, pay, benefits, all the usual components of the human resources scorecard. Even more important, however, is how we delegate and share responsibility, how we distribute leadership. We can value our people as a replaceable "factor of production" or as a renewable asset to be developed and cultivated. The choice is up to us.

Responsibility

We sometimes find leaders who want to assume a kind of absolute, unlimited responsibility for everything that happens in an organization. In fact, the leader's role is not to *take* responsibility so much as to *invest* it. Leaders must build subordinates who take responsibility for their own actions and are capable of independent action. That is the real sense of empowerment—not just the freedom to do one's job but the freedom to define it. Empowerment is not about "power" at all; it is about responsibility. It derives from a sense of responsibility without which the whole notion of empowerment is as meaningless as it is dangerous.

Integrity

Our use of the word "integrity" as an organizational value is not as a synonym for honesty, though honesty does tend to flow from integrity. Rather, we use it to mean a strong pattern of internal consistency. A colleague, a CEO of a large corporation, told us that in his judgment, he could raise prices 15 percent and still sell as much of his principal product as the company could produce. Alternatively, he said, he could produce more and hold the line on price but at the expense of quality. He said, "Either would be the wrong thing to do. In the short run, at least, we could make more money, but we have an obligation to deal fairly with our customers and to do what's best for the company in the long run." His statement shows a genuine integrity, a commitment to consistently doing the right thing for the long run, regardless of the short-term pressures or temptations.

SUSTAINING OUR VALUES WHILE DOWNSIZING

The bedrock of the Army's post-Vietnam renaissance was the realization, in the late 1970s, that a professional force could be achieved and sustained only by recruiting and retaining quality soldiers. Being a soldier in today's complex world makes unique demands on a young person, and the best indicators that a person can meet those demands are a high school diploma and above-average test scores. Recruits meeting those standards are more easily trained, capable of meeting higher standards, more easily socialized to their new environment, and more likely to spend less time away from their duties— in other words, bringing in quality recruits gave us better units and a better return on our recruiting establishment and training base. Achieving that objective required building a professional recruiting organization; ensuring an adequate quality of life for soldiers and their families; providing adequate pay and benefits, especially educational benefits; and creating advertising that stressed soldierly values. We were competing for the very best young people in America and offering them the opportunity to serve for a few years or a career, and to return to civilian life enriched by their experience. Every year got a little better until, by the end of the 1980s, virtually all our recruits were mature high school graduates with solid test scores.

The resulting organizational effectiveness has been extraordinary. It was evident in the performance of the Desert Storm Army. The magnificence of that Army was not simply that it performed well on the battlefield but that it conducted the entire deployment with very little of the indiscipline that had always characterized similar operations. Today's Army is essentially drug free and enjoys substantially lower levels of violent crime than the society it serves. Military offenses, such as desertion, have never been at lower levels than they are today. We knew we could not sustain that quality Army without attracting a constant stream of recruits that met the tough standards of the 1980s and without continuing to invest in education and training.

The second, equally important underpinning in rebuilding the Army after Vietnam was the commitment to formalized leader development, not just for commissioned officers but for all leaders, including the leaders of the Army's large civilian workforce. By the 1980s, the Army had put into place a structured program of leader development that related formal training and experience to selection, promotion, and assignment for all ranks. From the soldier's perspective, leader development was the ladder to opportunity. From the Army's perspective, competent leaders developed to uniform standards sustained quality across the force. A howitzer section chief at Fort Sill, Oklahoma, could now be relied on to perform pretty much like a howitzer section chief in Baumholder, Germany, or Camp Casey, Korea. That kind of leader stability enabled us to handle turbulence with much less difficulty than would otherwise have been expected.

As the extent of the downsizing began to be felt, the most important questions soldiers had concerned our ability to sustain the quality of the force and our enduring commitment to leader development. Sergeants—and many commissioned officers—remembered the "before and after" of the quality revolution, and they knew we could not sustain ourselves as the best in the world if we could not attract and retain the best America had to offer. They wanted to know that we would not walk away from quality programs to save a few dollars or to keep more units on the active rolls. Hence, the first step in transforming the Army was to sustain quality and leader development, and the first value we chose to reinforce was the value the Army places on people.

It is worth emphasizing that this was not mere rhetoric. Keeping the schools open, with most of the same courses, for a smaller force and keeping quality people coming in the front door took real money. Successful recruiting depends on having top-notch recruiters on the street, and the reality of the 1990s is that the cohort of eighteen-year-olds is shrinking. We learned the hard way that a one-third reduction in the force could not be matched by a one-third reduction in recruiters. We actually had to increase the number of recruiters in proportion to the size of the force. In leader development, the Army has been able to scale back some courses and leverage technology, but here also we could not make cuts that were proportional to the end-strength cuts.

Managing Downsizing

Maintaining this commitment to people while downsizing required implementing a number of policies. First, in an apparent paradox, *we continued to recruit while downsizing.* We also carefully balanced voluntary and involuntary departures to shape the future force. It would have been possible to shrink the Army by simply curtailing recruiting and by creating incentives for indiscriminate voluntary departures. But we had to look ahead five years, ten years, and try to visualize the force we would need. Creating a good sergeant or a competent commissioned officer takes years; the lieutenants the Army recruits this year are the pool from which it will select generals twenty-five years hence. A constant flow in and out was necessary to keep the force refreshed and to ensure an adequate pool of future leaders.

Second, we had to have the right skill mix for the future force. To achieve that goal, we curtailed voluntary departures of people with skills we needed while encouraging departures of those with surplus skills. We could see that by 1995 we would settle down at around

500,000 active strength, so in 1991 we started to structure the force to that number, to that skill mix, even though at that time our strength was still above 700,000. For example, we could tell approximately how many infantry battalion commanders we would need at 500,000, and we were able to adjust the number of infantry lieutenant colonels, from whom battalion commanders are drawn, so that today an infantry officer has the same opportunity to command relative to his peers that his counterpart had ten years ago. Although there are fewer battalions, promotions are coming on time, the very best can aspire to be advanced early, and competition for the most sought-after positions is reasonable.

We paid a price for that. It would have been easier simply to have pulled the plug on raw numbers, to have frozen promotions, or to have stopped recruiting lieutenants; but none of those easier-to-use tools would have led to a healthy environment for those who stayed. Getting the right skill mix for the future force was essential to maintaining both the effectiveness of the force and individual opportunity.

In all of this, we worked hard to treat people with dignity and respect. Everyone in the Army, be they active duty, Army Reserve, National Guard, or civilian, is a volunteer. By treating each departing soldier or civilian and his or her family with as much respect as possible, we affirmed both their importance and the importance of those remaining. We created an entirely new outplacement service to help soldiers relocate and assume new lives as productive civilians. It was an investment we could ill afford in the eyes of some, but doing otherwise would have been inconsistent with our view of the importance of soldiers. We wanted both those leaving and those staying to know that they were individually important to the Army. Even though the Army will eventually downsize by three quarters of a million (active, guard, reserve, and civilian) and in spite of an improving economy (which creates competition for the best recruits) and declining demographics, the 1990s have been the best recruiting and retention years in the Army's history.

USING STORIES TO REINFORCE COMMITMENT

The second basic value we consciously reinforced was *commitment*—the relationship among soldiers. The commitment soldiers make to one another and to the units to which they belong can be a life-and-death bond; this is different in the military than in most walks of life, but we should not trivialize the role of commitment in nonmilitary organizations. This was the most difficult of our basic values to affirm because commitment is something each individual internalizes in a unique way. We were able to do it by talking and writing about it, and we were helped by our history and tradition. One way we did this was by telling stories that reminded all of us of our commitment.

One such story concerned General Ulysses S. Grant and General William T. Sherman, friends who had first fought together in the western theater in the American Civil War. The story had been used by others, such as Major General Walt Ulmer, who used it with his officers in the 3d Armored Division in 1982. It is part of the heritage of Army values. Telling it was part of the process of handing down values from one generation to the next.

In his 1863 campaign, Grant was frustrated in his attempts to control the Mississippi River. His foes were formidable and the geography was even worse, making it very difficult for him to mass his effort. He realized that the North was becoming demoralized and that if his force was seen as faltering, as had happened repeatedly to the armies in the East, it would strengthen the hand of those seeking a negotiated settlement and the dissolution of the Union. Grant pressed his army into the field, overextending his logistics system. As he closed on Vicksburg in the spring of 1863, he relied on a fragile network of forward supply lines, ultimately cutting them all and living off the land, campaigning the final three weeks on five days of quartermaster rations. This put an enormous burden on his engineers and supply corps to open new bases and roads.

Grant's audacity paid off by giving him the freedom to maneuver, to mass his force, and to maximize its effectiveness. He succeeded in trapping his enemy inside the fortifications at Vicksburg, and in July 1863 the city fell. Vicksburg had been the last Confederate stronghold in the West, and its capture divided the Confederacy along the Mississippi, opening the rich agricultural areas of the southeastern states to invasion from the west.[5]

The following spring, General Grant was ordered to Washington to assume command over all the Federal armies, and General Sherman, Grant's subordinate throughout the battles in the West, took his place. Sherman wrote Grant a letter. He admitted to having had "points of doubt," but he said this to his friend: "I knew wherever I was that you thought of me, and if I got in a tight place you would come—if alive."[6]

The example of Sherman and Grant epitomizes personal commitment, the fact that soldiers can count on one another to perform to the best of their ability, to adhere to standards, to embody organizational values. It is this sense of commitment that we saw in the fighting in Somalia and that we see, displayed less dramatically, wherever we find American soldiers around the world. Talking about it as a virtue helped make it stronger. Talking about it helped people understand that it would not change—that they, when they needed help, could count on one another and on the United States of America.

REDEFINING SERVICE

Finally, we drew on our sense of history to make sure that soldiers understood that, in a democracy, *service* means much more than fighting and winning the nation's big wars. For a generation of soldiers steeped in the Cold War and the stories of our big wars, this was not an easy concept to grasp.

"Service to nation" became the basis of our vision. It means the dirty work of ambiguous little wars, long separations from family and friends, and stepping in when the people of America need help, as soldiers did, for instance, in the aftermath of Hurricane Andrew. The United States Army had done similar things in its long history, but they were unfamiliar to soldiers who, up to 1989, had experienced one of the least active periods in our history and for whom such operations had been a diversion from the vital business of deterring the Soviet Union.

THE TRUST BUCKET

The inner strength that derives from values gives each member of an organization strength and confidence; it motivates and inspires performance and builds genuine loyalty. People are motivated by personal rewards, but there are other, intangible motivations that are much more important. People aspire to identify with organizations that they can respect and to perform work that contributes value in a way that they can understand. Shared values foster both moral courage and self-confidence; they help people understand expectations; they help define acceptable behavior. Shared values provide strength for leaders to look beyond the "crisis *du jour*" and provide a sense of identity that is insurance against mindless fad surfing. This common set of values fuels an organization's self-confidence and provides a basis for genuine strategic alacrity, creativity, and boldness.

Ultimately, shared values foster trust. The basic pattern of an Industrial Age bureaucracy is checking and cross-checking to ensure that process complies with standards and that the organization makes its numbers. Such an organization is based on the assumption that getting the parts right will ensure the optimization of the whole. This leftover Newtonian world is deterministic and reductionist. Margaret Wheatley argues that better, more appropriate organizational metaphors are found in twentieth-century science, particularly quantum physics: "When the world ceased to be a machine, when we began to recognize its dynamic, living qualities, many familiar aspects of it disappeared. . . . In the quantum world, relationships are not just interesting; to many physicists, they are *all* there is to reality." [7]

Shared organizational values make possible the trust that underlies the relationships among the constituents of the organization. There is no simple recipe for building trust. In his book *Super Moti-*

vation, Dean Spitzer talks about the "trust bucket," suggesting that building trust is like filling a bucket of water drop by drop. Think how difficult that task would be and how valuable a bucket of water would be in a world where buckets were filled with eyedroppers. Trust begins by carefully defining individual and corporate expectations. Leaders can contribute to a climate of trust by demonstrating commitment, moral courage, honesty, respect for human dignity, and integrity.

Trust, then, in the sense in which we are using the word, is not about adherence to codes or procedures but rather about adherence to values. It is knowing how someone will act in a situation not because the employee manual contains a scripted example but rather because you know how that person will interpret his or her responsibility, think, make judgments, decide, and communicate intent. What the Army found as it brought in quality people and invested in their development is that our traditional approaches had far underestimated most soldiers' potential. From time to time, individuals do make errors in judgment, but the poor decisions are overwhelmed by the good ones. Today, we see that the very best organizations everywhere are learning the same thing: Leadership begins with values.

CHAPTER 5

Seeing the Elephant

★ ★ ★ ★

The Power of Vision

During the American Civil War, soldiers spoke of their first battle as "seeing the elephant." By and large, these were simple men, unsophisticated and young; many were newly arrived immigrants, and most had neither seen nor could imagine an elephant. Likewise, they could scarcely imagine the terror and confusion of battle, pitting hundreds, sometimes thousands, of men against one another at close range in an intense struggle to survive and win. They controlled their fears by nicknaming their tomorrow after the monstrous, fearsome animal of their imagination.

It is the leader's responsibility to see the elephant—to see the future. To create the future, you must first "see" it; then you must communicate it in a way that the organization can understand, calming its fears and boosting its confidence.

At the end of the Cold War, military leaders were faced

with the need to make major adjustments. In the years since Vietnam, the future for which we had prepared had been war in central Europe between NATO and the Warsaw Pact. Our unblinking focus on Western Europe had been correct, but it had narrowed some people's vision to simply beating the Soviets. That began to change in the summer and fall of 1989, when Carl Vuono began to talk about the Army as a strategic force.[1] But at the time, there were few such voices; for many reasons, most people were reluctant to give up their Cold War vision of the elephant.

In 1991, as the new Chief, I needed to harness the collective wisdom and energy of the Army to help people define and understand a new future. Fighting and winning the nation's wars would always be our core mission, but we had to come to grips with an understanding of what those wars would be. As I wrestled with the challenges of the post–Cold War world, I tried to mentally position myself in the future and, in my mind's eye, look back. It is a technique used by distance runners and other athletes—they "see" themselves at the finish line and "look back" to pull themselves along. Seeing themselves at the finish line, in the future, gives them the intense concentration needed to win and eases the constant pounding and pain of the event.

Imagining myself in the future enabled me to disregard the constraints of today and all the reasons why the future was impossible. Our people today are doing the best that they can with what we have given them. To imagine a new "best," you have to imagine a new context.

And as I tried to imagine what the Army would be like in the future, I attempted to "look back" from there and see the pathways leading to it. They looked very different looking back from tomorrow than they did looking out from today. From today, we see our paths linearly, making marginal improvement. From the future, we can more easily see which paths are the most important, which will lead to quantum improvements. This pattern of thought enabled me to think about the transformation of the Army in all its manifestations—not simply to create a vision but to connect the vision to today's reality in a meaningful way.

I know that my thoughts were at best imprecise. My imprecision was difficult for some of our people to handle. Many people would have been more comfortable with the precision of linear thinking. I knew that there would be many twists and turns in my imagined paths. But the mental exercise helped me create a vision of the future, and it helped me give it some substance that people could understand. I sometimes think that people expect their leaders to create certainty, but that is impossible. What a leader can—and must—do is create a vision, a context within which an organization can act to create its future.

—GRS

★ ★ ★ ★

Thinking and Doing

Vision is a sense of the future. It is an imagined possibility, stretching beyond today's capability, providing an intellectual bridge from today to tomorrow, and forming a basis for looking ahead, not for affirming the past or the status quo. The power of a vision is that it gives leaders a basis for positive action, growth, and transformation.

To be an effective beacon, a vision must describe the future in terms that people can easily grasp and understand. It must incorporate some concept of success that is simple enough for people to understand in operational terms; that is, they must be able to apply it to their role in the organization, to their job. This concept of success does not have to be measurable in a quantitative sense, though it can be; but it must be articulated in such a way that people can understand what it means to achieve it.

A vision empowers leaders by transcending day-to-day issues, creating a future context within which they can operate. A leader uses vision and values to mobilize people, to facilitate change and growth, to create a future for his or her organization. A vision is the first step in transforming the organization.

A Shared Vision . . .

- Provides a corporate sense of being.

- Provides a sense of enduring purpose.

- Incorporates a measure of success.

- Transcends day-to-day issues.

- Has legitimate meaning in both the present and the future.

- Empowers both leaders and followers to act.

RULE THREE: INTELLECTUAL LEADS PHYSICAL

The most important phase of the exercise of strategic leadership is the front-end work—the in-depth, serious thinking by a leader and his or her team—that results in the creation of an intellectual framework for the future. Imaging the future first takes place in the mind of the leader and then must be communicated throughout the organization. This intellectual change guides the physical changes—in process, structure, and output—that manifest the transformation. Without the tough up-front work of intellectual change, physical change will be unfocused, random, and unlikely to succeed.

Jack Welch, who since 1981 has led the ongoing transformation of General Electric as its CEO, describes it this way: "Good leaders create a vision. They articulate the vision, passionately own the vision, and relentlessly drive it to completion."[2] General George C. Marshall, the Army's World War II chief who was later secretary of state and secretary of defense, was such a leader. His extraordinary vision guided the strategy for the United States' participation in World War II, created the Army and Air Corps to achieve it, and then, in his crowning achievement, created the conditions for reconstruction and lasting peace in what came to be known as the Marshall Plan. It is hard to step back and create a vision of such breathtaking scope. But if you do not, your organization will drift.

It is not by accident that the Microsofts, the Wal-Marts, the Johnson & Johnsons, the Motorolas, and the Coca-Colas demonstrate market leadership year after year. The leaders of those companies are involved in a constant process of reflection and renewal, thinking about the future and doing the hard front-end work for change. Change must occur first in people's minds; only then can it take place in the structure, processes, performance, and output of the organization. Before you move bricks and mortar, you must move your mind. There is often a bias to shortcut the intellectual work—to "get on with it!" But you cannot act effectively without first developing an understanding of what you are trying to accomplish and how you are going to accomplish it, as well as some acceptance of what you know and what you do not know about the environment in which you will be operating.

You can think of this process of thinking and doing as being like an army advancing toward an objective on two axes (see Figure 5-1). The top axis—the "thinking," or intellectual, axis—is the more important. The bottom, or "doing," axis must take its cues from the thinking axis. The doing axis is the operating axis where successful day-to-day operations are executed and the physical changes that make an organization new and different are implemented.

There will always be tension between the two axes. Within an organization, there will be competition for resources, resistance to change, and a strong bias for current operations and short-term measures of success. Outside, there will be critics who want you to "get on with it," to "do something." At the same time as you are struggling

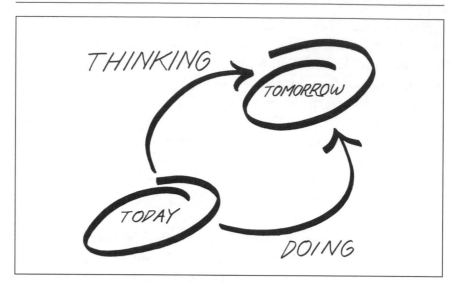

Figure 5-1—Thinking and Doing

to create the future, you *must* meet near-term expectations. The road to tomorrow leads through today.

But lots of roads lead through today, and you have to be sure you are on the right one. It is by this two-dimensional process of thinking and doing that you stay on the right road. A clear vision provides a rational context in which to change critical competencies, reengineer, divest, invest, and develop people capable of achieving the power of the vision. Actions such as cost cutting, downsizing, improving quality, and decreasing cycle time must be understood for what they are: dependent strategic variables. They can be useful, but without the serious intellectual front-end work needed to create a vision, they are only buzzwords with little enduring meaning or utility. Without the tough front-end work to provide direction, leaders truly are fad surfing at shareholder expense, but in fact there is little likelihood that they will ever catch the big wave.

PROJECT ANTAEUS:
WRITING THE HISTORY OF THE FUTURE

As General Frederick Franks, the former commander of the Army's Training and Doctrine Command, puts it, "How you think about the future influences what you think about the future, and, ultimately, what you do about the future."[3] Today's problems can be so close, so intense, that they become like blinders. Getting beyond today begins by imagining your organization out in the future. Ask yourself "What could be?" Postulate the new paradigm, and then imagine your organization in it (see Figure 5-2).

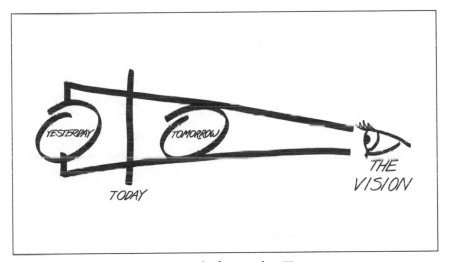

Figure 5-2—Looking Back from the Future

Many people seem uncomfortable with this process. They see it as being too much art and too little science—as irrelevant theology in a world that has deadlines to meet. It is not. It is how the Army's leaders of the 1970s and 1980s built the Army that was successful in the Persian Gulf War. It is how successful leaders in business, in all walks of life, in fact, operate: by keeping their eyes on today and on the vision—*always moving forward*.

Looking back from the future begins by going back to the most basic questions: What is your purpose as an organization; what business are you in? What will your purpose tomorrow be? What will the characteristics of your strategic environment be? What will it take to win decisively in tomorrow's markets? Don't ask yourself what the "next" organization will look like but rather what the organization "after next" will look like. The "next" organization is constrained by today; it must evolve from today's organization. By imagining the "after next," organization, you can take off today's blinders and imagine your organization in a world unconstrained by its present reality. This technique does not deny the reality of the present but rather helps you think beyond it.

A colleague in an organization most of us think of as an electronics manufacturer told us that by the turn of the century more than half the value added in its products and services will come from software. He said, "We are trying to come to grips with what it means to be a software company. We are finding out that it has enormous implications for everything from our investment profile to our personnel policies." That suggests the value of being able to create an intellectual construct for the future.

A longer example may be useful. In the late 1980s, we began planning the Army's future force structure. The arms control negotiations with the Soviets showed promise of being successful and downward budget pressures had already begun, but it was impossible to think about a world in which we would *substantially* reduce our forces in Europe or the size of the Army. The two U.S. Army corps on the ground in Germany were the linchpin of the NATO short-warning plan. The bias in the then-current paradigm was to increase troops on the ground qualitatively, if not quantitatively—certainly not to decrease them.

But in late 1988, General Carl Vuono brought together a small group of planners to think about the unthinkable. Called "Project Antaeus," it assumed that the Soviet Union would remain in place and that the Warsaw Pact and NATO would continue to provide the military framework. But economic pressures and the ideological thaw were portending reduced tensions and force reductions on both sides. What would this mean?

Antaeus started by looking at Berlin, where since the end of World War II we had maintained a brigade under the Four-Power occupation agreement. First the group looked at the "next Berlin" and asked "Will the Army be in Berlin ten years from now?" The answer was "Yes" (so much for prescience!). But then they asked about the "Berlin after next": "Will we be in Berlin forever?" That time the answer was "No." In fact, our planners, seeing the momentum building in arms control, argued that we would probably be able at least to reduce our presence in Berlin within ten to twenty years. While no one was prepared to commit to bringing troops home at that point, there was a consensus that we would begin to reduce force levels at some time in the future, probably sooner than later.

That kind of thinking opened the door to a contingency planning process that helped us think about the unthinkable so that by March 1989, seven months before the Berlin Wall actually came down, we had modeled a force posture for Europe that looks remarkably as it does today at one third its Cold War level. The "failure" of the project was only in its sense of timing. The Antaeus planners suggested that it would take ten to twenty years to accomplish what, in fact, took place in about four years under very different conditions from those they had assumed. Timing, however, is the most difficult and least important dimension of this kind of planning. The more useful dimensions are direction and what we called "signposts"—indicators that critical assumptions are failing and new opportunities developing.

While there is no substitute for a truly creative mind, there are some structured ways in which the paradigm after next can be envisioned.

One method we used effectively was to look very hard at the lessons of history. In the case of the Army, our history reminded us that there is a difference between that which is truly new and that which is merely unfamiliar. Disaster relief, for example, was a new mission to the soldiers who went to south Florida after Hurricane Andrew in 1992. But from a longer perspective, the Army had been involved in disaster relief since the last century. Army leaders in Florida and Washington actually used the historical accounts of the great Chicago fire and the San Francisco earthquake to help us think about the issues in Florida. The circumstances were different, but the human issues were remarkably the same: providing basic needs, ensuring public health, providing open communications, and assisting the rapid return of civil society with its duly constituted government.

As we contemplate the dawning of the Information Age, we can learn from the transition from the Agrarian Age to the Industrial Age. The Gatling gun, a multibarreled weapon that presaged the machine gun, made its debut in the American Civil War but failed because the enabling technologies were not in place. The technological concept was sound, but without better alloys, smokeless powder, and brass cartridges, and without considered employment concepts, it made little impact on the battlefield. It would be fifty years before the machine gun would be fielded in large numbers. Today we can process information much faster than we can apply it—is that an analogous growing pain? Only time will tell, but studying history helps prepare us to face the question.

Another way of seeing the future is by trying to interpret change that is taking place today. For example, the time interval between the introduction of successive generations of personal computer processor microchips has been remarkably consistent at just under four years since the 8088 chip was introduced in June 1978. Our ability to network computers and databases has grown in a similar fashion, with enormous improvements occurring at short intervals. The information capabilities we envisioned for the Army—shared situational awareness over large formations—were technologically unfeasible when we first envisioned them, but we expected them to be feasible by the time we could work out doctrinal and organizational concepts, which would not only have to leverage the next generation of technology and the generation after next but also be able to accommodate continuous change. Like computer software, our new systems must be both backward compatible and continuously improving.

Still another future-oriented technique is identifying the assumptions in the current paradigm and assessing their viability in the future. The Army's Cold War focus included an implicit assumption that we would not commit the force stationed in Germany to operations outside central Europe. There were literally no deployment plans for moving troops to the Middle East or Africa. As the Soviet threat evaporated and the former Soviet bloc stabilized, that assumption failed, creating the opportunity to use that part of the Army much more flexibly.

Regardless of the techniques you use to look into the future, your assessment must involve all the major systems of your organization. These include markets, raw materials, suppliers, physical plant, functional processes (value added), administrative processes (overhead), regulatory processes and agencies, technology, and other considerations that may be unique to your organization. All these elements must be brought together, in the future, simultaneously.

Articulating a Vision

When we applied that kind of "after next" thinking to the whole Army and asked ourselves "What business will we be in?" we saw four major roles for the Army. (1) We would fight and win on land, as we did in the Gulf. (2) We would deter war, as we are doing today in Korea and as we did for so many years in Europe. (3) We would provide reassurance to friends and allies, as we are doing today in the Sinai and Bosnia. (4) We would provide support—both international humanitarian support, such as in central Africa in the refugee crisis of 1994, and domestic support, such as in the aftermath of Hurricane Andrew in the summer of 1992. The common denominator of all these was service to nation, and that became the basis for our vision.

AMERICA'S ARMY
Trained and Ready to Fight,
Serving the Nation at Home and Abroad,
A Strategic Force, Capable of Decisive Victory—
into the 21st Century.

America's Army: A unique partnership of active, National Guard, and Reserve soldiers with their civilian employees, contractors, and families.

Trained and ready: So as not to atrophy in the manner of the 1920s or the late 1940s.

Serving the nation: A traditional, very broad concept of service.

Strategic: America's most flexible and decisive force for today's world.

Capable of decisive victory: On the battlefield, in central Africa, during hurricanes, whatever—success at whatever the nation calls upon us to do.

There are no hard-and-fast rules for what your organization's vision should look like. British Airways' recovery was sparked by a powerful, succinct vision: "The World's Favourite Airline."[4] On the other hand, we have seen visions that run to several pages, striving to be all things to all people and spilling over into the strategic plan, blurring both in the process. A short, simple vision is better because it is easier for everyone to grasp. But in the case of the Army, a short bumper sticker would have aggregated our thoughts at such a high level that people might have seen only the old and not the new. For example, we often used the phrase "To fight and win the nation's wars" as a slogan to help define our essence. More a core competency than a vision, that phrase did not sound like something different; thus it simply did not have the power to pull the organization into the future. Even more important, unless we happened to go to war, it did not lend itself to an unambiguous sense of accomplishment.

The perfect vision may be impossible to achieve. A somewhat weak vision that is well articulated and reinforced is better than constantly changing gobbledygook emanating from the executive suite. The critical test is not length or grammatical construction. The critical test is fit. A vision must fit the organization for which it was created, and it must be empowering, providing both the leader and the led a tool they can translate into strategy and action that result in real growth and change. The vision must pull the organization into the future.

ENVISIONING THE FUTURE: VISA INTERNATIONAL

One of our favorite stories about the power of vision is that of the creation of the Visa card. The story, as told by founder and CEO Emeritus Dee Hock, is a story of enormous vision, grounded in values and carried out by people.[5]

The Visa card had its genesis in a charge card called BankAmericard, created as a service of Bank of America in the 1950s and subsequently franchised to numerous banks. By 1968, as Hock says, "the infant industry was out of control." Losses were thought to be in the tens of millions of dollars, and those initial estimates turned out to be low by a factor of ten. Out of the search for a solution came a new perspective on money and a new concept of organization. As Hock puts it, "It was necessary to reconceive, in the most fundamental sense, the nature of bank, money, and credit card, even beyond that to the essential elements of each and how they might change in a microelectronics environment. Several conclusions emerged: First: money had become nothing but guaranteed, alphanumeric data recorded in valueless paper and metal. It would eventually become guaranteed data in the form of arranged electrons and photons which would move around the world at the speed of light. . . . Second: 'credit card' was a misnomer, a false concept. It was a device for the exchange of value."[6]

From this front-end work emerged a new way of thinking about money and, following that, a genuinely global network for the exchange of money. In 1970, it was a vision; in the 1990s, it is a worldwide network of more than 355 million people making more than 7 billion transactions annually,[7] in a wholly new kind of virtual organization that clears more transactions in a week than the Federal Reserve System clears in a year.[8] "Banker's hours" once meant 10 A.M. to 3 P.M. Today, thanks to Hock and his team, "banker's hours" means "anyplace, anytime," and the float we used to enjoy on our consumer debt has all but evaporated as the bill is on your account before you leave the store.

Could the Visa story have happened if the bank card industry had not been facing disaster twenty-five years ago? Is change possible in the absence of a crisis? A crisis is probably not necessary. The answer, rather, may be that real vision is (unfortunately) as rare in a crisis as it is in good times!

BUY-IN STARTS AT THE TOP

The vision for America's Army was authored by a study group of about two dozen people created to support the transition of chiefs in June 1991. People were selected so that their collective experiences would represent a broad range of skills and experiences; each member was a high-potential leader, and each brought along about twenty years of experience. It had top-down sponsorship but was junior enough and broad enough to have a healthy overall perspective. The senior leadership, including the leaders of the Army's powerful National Guard and Army Reserve constituencies, were brought on board quickly, and the vision began to spread throughout the organization. Even so, the process took several years of purposeful action and probably would have taken even longer if not for the serendipity of ongoing operations, which acted as a beacon lighting the way to the future.

Some would say that this kind of a "top-down" vision cannot be implemented, that "real" vision must somehow come "up" from "below." That view seems to miss the point. The point is buy-in and acceptance, not authorship or the source. In some organizations, the best knowledge about the future may lie several layers below the top; in others, the support of critical constituencies, such as suppliers or labor unions, may make a participative approach desirable. But authorship is not important; what is important is buy-in, and that does begin with the leadership at the very top.

It is the responsibility of the senior leadership to see the elephant and then to own it. A vision can be developed by a leader or by a group drawn from the organization to work with the leader. But if it is developed by a group, the leader must work with the group to make it his.

Once the leadership has taken ownership, the vision must be communicated and understood in a way that empowers people to seek to achieve it. That kind of buy-in is difficult precisely because a vision is intimately involved with the human dimension of an organization. *Vision challenges the people of an organization because, ultimately, it will force them to change.* It is hard to change culture. For example, for twenty years Nordstrom's growth has come from opening new stores populated by "trailblazing Nordies." They do that because in the 1970s, Nordstrom attempted an acquisition, buying three stores in Alaska, but found that changing the culture in the acquired workforce was too hard; the company has never attempted an acquisition since.[9] It takes time for a vision to become so imbedded in an organization that its ideas achieve a sustainable "critical mass." Such a process takes years.[10]

Once a vision has been articulated and the process of buy-in has begun, the vision must be continually interpreted. In some cases, the vision may be immediately understandable at every level. In other cases, it must be translated—put into more appropriate language—for each part of the organization. In still other cases, it may be possible to find symbols that come to represent the vision.

LITTLE RED APPLES: BRINGING THE VISION TO LIFE

The Army's vision was a complex set of ideas that expressed the Army's most basic competency (service to nation) but in a very broad context. Some felt that the emphasis on service would take the edge off battlefield skills. Others were troubled by the phrase "decisive victory" as evidence of backward, not forward, thinking. What is decisive victory, after all, when the mission is not combat?

We wrestled hard with that question when we put the Army onto the ground in southern Florida after Hurricane Andrew. The strategic issue was the collapse of civil society. When the military joint task force moved in, what we were really doing was propping up civil society—ensuring law and order and providing basic services—so that the relief agencies could do their work and government could be re-constituted. Soldiers brought stability, but success required more: the reestablishment of a viable, stable civil society. Realizing that, we decided our second objective, after establishing stability and provid-ing for basic needs, should be to reopen the schools. Opening the schools would get children out of the tent cities and other temporary housing and would reassure people that conquering the devastation was possible—that their lives were returning to normal.

To emphasize the importance of that objective, we went out and got several dozen plastic apples, the kind you see in inexpensive dis-plays of artificial fruit, and put them onto the desks of leaders in Washington. "An apple for the teacher" became a powerful focus both in Washington and in southern Florida. It helped the Army forces grasp that "decisive victory" meant working ourselves out of a job—and quickly. On September 14, twenty-one of twenty-three schools opened on time. People later called it the greatest demon-stration of hope they had seen up to that point in the crisis. Before then, people's main goal had been survival; after that, it began to be recovery.

There was lots more to be done. The teachers would later tell us that school that day, and that year, was not "great"; but opening the schools was the turning point. It was decisive victory.

Look for opportunities to define your organization's vision in a clear, concrete fashion, and use them to rally the energies of your people.

WHEN A VISION IS BLURRED

The leader must give clarity to the vision. If you are using a vision as a tool for distributing leadership throughout your organization, you must work hard to clarify it so that the independent actions of many people are powerfully aligned. Military history offers any number of examples of a lack of clarity of vision, one of the most dramatic being the Battle of Leyte Gulf in October 1944.

During World War II, the United States divided the Pacific region into two theaters of war, each with a strategic axis that came together at Japan itself: the Pacific Ocean Areas, commanded by Admiral Chester W. Nimitz, who made his headquarters at Pearl Harbor in Hawaii, and the Southwest Pacific Area, commanded by General Douglas MacArthur, who at the time of the battle made his headquarters with the invasion force in the Philippines. The two theater commanders shared the responsibility for engaging and defeating Japanese forces, but each was driven to a different vision by the circumstances of his theater. Nimitz's main effort was across the central Pacific, moving from island to island. For Nimitz, the critical Japanese target was its capital ships, the aircraft carriers and the fast surface ships that accompanied them. By decisively defeating the Japanese Navy, he could make the Japanese-held territory in his area of responsibility untenable and open the door to Japan itself. MacArthur fought a different kind of war. For him, the Japanese fleet was not the object so much as the islands themselves with their large garrisons and air and naval bases. From these islands, he could launch air attacks and stage even larger amphibious attacks as he closed his strategic axis on Japan.

The Leyte operation marked the first time that major forces of both commands had operated together. Admiral William F. Halsey's Third Fleet, which belonged to Nimitz, was assigned to "cover and support" MacArthur's invasion, with MacArthur's own naval forces under Vice Admiral Thomas C. Kinkaid providing the invasion fleet. The Joint Chiefs' intent was that MacArthur invade the heavily defended island of Luzon while Halsey protected him from the Japanese fleet if it appeared.

Anticipating this operation, the Japanese had prepared what historian Hanson Baldwin called "the desperate gamble, the all-out stroke—to conquer or to die." [11] In a complex attack on multiple axes, the Japanese sortied virtually all their operational combat ships to attack the flotilla supporting MacArthur's beachhead. Japanese Vice Admiral Jisaburo Ozawa led a diversionary force of four aircraft carriers and two hybrid battleship/carriers, with escorts and support ships in an "attack" from the northeast to draw off Halsey's Third Fleet and expose the invasion fleet to surface attack. But so poor was the operational capability of the Japanese Navy by this point in the war that Ozawa's force had only twenty-nine aircraft.[12]

As this complicated naval battle, the largest of the war, developed, Halsey took the bait and went after Ozawa's carriers, leaving the invasion force uncovered as the main Japanese surface attack was engaged. Disaster was averted only by the heroic action of Kinkaid's escort carriers and destroyers, whose actions created so much confusion and uncertainty that Japanese Admiral Takeo Kurita broke off his attack and withdrew before getting in among the transports and other ships supporting the invasion.

That day has been the subject of debate by military historians and serving officers ever since. Halsey's decision has frequently been blamed on poorly defined command relationships, critics charging that his relationship with MacArthur and Kinkaid had not been adequately defined. More fundamentally, however, Halsey was simply acting in accordance with the vision that had focused "his" theater, the Pacific Ocean Areas. Halsey took what in his judgment was an acceptable risk in order to defeat what he thought were the most dangerous elements of the enemy fleet. MacArthur and Kinkaid, on the other hand, shared a vision that would have kept Halsey's Third Fleet in closer proximity to the invasion force. Each saw a different elephant and acted accordingly.

"WITHOUT VISION, THE PEOPLE PERISH"

In the Book of Proverbs it is written, "Without vision, the people perish." Those words were written centuries ago, thousands of years before the first case was studied at the first business school, but they are as true today as they were then. When you find your organization in a crisis, you must have a vision resting on values to fall back on; otherwise your decisions will lack context. Failure to see the future can be attributed to many causes, but it always begins with a lack of vision.

CHAPTER 6

Creating a Strategic Architecture

Changing the Critical Processes

As important as values and vision are, they must be joined by a strategy—a set of concepts for action—before positive change can result. As we began, we did not know precisely how our strategy would evolve, but we knew the framework from which to start. In 1987, Chief of Staff General Carl E. Vuono had identified the six critical processes, which he called the "Six Imperatives,"[1] that had driven the transformation after Vietnam and into the 1980s: recruiting and retaining quality soldiers, developing leaders, training units, modernizing the force, creating the right kinds of units, and developing doctrine for the employment of the force. These were the processes the Army had used to build the Desert Storm Army. Together they form the basis of the

Army's core competence, conducting military operations on land—fighting and winning the nation's wars. We knew that our competitive advantage, our excellence in the marketplace, so to speak, comes from these critical processes.

To effect a transformation—to make a fundamental change—it was necessary to change the critical processes. But applying the barnstormer's first rule of wing walking, "Don't let go with both hands at once," our strategy for change was initially sequential, beginning with a decision to sustain Army values, readiness, and the quality of the force and to kick off the transformation by rewriting doctrine.

For an army, "doctrine" is its professional dialogue about how to conduct operations. Keeping in mind that armies spend most of their time preparing for, as opposed to actually conducting, military operations, doctrine provides a common intellectual context—how to think about operations, each one unique, so that soldiers can put them together when the time comes. Writing doctrine is analogous to documenting fundamental processes in a business.

It would have been easy to drive ahead, beginning a process of change in structure, organization, mission, or whatever without the initial emphasis on doctrine. In fact, there was pressure to do just that. Many outside the Army perceived our emphasis on doctrine as a kind of denial. Some saw us as monks retreating to our monasteries to consult the ancient tomes at a time when the world demanded action. Others cited the popularization of old theories of air and naval power and criticized the Army for a seeming lack of vision and an unwillingness to adapt to new realities.

However, I believed that moving pieces around without a clear sense of direction would be dysfunctional. That had happened immediately after Vietnam, when the Army's inability to establish a clear sense of direction quickly had discouraged many young leaders. By 1991, the Army was made up of men and women who had matured in an organization resting on doctrine. To leave that behind would have threatened both the quality of the force and the Army's sense of values—both of which were essential to our future.

I also believed that in the first two years after the Gulf War, when we were subject to severe stress as a result of downsizing and redeployment from Europe, the best way of sustaining an acceptable level of readiness was by making the initial stages of the transformation as transparent as possible. There is a limit to the amount of change an organization can absorb all at once, and with so much internal shifting going on we had time to do the less visible, less disturbing intellectual groundwork. Without a solid intellectual foundation upon which to rest training, education, leader development, equipment modernization, and organizational design, the Army could easily have become disoriented and unprepared.

Within two years, our work on doctrine had yielded a new capstone field manual, FM 100-5, "Operations," both in conventional printed format and on CD-ROM, as well as most of the "100 Series" of manuals. Together they define Army operations at the highest level; tactics and techniques of unit operations flow from these. The new doctrine included important work on strategic deployment and peacekeeping operations that had never before been published.

Over time, our work expanded to include each critical process. With the doctrine beginning to take shape, we applied it to training and leader development; we reshaped our modernization programs to integrate what we were learning about the Information Age in an empirical, and not strictly anecdotal, fashion; we began the process of developing new kinds of units; and we began to come to grips with the human dimensions of the future force. Over time, the change process gathered momentum, taking on a life of its own as people at many levels became empowered. What had begun sequentially became simultaneous, and coordi-

nated changes could be made on a broad front, all within the same coherent strategic architecture.

Transforming the Army was a process that emphasized maintaining continuity, making changes appropriate to the end of the Cold War, and growing to become a different Army: continuity, change, and growth.

—GRS

★ ★ ★ ★

What Is Strategy?

Vision without follow-through is a sure recipe for failure. In too many cases, what President George Bush called "the vision thing" goes no farther than the boardroom wall or the inside cover of the annual report. Vision and values get you to the starting line; it takes a lot of hard work to go from there to the finish line. The hard work is focused by strategy.

Strategy is the most misunderstood leadership concept today. Strategy is not about Attila the Hun or Sun-tzu; it is not about the management disciplines; nor is it about econometrics, numbers, or programmatic objectives. At its essence, strategy is an intellectual construct linking where you are today with where you want to be tomorrow in a substantive, concrete manner.

But strategy is a crossover word, used with varying degrees of precision in several disciplines. Like "new and improved" or "less fat," it too often means whatever the writer wants it to mean—and let the buyer beware. Its Greek root, *strategos*, refers both to the army (military force as an instrument of the state) and to generalship (the leadership and application of military force). Most common dictionaries frame their definitions of the word in military terms. Management literature tends to be less precise, often confusing strategic planning with what we would call programming—the setting of production, marketing, or financial goals along with precise plans to achieve them. Programming tends to be linear, extending today into tomorrow. In its correct formulation, however, strategy begins with tomorrow—the vision—and is the process of looking back and identifying the critical paths to the future.

The essential character of strategy is that it *relates ends to means*. Strategy is the set of concepts for action that relate where you are to where you want to be. Think of strategy as a bridge: values are the bedrock on which the piers of the bridge are planted, the near bank is today's reality, the far bank is the vision (see Figure 6-1). Your strategy is the bridge itself.

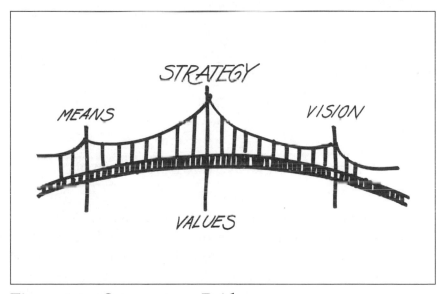

Figure 6-1—Strategy as a Bridge

Taken together, values, vision, and strategy form the strategic architecture of the organization (see Figure 6-2). Your values capture who you are and how you will operate. Your vision illuminates your purpose; it is the spark that ignites everything else. Your strategy outlines how you will achieve your vision within the context of your values. Strategy without vision is meaningless, just as vision without values has no legitimate basis. Taken together, however, they create a gestalt that is the basis for successful action.

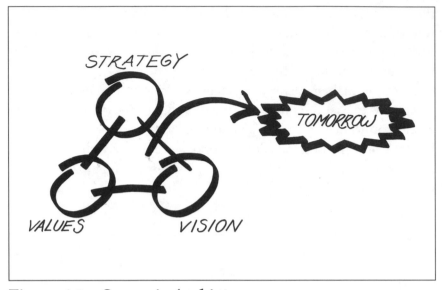

Figure 6-2—Strategic Architecture

GRANT AND THE POWER OF STRATEGIC ARCHITECTURE

Ulysses S. Grant's 1864 campaign is an instructive example of the formulation of a strategic architecture for victory. In early 1864, Grant was summoned to Washington and given command of all the Union armies. Grant was driven by his vision to restore the Union. His genius was in forging a strategy to achieve that vision. At that time, the dominant theory of victory in war was a theory of decisive battles: the objective was to win one *decisive* battle and force either the surrender of the enemy or a negotiated settlement on favorable terms. Even Lee, Grant's most formidable adversary, was guided by the theory of decisive battle. In his two invasions of the North, he sought not to crush the Union but rather to beat the Army of the Potomac in battle, to threaten Washington, and to force recognition of the Confederacy and a negotiated end to the war.

Grant's genius was in understanding that preservation of the Union could *not* come from a decisive battle. Grant realized that, for the Union to be preserved, he would have to crush the warmaking capability of the Confederacy. With Lincoln, he fashioned a strategy using the industrial power of the North, the blockade, diplomatic isolation, and the power of his armies. By 1864, the Union Army, backed by the industrial power of the North, was qualitatively superior to the Confederate Army, and Grant was able to leverage that qualitative superiority by synchronizing a massive offensive. In this last series of campaigns, Grant commanded five armies in the field:[2] those of George G. Meade in Virginia; Sherman, his most trusted lieutenant, who was attacking from Tennessee into Georgia; Benjamin F. Butler on the Virginia peninsula; Franz Siegel (later Philip H. Sheridan) in the Shenandoah Valley; and Nathaniel P. Banks in the Red River Valley.[3] This holistic approach prompted Lincoln to remark, "Oh, yes! I see that. As we say out West, if a man can't skin he must hold a leg while somebody else does"—a good assessment of Grant's comprehensive strategy.

To military historians, this is the first campaign of the modern period. In crushing the Confederacy, Grant crushed the theory of decisive battle. Massing the industrial power of the North in a relentless crusade, he carried warfare to a new level, where technology and national power could be concentrated with hitherto unprecedented effect. In terms of military theory, Grant shifted our thinking about the power of armies to a focus on the total power of the state—not for the sake of battles themselves but for their combined effect.

Grant achieved success where, for three bloody years, his predecessors had failed. In his campaigns, we can see the elements of strategic architecture: His actions were grounded in basic *values* centered on the sanctity of the Union and his loyalty to those he led. His *vision* was expansive: not merely winning battles, but preserving the Union. His *strategy*, focusing and synchronizing his powerful armies in concert with other national strategic means (e.g., the blockade), gave him an insurmountable edge when pressed to advantage. His success was absolute.

Grant changed the way wars are fought by changing the critical processes for the generation, employment, and sustainment of armies. By force of will and clarity of intent, he synchronized the actions of huge armies separated by hundreds of miles. He and his generals transformed logistics processes, which in turn enabled ever-greater changes in operations. They capitalized on emerging technologies such as the telegraph, railroad, and processed food-stuffs to effect nearly continuous operations. And he acted not by virtue of any analytic process but intuitively. Such is the nature of genius.

RULE FOUR: REAL CHANGE TAKES REAL CHANGE!

Your critical processes provide the link between thinking about change and actually effecting change, because by changing the critical processes—not simply making adjustments at the margin—the leader creates a pattern, a structure, for doing things differently at the most basic level of the organization. Only by making change at this fundamental level is it possible to effect substantive and enduring transformation.

THE SIX IMPERATIVES: MAKING FUNDAMENTAL CHANGE

The Army's Six Imperatives were the basis for transforming the organization after Vietnam. There is very little evidence that the process was conscious from the beginning; rather, like Grant, the leaders who sparked the post-Vietnam renaissance were at least as intuitive as they were analytic. But by the end of the 1980s, the patterns ingrained by the critical processes were very clear. Our task in 1991 was equally clear: we had to get inside these processes in a rational way and change them, preserving the goodness but transforming the Army.

The Army's critical processes are illustrated in Figure 6-3. The six-pointed star with its connecting lines demonstrates that each critical process relates to all the others. For example, it is not possible to realize the potential of a quality force if modernization collapses so that Information Age hardware and software are not available to put

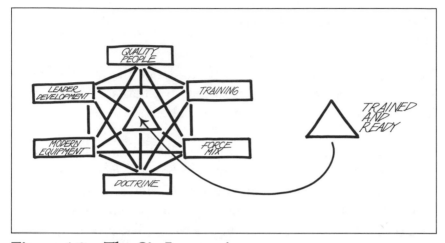

Figure 6-3—The Six Imperatives

in the hands of soldiers. The triangle in the middle is a "delta," a symbol of the quantum increase in performance that results from the processes interacting. It is the synergy of the critical processes coming together that makes America's Army the best in the world.

Enduring transformation would have to be effected through these processes. It began sequentially, with a conscious affirmation of quality and a conscious commitment to write new doctrine; it spread to training and leader development as the doctrine began to be developed. As we learned more and more about the impact of changing technology, transformation spread to modernization. Finally, applying both new doctrine and new technology, the focus of transformation spread to the redesign of tactical units, a process that will go on for a decade or more. The "lead" element in the strategy shifted over time, but at every stage all elements were involved. Together with a reaffirmation of the Army's basic values and the vision statement, the Six Imperatives completed the strategic architecture for change.

THE LANGUAGE OF STRATEGY

Before going any further, it is useful to define the family of terms that relate to the formulation of strategy but that are often defined loosely or not at all in the management context.

1. *Strategy* is the set of concepts that relates means (where you are today) to ends (where you want to be). The word generally applies to an organization as a whole. However, it may be equally applied to a subordinate element, provided it encompasses the subordinate element as a whole. The process of ensuring that the subordinate strategy supports the overall strategy is strategic alignment.

2. The *strategic environment* is the context within which an organization operates. For most organizations, this will include factors such as market conditions; the growth and expansion of technology; access to resources, including financial resources; political and regulatory dimensions, especially if operating across political boundaries; and cultural dimensions. The strategic environment may also include unique competencies or other internal factors.

3. *Strategic intent* is *what* you are working to accomplish. Strategic intent is more specific and limited than vision, as well as more quantitative.

4. Your *strategic concept* is *how* you intend to accomplish your strategic intent. It explains key roles and assignments, timelines (or at least sequences), and key relationships. The strategic concept also assigns resources and establishes priorities.

5. *Strategic objectives* are specific goals whose achievement is tantamount to the accomplishment of the strategic intent or of some major dimension of it. For example, if the strategic intent is to become the dominant provider of a product or ser-

vice, a certain level of market share could be established as a strategic objective. Accomplishing strategic objectives is usually necessary, but it is not always sufficient to accomplish the strategic intent. Significantly, it marks progress toward the vision that can be easily grasped and understood by the members of the organization and the leadership team.

TASK FORCE 51: IDENTIFYING THE STRATEGIC OBJECTIVE

In July 1994, U.S. forces were sent to central Africa to relieve the suffering in refugee camps outside Rwanda. Hundreds of thousands of Rwandans had fled their country in the wake of tribal violence and genocide. Cholera and dysentery, spread by unsafe drinking water and unsanitary conditions, were taking the lives of thousands daily, creating conditions beyond the control of the United Nations High Commissioner for Refugees (UNHCR) and other international relief organizations. These problems were compounded by the primitive infrastructure and mistrust between neighboring nations and tribes.

The strategic intent was to create conditions under which the United Nations and other agencies could facilitate the repatriation of Rwandan refugees—in other words, to reduce the crisis to manageable limits. The few thousand U.S. servicemen and women on the ground had a central role in accomplishing this.

The initial strategic objective was, in the words of General George A. Joulwan, U.S. commander in chief, Europe,[4] "to stop the dying." The key was a water purification unit called Task Force 51. Made up of engineers equipped with reverse-osmosis water purification units (ROWPU's), military police, and medical personnel, Task Force 51 deployed from Frankfurt, Germany, on July 23 and began distributing potable water to the camps around Goma, Zaire, less than thirty-six hours later. After U.S. forces took control of the airstrip at Goma, stability began to return and Task Force 51 was joined by teams from nongovernmental organizations with an even greater capacity to pump, purify, and distribute the abundant lake water. In spite of almost unbelievable overcrowding, the death rates in the camps quickly descended to well below precrisis levels and well below UNHCR standards.

Accomplishing this first strategic objective fundamentally changed the conditions on the ground, shifted the initiative to those providing assistance, and made longer-term success possible. The second strategic objective was to get the UNHCR and other agencies back in control of the situation. That was accomplished nearly concurrently by opening the airstrips and roads and putting emergency communications into place to manage the heavy flow of foodstuffs, medical supplies, and other life support. The third was to reverse the flow of refugees out of Rwanda, a process that depended on diplomatic and other action but that was aided by the cleaning up of the refugee camps, which, before Task Force 51 arrived, had become little more than places to die.

Today there are still refugees in and around Rwanda, as there have been since the 1950s, when the breaking up of European colonies unsettled political boundaries. Operation Support Hope did not solve those problems, nor was it intended to. It did reduce the crisis and enable the resumption of what, in that part of the world, can be called normalcy. Success was possible because of a small group of young Americans pumping clean water. *Selecting an initial strategic objective that is achievable and will yield immediate benefits is a crucial first step in carrying out any strategy.*

STRATEGIC ALIGNMENT

Professors Christopher A. Bartlett and Sumantra Ghoshal, in an important 1994 *Harvard Business Review* article, "Beyond Strategy to Purpose," argue compellingly that today's enterprises are built on an archaic paradigm of systems driven by structure driven by strategy.[5] At one time, the critical processes of the enterprise generally conformed to traditional management disciplines, and it was easy to create corporate strategy as a composite of marketing, finance, production, distribution and other logistics functions, research and development, and so on. Demonstrating the inappropriateness of this model to today's world, Bartlett and Ghoshal conclude, "The great power—and fatal flaw—of the strategy-structure-systems framework lay in its objective: to create a management system that could minimize the idiosyncrasies of human behavior."[6]

The power of a complete strategic architecture lies in the linking of values and vision with deliberate concepts for action that adhere to the critical processes in an organization, precisely so that the idiosyncrasies of human behavior can be realized. The vision aligns both strategic plans and action plans; values keep them within acceptable bounds. The strategic architecture becomes the basis for decentralized execution and empowerment because it gives people a foundation from which to be self-directing.

In putting the strategic architecture into place, the importance of a well-articulated concept and intent cannot be overstated. They are the essence both of communicating and of planning to achieve the vision. As General William DuPuy wrote, "The commander's concept is his supreme contribution to the prospect of victory. . . . Without a sound and dominating concept of operation, no amount of command presence, personal flair, years of rectitude, demonstrated integrity, advanced degrees, perfectly managed assignments, warrior spirit, personal courage, weapons proficiency, or troop morale can hope to compensate."[7] *In the military and elsewhere, concept and intent must be clearly and unambiguously stated and then emphasized, over and over and over.*

BRITISH AIRWAYS: A STUDY IN STRATEGIC ALIGNMENT

The 1980s turnaround of British Airways is a remarkable example of creating and aligning strategic architecture, taking decisive action, and effecting a successful transformation.

British Airways (BA) was in many ways stillborn. It was formed in the early 1970s by the merger of British European Airways (BEA) and British Overseas Airways Corporation (BOAC), both of which had deep roots in the Royal Air Force culture of World War II. The merger was intended to create a more efficient carrier by eliminating redundancies and inefficiencies, thereby providing a basis for privatization, but in practice the two predecessor companies continued to operate pretty much as before under the new corporate umbrella. Increased competition in the international market stymied their growth, and, although they were marginally profitable, they limped along with too many people and increasingly obsolescent aircraft and infrastructure. Recession, coming at the end of the decade, crippled the already weakened company.[8]

The result was a downward spiral that, had the company been in private hands at the time, probably would have led to receivership. By 1981, BA chief executive Roy Watts reported that "our money is draining at the rate of nearly 200 pounds a minute. . . . No business can survive losses on this scale. Unless we take decisive action now, there is a real possibility that British Airways will go out of business."[9] Later that year, Watts and BA chairman John King announced a "survival plan." The essence of the plan was to cut costs by cutting the workforce. Eventually, 23,000 people were taken out of the system.[10] Downsizing the workforce and eliminating many senior people who would have been resistant to change was a necessary first step toward "stopping the dying," but it was only a foundation—a "step zero"—for real transformation. But with that more realistic cost basis, the leadership, joined in February 1983 by a new chief executive, Colin Marshall, created a strategic architecture for growth and change.

Values. The transformation was grounded in a blend of old and new values. National pride, "keeping the British flag aloft," had guided both British Airways and its predecessor companies since the beginning. But the business, dominated by pilots schooled in the early days of commercial aviation and World War II, had grown too large and too troubled to be run by "those magnificent men in their flying machines," whose focus had been on keeping planes in the air and routes open, not on fiscal soundness. Spurred by the government's desire for privatization, which would be possible only if the firm gained vitality in a business sense, new values included a greater re-spect for profitability. The leadership, however, was committed to a wider constituency of stakeholders than simply future investors and strove to transform the company for its customers, its employees, and the British people as well.

Vision. The vision was captured in Saatchi & Saatchi's advertising slogan "The World's Favourite Airline," an almost ludicrous thought when it was rolled out. It proved to be a powerful magnet to pull the organization forward by empowering people and signaling change in a culture that had been focused on getting planes up and down with little regard for customer satisfaction. Marshall, the leader, was ab-solutely committed to the new vision. The business was to become getting people from place to place pleasantly, comfortably, and on time—not just getting planes into the air.

Strategy. The set of concepts that enabled King and Marshall to achieve their vision began with an extensive training program called "Putting People First" that resulted in a more empowered workforce with a commitment to customer service. The strategy grew to encom-pass aircraft modernization and revitalization of ground facilities, even to include such things as attractive new uniforms; implementa-tion of a responsive, computer-based reservation system that nearly eliminated irritation caused by misbookings; quality in operations at every level; restructuring of routes to reduce internal frictions and better serve customer needs; and the formation of strategic alliances with other global carriers that enabled BA to divest its marginal routes while retaining a global reach.

The turnaround was aided by an improved economy, but that only accelerated the transformation already in place. In about five years, British Airways truly did become a synonym for quality and customer service, and the firm also became viable financially. In the words of *Business Week*'s 1989 review, British Airways had gone "From Bloody Awful to Bloody Awesome."[11] Privatization was accomplished to great fanfare in the late 1980s, and today British Airways is a re-spected firm competing favorably in a difficult industry.

"Steady . . . Steady"

Changing everything at once adds to the ambiguity and uncertainty of the strategic environment and can easily overload the organizational coping mechanisms. Successful implementation of a strategy for transformation requires prioritizing the elements, determining which are the most critical (a situational judgment), and executing the most important elements first. For example, if new, decentralized production techniques are the best way of achieving new results, it may be unwise to change the personnel system at the same time because of the risk of losing maturity and experience in the workforce, which would make such a shift in production impossible.

A corollary to this principle is to settle on a strategy and execute it. Difficult as it is for an organization to handle too much change, it is even worse to try to handle a constantly changing strategic direction. This is precisely why the front-end work of strategic planning is so important, to enable the organization to settle on a strategic architecture and hold it, making adjustments, if necessary, rather than big shifts. An organization has only so much energy, and it can be too easily dissipated if the direction from the top appears to be ambiguous and constantly shifting.

The journey to change, especially in large organizations, can be long and difficult. There will be times when a leader's role is neither to push nor to pull but simply to stick to the strategy and counsel, "Steady . . . steady."

CHAPTER 7

Building a Team

★ ★ ★ ★

Team of Teams

On April 25, 1991, in the Saudi Arabian desert, I was presented with a tattered American flag and a meticulously printed letter explaining that the little flag had flown from the antenna of the tank of the commander of Task Force 3-37 Armor. What made the memento especially significant is that the note was signed "The men of Task Force 3-37 Armor."

I had known the commander for years, so I was both surprised and pleased that he had signed the note the way he had. This was not a personal gift; it was a gift from his team and an acknowledgment of their success. The commander, my friend, was proud to have commanded troops in battle, proud of what they had accomplished, and his personal pride was sublimated in the pride of the team.

This little episode was all the more meaningful to

me because the 37th Armor had been commanded by General Creighton Abrams, in the Battle of the Bulge—the same Abrams who had begun the Army's long march back after Vietnam. The same Abrams who, when feted as a hero by *Time* magazine after the 37th relieved the 101st Airborne Division at Bastogne, had dismissed the heroic accounts of his personal role as "hopeless dribble."[1]

The flag and the letter have hung together in my office ever since as a manifestation of courage and selflessness. I use them to remind people that the practice of leadership is about building teams. Your first task as a leader is to build your leadership team.

Like every new senior executive, I inherited a leadership team that was in place and functioning. As vice chief, I had been a part of that team, and its members and their views, as well as their strengths and weaknesses, were known to me. It was a great team, and we were justifiably proud of our success. Nevertheless, the nature of the Army is such that normal reassignments and retirements caused the team with which I started to turn over by more than half within a year, making it necessary to rebuild the team constantly. The choices were not entirely mine; they were made with the concurrence of the secretary of the Army, and the most senior were subject to Senate confirmation. Once the decisions were made, I had to bring each new team member on board, helping them all come to grips with greater responsibility and understand my thoughts and intentions.

The Army team is part of America's team. As chairman of the Joint Chiefs of Staff, General Colin Powell published a small doctrinal publication, JCS Pub. 1, *Joint Warfare of the US Armed Forces*, to set the tone for that bigger team. In it he wrote, "When a team takes to the field, individual specialists come together to achieve a team win. All players try to do their very best because every other player, the team, and the home town are counting on them to win."[2] In the aftermath of the Berlin Wall and the Persian Gulf War, Colin correctly saw that if the chiefs and the services were not seen as a cohesive team, with the common interests of the nation preeminent, the results could have been disastrous. Service parochialism is as dysfunctional in peace as it is in war. He was a master team builder. He made his policies unambiguous; then, working one on one and with the team as a group, he kept the team focused on the task of transforming America's armed forces.

For any organization, the "team" includes people who are not in the organization but who influence it. In the case of our team, this included not only the chairman and the other service chiefs but also key leaders throughout the interservice community—principally the Joint Staff and the regional commanders in chief, including Navy, Air Force, and Marine officers whose perspectives were sometimes very different from mine. The Army team also included key officials in the Department of Defense and the Congress, influential members of the Pentagon press corps, noted academics, White House staffers, and many, many others. I was an important link between many of these team members and my key staff people. Consequently, I devoted a substantial amount of time to ensuring that they understood what the Army was doing. I wanted them to see the Army as a part of their team and to tell our story.

Teams come naturally to my mind when thinking about military organizations. Commanders who isolate themselves in the "loneliness of command," keeping their own counsel and not having the strength of a leadership team to draw on, are less effective. We live and lead others through the power of teams. As much as anything else, my intent was to foster team building throughout the Army. When I found effective teams at lower levels, as I had the day the men of Task Force 3-37 Armor presented me with the little flag, it reinforced my understanding that the strength of the Army is as a team of teams, all pulling toward a common goal.

We live and lead others through the power of teams.

—GRS

BUILDING A TEAM

Our colleague Lou Lataif, dean of the Boston University School of Management and former president of Ford Europe, tells a story of two children arriving home after a ball game. The first is asked by his mother, "How was your day?" To which he replies, "I had a great day, I scored two runs." The second, asked the same question, replies, "I had a terrible day, the team lost." The first was consumed by his own performance; the second had sublimated himself to the team.

Because we work in teams, the "I" focus is dysfunctional. Our organizations do not exist for the aggrandizement of some particular "I," least of all the leader. They exist for a common good that can be achieved only by the sublimation of self. The heroes of the organizational folklore have become anointed as heroes because of what they did *for the team*. But regardless of the willingness of team members to sublimate their personal or institutional agenda to the collective good, there will be lines that will not be easily crossed. When faced with disappointing performance, even the strongest team may waiver. Those realities taken into account, one of a leader's most difficult and time-consuming challenges is building and maintaining teams.

> RULE FIVE: LEADERSHIP IS A TEAM SPORT
>
> Effective leaders forge alliances and build teams. They break down walls, floors, and ceilings, distributing leadership throughout the extended organization. Team building empowers people with a sense of responsibility so that the momentum for growth and transformation originates throughout the organization, not just from the top. Effective leadership is not about controlling from the top; it is about unleashing the power of people.

TALKING TO OURSELVES

The Army has always emphasized teamwork. The Army's present ideas about teams lie in its experience in combat, but they have been tempered by study and practice across a much wider range. In the late 1970s, Chief of Staff General Bernard Rogers[3] sponsored a group of studies in organizational effectiveness. In the immediate aftermath of Vietnam, we had tried a number of techniques to tap into the force, such as town meetings and advisory councils, but they had not worked very well. Nevertheless, Rogers and others knew we could create more effective units if we could find the right ways to engage the power of our people.

At that time, the guru of the Army's organizational development efforts was Colonel Dandridge M. Malone. Mike Malone's experiences as an infantryman and a scholar had shown him that we had all the power and energy we needed to build the best army in the world—and that it was locked up in our people. Our best leadership efforts were all too often inhibiting, not liberating, our people. He saw the potential, in a professional volunteer force, of developing and using people in completely different ways than had been possible in a draft army, and he suggested that the best way to draw out the unrealized effectiveness in our organizations was to be "organized by information."[4]

Mike helped us see that high-performing organizations "talk to themselves." Information is the most empowering resource available to any leader, and sharing information, starting with the strategic intent, is the critical first step of truly effective leadership. This early work, by Malone and others like him, was not focused on computers and computer systems, though the day would come when technology would help realize their ideas. They taught us that the first steps in building effective teams are breaking down walls and realigning functions so that information can be shared.

"Weekly Summary": Building Teams-at-the-Top

Since the 1950s, one way the Army Chief of Staff has shared information with the Army's top-level teams is by means of a "Weekly Summary" distributed to each general officer in the Army and the most senior civilian leaders in the department. It is a small booklet, seldom more than twelve or sixteen pages long, containing a short operations update, an intelligence summary, news about developments and activities throughout the Army, and a summary of personnel actions involving the generals. The chief has often included personal letters to the leadership and attachments ranging from articles of topical interest and important speeches to such things as videotapes and copies of new publications, such as important new field manuals. The chief's letters, printed on a distinctive yellow paper and hence called simply "yellows," appear only when the chief feels compelled to share his views on some particular issue. Yellows have been used to help facilitate the Army's campaign on values, to further the training revolution, to imbed the Six Imperatives, and, more recently, to explain the Louisiana Maneuvers, Force XXI, critical budget issues, personnel policies contributing to the reshaping of the force, critical lessons learned, and other specific issues. By publishing them, the chief personally plays a role in the continuous development and shaping of the leadership team.

Interestingly, after the chief's letters, the most popular section of the summary is invariably the personnel notes that report the promotions, reassignments, and retirements of the generals—the same group that receives the summary. In an organization as large as the

Army, this contributes to the sense that these men and women are part of a special team and that the life of each of them is important to the team as a whole.

Today, the "yellows" are being carried on an interactive computer net. This provides an even more rapid means for the chief to communicate with his leadership team, and the medium sends a message about the importance of the Army's growth into the Information Age.

Battle Laboratories: Building Horizontal Teams

The development of Battle Laboratories provides an example of a completely different kind of team—a horizontal team that can break down walls. These amoebalike organizations are made up of people from multiple commands who can quickly be focused on critical needs or emerging technology relating to the fielding of new equipment. The laboratories have created horizontal links across the Army and broken down bureaucratic walls, making it possible to make hardware and software changes faster than ever before. As opposed to a traditional functional orientation (e.g., artillery, armor, infantry), the Battle Laboratories were organized to align what we saw as the most rapidly changing dimensions of the battlefield: battle command; depth and simultaneous attack; mounted combat; dismounted combat; combat logistics; and early entry, lethality, and survivability. *By avoiding functional alignment, closer functional associations actually resulted.* For example, because there was *not* an aviation laboratory, the aviation community was led to participate in each of the others.

Combined with wider use of commercially available equipment, innovative evaluation techniques relying heavily on simulation, and streamlined acquisition procedures, Battle Labs have made it possible to put state-of-the-art equipment into the hands of soldiers faster. As a new kind of team, they have demonstrated the power and responsiveness of organizations without boundaries, concentrated on a task and organized around information.[5]

One Team, One Fight: Building a Team of Teams

One need only spend a few minutes in the company of General George A. Joulwan to hear him say, "One team, one fight!" It is his way of announcing that the task at hand is a shared responsibility and that as the leader, or as a supporter, his orientation is on the team's performance and not on that of individuals or individual agencies.

As the commander of the U.S. V Corps in Frankfurt, Germany, when the Berlin Wall came down in 1989, Joulwan led a team composed of U.S. Army soldiers stationed in Germany, as well as members of the Air Force, the German territorial forces, reinforcing units from the United States, and others. In his next assignment, as the senior U.S. commander for South and Central America, his task was promoting democracy and combating drug trafficking. The team included host countries throughout the hemisphere, the Drug Enforcement Agency, the other military services, U.S. ambassadors throughout the region, and many others. In neither case did he *command* all these elements, but he understood that all were part of a single team. Today, Joulwan is the senior U.S. commander in Europe and NATO's Supreme Allied Commander, Europe. Today his "team" includes all the armies of central Europe, former Warsaw Pact adversaries, and nongovernmental agencies. His role on this team is every bit as ambiguous as his role in South America was. "One team, one fight" gives him and his staff a way to focus, to build ad hoc teams, and to influence their success.

"One team, one fight" is a simple-sounding phrase, but it captures the complexity of today's world, in which teams and team members can extend far beyond the boundaries of the formal organization and can shift dramatically over relatively short periods of time. Joulwan's admonition causes us to look first at the task and the structure: What is the task? Who is on your team (who can influence the outcome?)? Whose team are you on? The answers tell us who we have to recruit to build the team and what we have to do to keep it focused.

DISTRIBUTED LEADERSHIP

Team building is a process of distributing leadership. Recall the leadership trinity: creating, managing, and building teams. Distributing leadership empowers people to act within boundaries of acceptable behavior as defined by the values, vision, and strategy of the organization. Distributing leadership, however, also means distributing responsibility. To be a team member is to accept responsibility, both for the team's performance and, in a more general way, for the team of teams. We want all our people to be leaders in the sense that we want each to feel an acute sense of responsibility for the performance of the whole organization. We want our people to say: "The team won/lost" not "I hit a home run." Being a leader in this sense is not about rising to the top; it is about accepting and discharging responsibility.

ESTABLISHING EXPECTATIONS

In talking to many leaders over many years, we have found that most admit, "If I could do it all over again, I would try to do a better job of establishing expectations." To be effective, each team member must know what is expected of him or her individually as well as what is expected of the team. Giving them this information is difficult for many reasons, not the least of which is that, as leaders, we often do not know precisely what we do expect. So we tend to retreat into jargon, say vague-sounding things, and then walk away. As soldiers we tend to say things such as "Defend along this line" when what we should say is something like "Do not allow the enemy to get south of this line with anything larger than a company, and do not allow him to get into position to fire into this area; you may give ground to the south of this mountain temporarily, but you must eject any enemy force that gets in there."

We see people saying things such as "Fix the problem in Dallas," when they should be saying, "We're losing market share in the South-west because we're losing our grip on customer service. I want you to go down and take charge of our operation in Dallas, get to know our major customers, focus on putting quality back into our operation, and reverse that trend. I expect things may continue to slide a bit at first, but when you think you have a handle on what you need to do, come back and let's talk it over."

Leaders often do not know what they want because they have not thought it through. In our combat orders process, we taught commanders to develop their concept in great detail, to tell people how the plan is to be executed and what to do at critical stages if certain things happen—in other words, to establish expectations. In that process we have come to understand that *expectations are established in a dialogue*. You do not give orders and walk away, you dialogue—not to debate intent but rather to develop a clear, common understanding of the fine points and ensure that there is a basis for reasonable, shared expectations.

Letters to Commanders

At the top level of the Army leadership, as new team members came into place, I talked with them one on one. Often I also sent them a letter explaining my views on the areas for which they were assuming responsibility, defining my expectations, and opening a dialogue. This was not something I felt to be unique; I had learned the technique from mentors such as Lieutenant General Julius Becton and Major General Walt Ulmer.[6] Both men—and there were others, too—helped me realize the importance of establishing common expectations, although, like so many others, if I had it to do over again, I would have spent more time on this critical task.

The men to whom I was writing were not strangers to me, but my letters helped me organize my thoughts and, especially for those stepping onto my personal leadership team for the first time, the letters were a way of strengthening our new relationship. These letters were useful to the recipients because they emphasized their new and expanded responsibilities. Most used them in directing their transition to their new position, some circulated the letters as a foundation for their own team building, others wrote letters of their own to their new direct reports—but that was always their choice. My intent was simply to foster a clear, straightforward dialogue with the people who reported directly to me.

The letters were usually three or four pages long, and I wrote them myself, usually in several drafts. As I look back on them, I find I was often normative, legitimizing team values; I was sometimes directive, when I wanted to personally emphasize the importance of some specific project—but these letters were not job descriptions; I was sometimes very personal, inviting a closer relationship; and I was often a mentor, trying to share some of what I had learned—often the hard way. I wrote things like this:

> The ability to rapidly gather, manage and distribute information will provide a decisive advantage on the 21st century battlefield. . . . You must be personally involved in the Force XXI process of changing our Army. . . .

> It will be helpful for you to know that I see us engaged in three sets of critical issues. I have not set this out on a chart or in a speech, nor will I; but it may be useful to us both to organize our thoughts in these terms. First, there are operational issues. . . . Second, there are "inside the beltway" [political] issues that relate to the future of the Army. . . . Third, there are "outside the beltway" issues that relate to changing the Cold War Army into a 21st Century Power Projection Army. . . .

> My intent is to tell you how I view . . . your responsibilities in terms of four strategic challenges: Reshaping—You

need to stay in the lead to ensure that [the smaller Army] is built upon sound, supportable doctrine. Resourcing—Your major challenge, as I see it, will be to ensure smooth transitions to new systems. Integrating—You must . . . ensure that all components of the force understand and comply with a single standard. Maintaining Readiness—You must ensure that the Army—the total Army—is prepared to go to war tomorrow. I am suggesting that we move beyond our current state so that we have [information] systems which project . . . and allow us to anticipate problems before they occur. . . .

. . . While I want to be involved and to provide cover for you, you must work the nitty-gritty details of change. I neither have the time nor inclination to do your job. What you are about to undertake has the potential to be a major turning point for our Army and the enduring legacy of our leadership. . . .

This brings me to my second point—the relationship that you and I have with each other. Simply stated, you have total access and I expect you to exercise that privilege continually—this means day and night and weekends. To truly know my position on various issues and act on my behalf, you must have a close working relationship with me. . . . Bring me good news; bring me bad news; be my eyes and ears. . . .

Your major task during this critical time for the Army is to execute the personnel drawdown of the total force in a timely manner with appropriate concern and compassion for soldiers—collectively and individually. This one task is so all-encompassing that it subsumes all others. . . .

And invariably, I said something like "I would like you to brief me on your concept and plan sometime within your first ninety days in command." That requirement for feedback, not a big staff presentation but the two of us talking one on one, helped ensure that our dialogue about important issues, about the future, did not atrophy as we both worked the tough day-to-day issues of our jobs.

Often, before I felt I was finished with the letter, someone from my personal staff would hand-deliver it to the ultimate recipient and explain what I was doing. I wanted the recipient to look at it in draft to see if there was anything he wanted me to add. My intent was to strengthen the notion that he and I were a team, that we were establishing expectations as opposed to my giving orders. Sometimes the recipient would ask for some particular emphasis, suggest a task, ask for support on an issue, or whatever. I was generally accommodating.

Finally, it is important to stress that these letters were the beginning of a dialogue. They were not a contract or a checklist or the basis of a future report card. The recipients knew, and I knew, that circumstances would change and that our expectations would change accordingly. But the letters gave us both a starting point.

—GRS

★ ★ ★ ★

EMPOWERING SUBORDINATES

Clear communication, beginning with the establishment of expectations, empowers subordinates. When they know what is expected and when they understand the vision and strategy for transforming the organization, they can act with much more confidence. When empowered this way, subordinates have a freer rein to seek and accept responsibility, within the bounds of acceptable risk. It was in this sense that President Lincoln empowered his new commander, Grant, in a letter just before the beginning of the 1864 campaigns. Lincoln and Grant were comfortable that they understood each other, the vision and the strategic concept and intent. In this letter, Lincoln told Grant that he was empowered to execute the plan.

> Executive Mansion
> Washington, April 30, 1864

Lieutenant General Grant,

Not expecting to see you again before the Spring Campaign opens, I wish to express, in this way, my entire satisfaction with what you have done up to this time, so far as I understand it. The particulars of your plans I neither know or seek to know. You are vigilant and self-reliant; and pleased with this, I wish not to obtrude any constraints or restraints upon you. While I am very anxious that any great disaster, or the capture of our men in great numbers, shall be avoided, I know these points are less likely to escape your attention than they would be mine.—If there is anything wanting which is within my power to give, do not fail to let me know it.

And now with a brave Army, and a just cause, may God sustain you.

> Yours very truly,

> A. Lincoln

A more contemporary story, but one no less substantive, was told by Roberto Goizueta, chairman and CEO of Coca-Cola. He tells of a phone call in the middle of the night from Coca-Cola Russian manager Alexander Leontiev to Greater Europe Group President E. Neville Isdell. Leontiev called with an opportunity to purchase an interest in a bottling plant in the remote southern Russian village of Nagutsky, an opportunity not expected to last long enough for the formal process of consideration and approval. The two men discussed the situation and acted immediately. They knew the concept and intent. They knew what was expected of them as part of the team. As Goizueta reports, "And nine months after that, every hour 60,000 bottles of Coca-Cola and 36,000 cans of Coca-Cola, Fanta or Sprite were rolling off a modern assembly line in a refurbished Nagutsky plant—a key component of a plan to serve a regional market of 40 million consumers."[7] Leontiev and Isdell were able to take responsibility and act because expectations had been clearly established, even though the precise execution had to be developed as the situation unfolded.

SUCCESSION PLANNING: LOOKING TWO UP AND TWO DOWN

Building a team includes succession planning, and this, too, can be difficult. Picking people is difficult because it is difficult to evaluate potential. It is much easier to measure past performance, so most promotions, in spite of our best intentions, are based primarily on performance. But as you go up the ladder, your task does not get harder so much as it becomes different, and past performance becomes less and less valuable as a predictive tool.

As a junior officer or manager, you are running things. As you become more senior, the creative dimension of your job begins to dominate the managerial dimension, and your adaptive and generative skills become more important than your technical skills. You become more involved with creating the future. You are team building at every level, but that too becomes more complex as you get nearer the top.

This difficulty notwithstanding, a leader must spend countless hours building and rebuilding the team—doing succession planning. The depth to which you plan depends somewhat on the turnover in key positions, but we suggest planning "two up and two down." In our case, as we looked at an individual, whether a junior captain or a senior general, we tried to look at least two moves beyond his or her present position. For our junior people, it was at best a generalized process, centrally controlled but somewhat decentrally executed. For our senior people, it was a much more precise process including trying to have a follow-on assignment in mind when we made each selection. This process was joined in by all of the senior generals; essentially, the top team assisted in the selection of those who would join its level or the next two levels down. For critical jobs, we attempted to keep available a bench of qualified people, always more than one, so that when the time came to make a choice, we had options. That kind of succession planning was our way of dealing with the challenge of evolving skills as people go up the ladder. By trying to look ahead several years and by always thinking in terms of options and not necessarily in terms of individuals, we could help people grow at the same time that we could, however subjectively, evaluate potential.

Leaders cannot do it alone. Creating the future is truly a team sport. Mike Malone's lesson for the Army is a lesson for everyone. The power to achieve is at our fingertips—it lies in the people in our organizations. By forging them into teams and by building teams of teams that are empowered by values, vision, and a strategy to grow, they will turn our visions into reality and create the future.

CHAPTER 8

Campaigning

★★★★

Expect to Be Surprised!

On November 9, 1989, I was a keynote speaker at a conference sponsored by the Fletcher School of Tufts University. As I went onstage to make my talk, I was handed a note telling me that the Berlin Wall had just come down, news that I shared with the audience. During the question-and-answer period, the first question was about the unfolding events in Europe: "General, what does it mean?" I was tempted to speculate, but what was happening was too profound to be addressed in a quick answer from the podium. My answer was simply "I don't know what I don't know."

No one had predicted that the Berlin Wall would come down. No one predicted that the Warsaw Pact and the Soviet Union would implode. No one predicted that we would go to war in the Persian Gulf, use forces from Europe, fight with Syria as an ally, and win a decisive victory. As we watched the victory parades after Desert Storm, no one predicted that George Bush would be defeated for a second term. Yet in the middle of what we thought was our downsizing plan, we made a transition to a Democratic administration that made additional, deep cuts in defense resources. No one predicted that we would deploy soldiers to Africa, to the Balkans, or to Haiti, that the U.S. 3d Infantry Division would train in Russia, or that Russian infantry companies would visit Fort Polk, Louisiana, and Fort Riley, Kansas. Yet all those things and more have come to pass.

Life is a journey with many unexpected twists and turns. The challenge for the Army was not to make better guesses about the future—which is impossible—but to build more flexibility and versatility into our planning and into the force so that when the time came we could tailor a response and get it about right.

We had a pretty good sense that the precision of Cold War–era strategic planning, programming, and budgeting was no longer relevant. Untold thousands of hours had gone into the development of the assumptions and databases in our Cold War models. The models and scenarios had been debated over the years, and while in hindsight they appear somewhat suspect, they had at least provided a common language and context for the development of the nation's military forces. Suddenly those models no longer had any relevance, and there were few analytic tools at hand with which to replace them. We were planning, programming, and preparing future budgets under uncertainty, something with which the bureaucratic structure of the Defense Department has yet to come to grips.

Opting out of the formal planning processes of the department was not an option. So we attempted to keep things in context by directing our journey as if it were multiple campaigns—both sequential and simultaneous. Like Grant leading five armies, we were directing several campaigns; preparing for new missions, incorporating new technology, getting smaller, coming home from Europe, and writing new doctrine were only the major ones. On top of those came the missions we were actually performing around the world, each taking us another step further from the Cold War, each leaving its mark on the new Army.

Like me, most people want to "finish" things; but in an organization such as the Army, at a time like this, there is no "finish." My tenure as chief coincided with the fiftieth anniversary of the United States' entry into World War II. I thought about that a lot. World War II ended in V-E Day and V-J Day—clear marks of a successful conclusion. For today's Army, and for most of our organizations, there are no such clear-cut finish lines, no perfect, enduring solutions. The campaigns I was leading could not be managed as projects with a beginning and end.

The demands of our world are constantly changing, and structuring things too rigidly can leave you ineffective at the next bend in the road. Part of us wants to believe that we can somehow get our organizations perfectly right so that, like the Great Wall of China, they will endure for centuries. As leaders, we must avoid the temptation to attempt to build such walls.

To be able to handle this journey, leaders must condition themselves and their people to be surprised, to handle the unexpected. We must build into our organizations the expectation that they will be surprised. I am convinced that no matter what path of life you walk, there will be surprises. Competitive advantage will come not from more precise planning but from planning that anticipates surprise in an active way. Good organizations become adept at what infantrymen call "developing the situation."

When Ulysses S. Grant left Culpeper Court House in the spring of 1864, he did not know, in a specific sense, where he was going—but he knew what he wanted to accomplish. Grant's road led through the Wilderness, Spotsylvania, Cold Harbor, Petersburg, Five Forks, and only then to Appomattox. In November 1944, when Eisenhower held a council of war at Maastricht and approved the final plans for the invasion of Germany, he did not know that the German counteroffensive, the Battle of the Bulge, would erupt only weeks later. Omar Bradley and George

Patton did not know that they would have to move north to go east. Eisenhower's strategic concept was not a precise blueprint, planning chart, or timeline; but his campaign plan, in the hands of competent commanders and courageous soldiers, accommodated the Battle of the Bulge and provided the framework for moving on, leading to victory only six months later.

There is no substitute for insight or genius, but, when all is said and done, most of us do not see into the fog much better than our competitors. The competitive advantage we need is neither clairvoyance nor precision in planning. The competitive advantage we can build into our organizations is people who react faster than their competitors do.

The United States Army had no units specifically designed to go to Haiti or Bosnia. There are no books at the Staff College that tell precisely how to create such units. Instead, the Army was able to put the pieces together—not like Henry Ford but like an artisan, individually crafting each piece—and do it faster and better than anyone else.

It is comforting to think of this metaphorical journey as downhill stretches on sunny summer days, but my experience suggests otherwise. There will be potholes and uphill stretches; there will be ambushes, flooded rivers, and winter storms. There will be resource challenges and tough trade-offs. Leaders must prepare their people to appreciate the uncertainties and random nature of life and the necessity of anticipating the unexpected, always keeping the organization positioned so that it can respond. Successful organizations accept uncertainty and are not surprised to be surprised. Winning organizations are poised to find opportunity and to act faster than anyone else.

Expect to be surprised.

—GRS

★ ★ ★ ★

STEERING FROM POINT TO POINT

In his biography of Lincoln, Pulitzer Prize–winning author David Donald tells of an exchange between Lincoln and Congressman James G. Blaine. Asked his plans about the postwar South, Lincoln responded with a story: "The pilots on our Western rivers steer from *point to point* as they call it—setting the course of the boat no farther than they can see; and that is all I propose to myself in this great problem."[1] The pilots knew where they wanted to go, be it Corinth, Cairo, or New Orleans. In our terms, they had a vision. But they worked to achieve it a piece at a time. They did not give orders and go to bed saying "Wake me up when you get us there"; they stood in the pilothouse and worked from point to point. In the ever-changing vastness of the Mississippi, every trip was a unique journey.

Thus, for an enduring organization there is no finite end state, only a journey—always becoming, never being. An institutional vision is not an end state, like reaching New Orleans. Rather, it is our guide as we go from point to point, dealing with the world's uncertainty and ambiguity.

A leader must accept these realities and grow the organization to survive and prosper in an ambiguous, uncertain world that makes precise planning a business school exercise. With a strategic vision out in front, pulling the organization forward, the leader can focus on the journey one segment at a time. The journey will have unexpected twists and turns; actions will have unintended consequences; there will be "lucky" and "unlucky" events. But it is possible to direct a journey in such a way as to accommodate the unexpected.

RULE SIX: EXPECT TO BE SURPRISED

The paradox in creating the future is that you cannot predict the future. Success will come from being able to accommodate the unexpected, exploiting opportunity and working through setbacks. A leader must build flexibility and resilience into the organization, conditioning it *not to be surprised to be surprised* so that, when the unexpected occurs, response is prompt, action is deliberate, and the organization stays on course. The organization that is successful is the one that can best deal with surprise.

Campaigning

• Use shared values as the foundation for action.

• Create a vision that provides a sense of direction and purpose.

• Build a strategy that is grounded in your basic competencies and processes to focus and direct your actions.

• Communicate constantly; make change part of the culture.

• Structure for success; create options to provide strategic flexibility.

• Integrate and synchronize actions and events to achieve decisive results.

• Expect the journey to take unexpected twists and turns; translate them into effective action.

THE CAMPAIGN PLAN

Strategic plans must be inherently flexible, organized as a campaign—a series of related activities, events, or operations aimed at accomplishing a strategic objective or a series of strategic objectives within a specified time frame or market. Campaigning is *opportunistic*, not deterministic, planning; it enables an organization to move quickly in response to a changing environment. Campaigning is inherently flexible, enabling a leader to seize and maintain the initiative by setting the terms for confrontation as opposed to reacting to terms and conditions created by others. The journey to the future is such a campaign or series of campaigns. Like political or military campaigns, it links strategic objectives to achieve the vision; it is structured to integrate and synchronize the means; and, while never ambiguous in its intent, it accommodates uncertainty by its inherent flexibility.

For a campaign plan to have real substance, it must include (1) a clearly stated and well-understood intent, (2) a clear concept, (3) an orientation articulated as a strategic objective or series of objectives, (4) identified resources, (5) a mechanism to integrate and synchronize the plan's execution, and (6) branches and sequels that will enhance the plan's flexibility. The campaign plan lays this out in terms of the basic competencies or processes of the organization. Thus, applied to a business, the campaign may have a product development dimension, a marketing dimension, a logistics dimension, a financial dimension, and so on. *The campaign plan may be supported by analysis and financial projections, but it is the ideas behind these elements—not the numbers—that are its essence.*

Questions to Ask in Developing a Campaign Plan

- What do we want to accomplish? (intent)

- What are we going to focus on? (concept)

- What steps are we going to take? (objectives)

- What do we have to work with? (resources)

- How are we going to pull it all together? (integration and synchronization)

- What do we do next? (branches and sequels)

Intent

The *intent* translates the vision into very specific terms that can guide your actions. In articulating the intent, the leader stretches the organization, both pushing and pulling toward success. It is important to understand that intent seldom leads directly to realization of the vision but carries the organization in the direction of the vision. Achieving the vision will generally be the result of several simultaneous or sequential campaigns. For example, in World War II, Churchill and Roosevelt shared a *vision* of the unconditional surrender of the Axis powers. Eisenhower's *campaign* to liberate central Europe was only one part of that, along with operations in the Mediterranean, on the eastern front, in the Pacific, in the China-Burma-India theater, in the North Atlantic, and elsewhere. Eisenhower's campaign in the European Theater of Operations was necessary to the accomplishment of the grand strategic vision, but not sufficient.

Concept

The most important part of the plan is the *concept*, because, in the concept, the leader describes how he or she visualizes the campaign unfolding. In the concept, the leader explains how he or she will mobilize and deploy the means of dominating the enemy, the competitor, the market, or whatever. It describes what the staff and subordinate elements are to accomplish, identifies the main effort, and prioritizes supporting efforts. Finally, the leader describes how he or she sees the elements of the campaign coming together.

At its essence, the concept orients the organization on what military theorists describe as the enemy's "center of gravity," defined in Fm 100-5, "Operations," as the "hub of all power and movement upon which everything depends. It is that characteristic, capability, or location from which the enemy . . . forces derive their freedom of action, physical strength, or will to fight. Several traditional examples include the mass of the enemy army, the enemy's battle command structure, public opinion, national will, and an alliance or coalition structure."[2]

"Center of gravity" is a nineteenth-century idea couched in nineteenth-century terms. But it leads one to think about one's sources of strength and weakness relative to the opposition's. You must ask yourself "What must I accomplish to trip the scales overwhelmingly in my favor so that I can win?" The answer might be development of a new process or distribution channel that establishes a new standard of performance, thus superannuating the present ones. For example, when Henry Ford set out to create Ford Motor Company, the center of gravity was producing inexpensive, simple automobiles. When Steve Jobs and Steve Wozniak set out to develop a market for personal computers, the center of gravity was making a user-friendly machine. When Sam Walton set out to revolutionize discount retailing, the center of gravity was distribution, which he solved by his innovative cross-docking warehouses and by demanding alliances with suppliers. Just as military commanders must appreciate the enemy and friendly situations and the relative strengths and weaknesses of each, so must an organization understand how it will transform the nature of its competitive environment. The answer to this question becomes the focal point of the concept.

Objectives

The *objectives* define the path to successful execution of the campaign as a series of specific major actions to be accomplished. Objectives should be quantified and, therefore, measurable. To return to the World War II example, Eisenhower's concept was to attack across the English Channel into France, break out of his initial lodgment, conduct a supporting attack through the South of France, and then attack through France and the Low Countries into Germany on two axes—Montgomery on the left, in the North; Bradley on the right—to destroy the German Army, occupy Germany, and link up with the advancing Red Army. His strategic objectives followed his concept: invasion and lodgment in Normandy, breakout into France, opening of the Channel ports, liberation of Paris, and so forth. His objectives gave him a basis on which to constantly adjust his plan, using branches and sequels to optimize its execution. The concept is the leader's visualization of the campaign; the objectives give him his point-to-point orientation.

Resources

The campaign plan must identify the *resources* to be used. Resources include the people, money, and time that are allocated to the campaign, including "reserves" that are earmarked for use if needed to exploit success or avert failure. More important, however, are critical capabilities, or competencies that give you an asymmetric advantage: the speed with which you can deploy into the targeted market, superior quality, technological leadership, unique customer service, or some other advantageous capability that you possess. Asymmetric advantage facilitates taking an indirect approach: not simply slugging it out head to head for smaller and smaller margins but establishing a wholly new future basis for competing, a basis on which you are dominant. By exploiting your unique competencies, you can control the conditions of the campaign and gain and retain the initiative.

We can see the application of asymmetric resources in the campaigns for the North American automobile market in the 1980s. The Japanese companies' asymmetric advantage was what James Womack and his coauthors called "lean production" in their book *The Machine That Changed the World*. Striking a balance between craft and mass production by organizing production around multi-skilled teams that were networked from supplier to production to market gave the Japanese increasing quality at decreasing costs and enabled them to be more responsive to the market. Thus, Japanese automakers could produce an attractive, high-quality automobile and deliver it to the North American consumer at a lower price than could Detroit. As the campaign played out, the U.S. Big Three automakers responded, under pressure, with their own versions of lean production—Team Taurus, the Saturn project, and Chrysler's Technology Center—neutralizing the asymmetry (essentially creating a new symmetry), but only after the whole marketplace shifted dramatically.

Some portion of total resources should be held in reserve to be employed only as the situation develops or as a need arises. The reserve is a hedge against uncertainty. Reserve resources give a leader the flexibility to sustain the initiative, to reinforce success, or to prevent defeat. There is a tendency in planning to disregard the need to retain a reserve, to want to use all available resources all the time. Planners should recognize that reserve resources are *committed* resources and provide accordingly. Examples of retained reserves would be financial resources, including unused credit lines; surge production capability; resources being used on lower-priority projects that could be diverted; skilled people who could be used to "pile on" at a critical point; even extra time that can be allocated to let a campaign mature more satisfactorily.

Integration and Synchronization

The issue in controlling the plan is not managing day-to-day execution, which should be delegated, but rather monitoring, so that the plan can be adjusted from the strategic level. At that level, the leader must perform two functions. First, he must integrate and synchronize the actions taken. *Integration* is the arranging of events so that they support one another effectively, making everything fit together; *synchronization* is the arranging of events so that their effect is massed at the critical point, making everything happen at the most advantageous point and time.

Branches and Sequels

The leader's other major function in providing strategic direction during execution is modifying the plan as it unfolds, primarily through branches and sequels. "Making it up as one goes along" is not good enough. Nor is a process of constant tinkering or successive approximation. But carefully timed options, built into the concept, give flexibility and balance to the campaign. *Branches* are options built into the basic plan to anticipate situations that could alter the plan or the outcome. *Sequels* are subsequent actions based on possible outcomes. Branches address the "What if?" questions; sequels address the "What next?" questions. Neither needs to be robustly developed during planning: what counts is not the level of detail but rather the depth of thought. Branches and sequels may involve the employment of reserve resources, or they may simply involve the redirection of resources already employed.

Richard Pascale, in his assessment of transformation at Ford in the 1980s, tells this story of the Taurus project:

> *Planning had projected gasoline prices of $3.40 per gallon for the late eighties, and Taurus' configuration was based on that assumption. By spring 1981, fuel price projections were converging on $1.50 per gallon. Did the revised projections point toward the feasibility of a larger car? . . . Discarding an entire year's work, the team increased Taurus' wheel base, upped capacity from five to six passengers, widened its tread, and shifted from a four-cylinder engine to a V-6. In the circumscribed world of car design, this is like telling the carpenter you want a new kitchen in the place he's halfway through remodeling as a bathroom. Yet Ford was agile enough to make this shift and still meet Taurus' targeted introduction deadline.[3]*

As we see, a fundamental assumption of the Taurus campaign plan failed, creating opportunity: Ford was learning even as it was executing. The campaign continued but shifted to a branch—a larger configuration—leading to the most successful new-car launch in the modern history of the automobile industry.

Sequels give you flexibility once you obtain a strategic objective. The campaign plan, for example, may call for a given level of market penetration within a specific period of time. If that objective is achieved more easily or more quickly than anticipated, preplanned sequels can help a leader exploit success by pressing toward a greater share, shifting resources to another market segment, or simply consolidating on the objective to build a more sustainable position. Thinking through sequels early in the campaign-planning process gives the leadership team immediate options for exploiting success. The epitaph for too many successful plans that ended up going no farther than the first major objective is "No one was more surprised than we were."

When the Army began its experiments in using information technology to create a common situational awareness, each experiment—each objective in the campaign—was designed with follow-on experiments in mind: sequels. When we reviewed the results, we always had options: stopping and redirecting our effort, going back and refining our results, or going on to a more complex experiment. This gave us a degree of control over the journey; it was not a process of random discovery but rather of structured learning.

Trigger Points

Timing of the employment of branches and sequels is controlled by using *trigger points*. A trigger point is a set of conditions for making a decision. The most obvious are decision sets built around the assumptions in your plan; others are based on the actions of your competitor or a major shift in the strategic environment. In the first case, you begin by identifying the critical assumptions in your plan, the assumptions that must hold up if your concept is to hold up. In the Taurus case, one key assumption was high gasoline prices, which made smaller cars desirable. Had Ford persisted in building Taurus as a small-car entry, it is unlikely it would have captured the imagination of the market as it did. As another example, if one of your objectives is to open a new international market, you will need to make assumptions about the regulatory and legal climate in the relevant country. In your planning, you should identify indicators that these assumptions may be incorrect. If those indicators appear, you have a trigger point based on a discrete decision set. Your options then may be, for example, to step up your efforts to accommodate the host nation's concerns, to emphasize the benefits the host country will derive from your investment, to back away from your investment altogether, or to seek a strategic in-country alliance that would shift your legal and regulatory posture. It is possible to "war-game" these kinds of eventualities in such a way that you will be able to see them coming more clearly and respond more quickly, before they reach crisis proportions.

The second kind of decision set associated with trigger points for branches and sequels involves strategic "counter-counter" moves. You do "A"; your competitor responds with "B," "C," or "D." Your trigger point should be structured to identify the critical information that will tell you, as early as possible, which option your competitor has taken so that you can make your next move against its relative weakness, not its strength. Even if your competitor responds with "None of the above," this kind of analysis will leave you in a better posture to respond. Trigger points create a focus for control from the strategic level and give you a rational basis for initiating branches or sequels.

Trigger points should not be set on autopilot. Their purpose is not to preset your responses. Trigger points are sets of conditions that *might* lead you to shift the campaign plan one way or another. The important word in that sentence is "might." Trigger points keep "What is happening?" in context. Leadership teams that have learned to work using trigger points are invariably able to react faster than teams that wait for things to develop. Even in situations where there is no trigger already established, a leadership team trained to think and act in anticipation will outperform a team conditioned only to react.

The Jayhawk Corps: Campaign Flexibility

The Army's VII Corps, nicknamed the "Jayhawk Corps," was headquartered in Stuttgart, Germany, throughout most of the Cold War. By 1990, it had been picked for inactivation as part of the Army's downsizing campaign, although public announcement had been withheld because the actual inactivation date was envisioned for 1992 or even later. In 1990, the Army went to the Persian Gulf. The unexpected had created an opportunity to overlap the Gulf War campaign and the downsizing campaign. The Army sent VII Corps, with its divisions from Europe, to the Gulf, where, reinforced by units from the United States, then Lieutenant General Fred Franks led it in the largest and most rapid armored assault in our history. Immediately on the heels of the Gulf War, the Army inactivated the units and brought the troops and equipment directly back to the United States. In about eight months, the corps had deployed to the Middle East, integrated new units, moved thousands of miles in the most difficult conditions, engaged and defeated a larger force, redeployed, and inactivated. But difficult as it was, it made sense because it all fit into the context of the Army's ongoing campaigns. Thus the Army actually reduced the turbulence induced by both the war and the downsizing and saved the costs of reestablishing the Jayhawk Corps in Germany, only to have to take it out a year later.*

LEADING THE CAMPAIGN

The leader alone bears the responsibility for taking risk. But a well-conceived plan, by its very nature, mitigates risk. Branches and sequels provide a means of dealing with the unexpected. But the leader must not assume that a thick and impressive strategic plan, the details of which may be of little value once the execution is under way, will completely eliminate risk.

The leader must structure the plan for success, first by developing a good plan and then by selecting objectives that help to build momentum, sustain the initiative, and demonstrate the strength of the

---

* The entire redeployment from Europe, a monumental task tantamount to moving the city of Raleigh, N.C., to California, was performed under the direction of General Crosbie E. Saint, then U.S. Army Commander in Chief Europe, whose foresight and planning made possible the movement not only of people and units but also all the Army's nuclear and chemical weapons and hundreds of thousands of tons of war material stockpiled in Europe, and the closure and return to Germany of hundreds of bases and facilities.

campaign to all its constituents. The initial goals may be relatively modest in absolute terms, but they are nevertheless "strategic" because early success is so important.

Executing the plan is a process of learning that involves the entire leadership team. It requires feedback (including bad news, which never improves with age) and a continual assessment of that feedback so that adjustments can be made as new and better information becomes available.

Executing the plan requires a constant trade-off between today and tomorrow. The organization must operate and it must grow—the leader must keep these in balance (Figure 8-1).

Figure 8-1—Balancing Today and Tomorrow

Robert E. Lee's Six-Pounders

The opportunity cost of investing in the future is seldom as apparent as it was for Robert E. Lee in the winter of 1862. Lee was troubled by the fact that the Union artillery was superior to his own. The Union, possessing the preponderance of American ordnance factories, had equipped its force with modern fieldpieces while the South was forced to make do with older models supplemented with what it could purchase overseas, capture on the battlefield, or manufacture in its few foundries. Thus, a year and a half into the war, Lee wrote to the Confederate secretary of war recommending modernization and simultaneously issued instructions to the chief of ordnance to "improve our field artillery." He wrote, "I have also recommended, should metal be wanted . . . that our bronze 6-pounder smoothbores and even our bronze 12-pounder howitzers, if necessary, should be recast. This would simplify our field ammunition, save horses, and place our batteries more nearly on an equality with those of the enemy."[4] In other words, he gave up his smaller guns to be melted down and manufactured into better ones. When he began the 1863 campaigns, Lee had a newer and better artillery train. His logistics requirements were reduced, and his firepower was increased. (We can guess that there must have been some long faces as his gunners packed their cannon off to be melted down before the Yankees came back. But Lee knew that the risk of attack in the winter was small. His decision paid off.)

Few leaders will be faced with decisions as difficult as Lee's, but the same dilemma—balancing today and tomorrow—is faced by leaders every day. How to allocate scarce capital, where to assign people, how to prioritize new products or services, how much to spend on basic research, how to establish resource levels for market development—all are examples of today versus tomorrow. If you put too much emphasis on today, you preordain your tomorrow to being a shallow extension of today. If you put too much emphasis on tomorrow, you undermine the foundation on which tomorrow is built. Overconcern about short-term results can undermine the future. But indifference to short-term results can leave an organization too weak to create the future, no matter how desirable that future may be.

RULE SEVEN: TODAY COMPETES WITH TOMORROW

An organization has only so much energy, so many resources, so many bright people capable of leading. Most of that organizational energy must be focused on today's requirements— meeting the needs of the market in real time. A certain amount of resistance to any change campaign is not disagreement so much as exhaustion. But the leader knows that some of the resources—time, energy, the best people—*must* be directed toward the future and that he or she must find a balance between the two.

As Xerox's CEO, David Kearns led the transformation that brought the company back from near ruin. He became convinced early on that the most pressing strategic issue for Xerox was quality in all of its dimensions, from basic product reliability to customer service. Xerox had rested too long on its laurels as the industry pioneer and was producing an inferior product, causing it to lose badly in the marketplace. In his book *Prophets in the Dark*, Kearns reflects on an early, two-and-a-half-day meeting at the Xerox Training Center in Leesburg, Virginia, far from corporate headquarters, as a major milestone in the quality revolution that fueled the turnaround. But, he writes:

> By no means was there widespread eagerness to attend. . . . After all, we were running a nearly $9 billion business while all this was coming up. . . . A lot of people wondered why we should spend a lot of time and money on a quality program when there was so much to do. . . . Some other people saw this as totally incompatible with all the cost-cutting we were engaged in. . . . There were any number of attempts to get this whole exercise wiped off the calendar. "Why do we need this?" someone would ask. "Let's spend a half day in Stamford [corporate headquarters] and that'll do it. We'll go nuts spending two and a half days in Leesburg."

That kind of resistance is both typical and predictable. Each of the people who attended that meeting had difficult, demanding day-to-day challenges; their today competed directly with their leader's vision of tomorrow. But Kearns found the essential balance. The meeting was only a step, only the tip of the iceberg of commitment; but it was essential to what is today seen not simply as a successful turnaround but as a successful transformation.[5]

For each of the Army's experiments with the future, there were critics who would have spent the money for maintenance or for a conventional training exercise. For every dollar spent to ensure that the skill mix in the smaller force was tailored properly, there were critics who would have "saved" it by slash-and-burn downsizing. For every dollar spent keeping the technology base alive, there were critics who would have bought badly needed trucks or repaired infrastructure. You will face similar criticism of any change effort you launch. In the final analysis, it is leaders who must make the tough calls and balance the demands of today and tomorrow.

CHAPTER 9

Transforming the Organization

⭐⭐⭐⭐

Better Is Better!

Downsizing the Army was hard. In our hearts, we were reluctant to see old units inactivated. Many of us had served
in those units, and it was hard to see them go away. It was
harder still to see our friends leave. But all of us appreciated that America's Army, both active and reserve forces,
could safely become smaller in the absence of a clear threat
to NATO, and so there was never any serious resistance to
getting smaller. But the strategic issue was not getting
smaller. We appreciated that we could not shrink to greatness. The strategic issue was to create a better Army—
better for the world as we were coming to know it, not as it
had been.

Working with the chairman of the Joint Chiefs of Staff,
the senior Army generals, and the political leadership, I
had to decide whether the Army's course should be one of
gradual change or transformation. Some thought we could

simply get smaller and keep doing what we had always done, making measured improvements in the efficiency of the department by using the tried and true processes of the past. We had created the best Cold War Army in the world by continuous process improvement—gradual change—along a well-defined path. But the existing processes, which had been appropriate for their time, did not seem sufficient to propel the kind of growth the Army needed.

Thus our decision to attempt a transformation was a deliberate one. Transformation is moving an organization to a higher plane, leading it to become something qualitatively different while retaining its essence. We faced discontinuities both in our mission (what we were being asked to do) and in technology (the means by which we were to do it), as well as the challenges of greater uncertainty, new partners, and whole new relationships within the Army and defense community. The changes in our environment were too severe to be handled by gradual change.

Ours was to be a transformation in two primary dimensions: we had to transform from the Industrial Age to the Information Age and from a bipolar world with a single, narrowly defined threat to a multipolar world with a seemingly infinite variety of threats. Combined with getting smaller by one third, it was a very demanding requirement.

In attempting such a shift, keeping your organization with you is not an inconsequential issue. We knew enough about the Army to know that it would not accept trendy change. During our initial experiments with the all-volunteer force in the 1970s, we had tested some policies that had not worked out because people found them dysfunctional. We had seen the Navy and the Air Force grapple with similar issues. Thus, we knew that if we got too far off course the changes we made would be transitory. Our experiences in the 1970s had also taught us that high-performing organizations depend on a very high level of internal communication. As leaders, we could make change more acceptable by being personally involved and by constantly talking to people, explaining both what we were doing and why.

In short, we needed a program of transformation that would take us to a new level while reflecting what the professionals in uniform saw as legitimate. For me, it was a question of balance: making a real transformation but keeping the support of the organization.

I also had to find a balance point in the rate of change. We had to move "fast enough" but not "too fast." Initially, I spoke of "maintaining continuity while accommodating change." That language was an acknowledgment of past success, as well as an endorsement of my predecessor's approach to downsizing and change. We soon added "growth" to the message: continuity, change, and growth. I was concerned that without a strong emphasis on growth, getting smaller could in itself become our objective in spite of our best intentions to the contrary. It was important to build the mind-set that we were not out to accommodate anything, but to sustain our position as the best army in the world by growing. People are inclined to think about growth in physical terms, and in an atmosphere of downsizing, the idea of "growth" was counterintuitive to many. But we persisted. Gradually, "change" came to be associated with the adjustments made necessary by the end of the Cold War (e.g., base closures, downsizing, coming home from Europe), which were necessary but insufficient conditions to realize the vision. "Growth" came to stand for building the future Army, actually realizing the vision, while "continuity" was a constant reminder that our history was important and our values would not change.

Over time, things came together in a coherent vision for the future force, Force XXI; but it was a time-consuming process, more difficult and time consuming than any of us envisioned in 1989 or even 1991. As I look back, the key to whatever success we did achieve was not so much our commitment to transformation but rather achieving balance: striking out to achieve a true transformation while keeping the **pace and amount of change within the bounds the Army could handle.**

—GRS

★ ★ ★ ★

RAISING THE BAR

We hear a lot today about "raising the bar," which implies that standards are getting higher and higher and that it is harder and harder to succeed. A colleague, sports enthusiast General Lee Salomon,[1] showed us one day exactly what raising the bar means. He sketched out the high-jump record for the last century, and, sure enough, we could see that, for high jumpers at least, the bar had been rising for a long time (see Figure 9-1).

There are two important lessons to be learned from Figure 9-1.

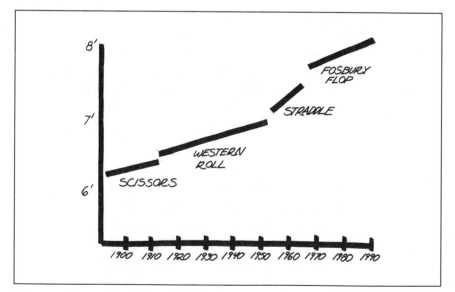

Figure 9-1—Raising the Bar

The first is the difference between process improvement and transformation. High jumping has had very stable periods separated by periods of instability. In the stable periods, athletes were using a given, accepted process, and becoming the new champion meant improving on that given process—doing a western roll or a straddle better than anyone else had ever done it. The discontinuities occurred when somebody *transformed* the process—the accepted process was the straddle, and then Dick Fosbury came along with the Fosbury Flop. At those times the bar did not go up a little, it went up a lot, and to remain competitive, everybody had to make the adjustment.

The second lesson is that the challenge is to be the next Dick Fosbury. If you keep struggling along, trying to benchmark someone else's process improvement or trying to squeeze better performance out of an old process, you will always be at the mercy of the innovators, those who see an opportunity to create a transformation and break away from the pack. Raising the bar is not something your environment mysteriously does to you; it must be something you do for yourself.

The final thought one can take from this metaphor is the nature of the event itself. The high jump is an individual sport, in which technique (process) is all-important. But transformations can be driven by other factors. Think, for example, of the pole vault, in which the discontinuities have been created by the available technology as the pole evolved from wood to composite materials. Think of basketball, in which rule changes made the three-point shot a reality; it became, as they say, a whole new ball game. The discontinuities that provide an opportunity for transformation can come at you from many sources.

NEW MAPS

Change is taking us into a new world, a world our old map does not fit, a world in which in some cases there are no maps. In the case of the Army, that was literally true when we moved troops from Germany to Africa in December 1992, during the Somali crisis. We had to bring in maps from the United States, and we had to make our own maps of much of the interior. But the figurative maps are even more challenging. Today, we face fundamental shifts in technology, markets, human resource development, global distribution, information management, government intervention, and other critical dimensions of the strategic environments in which we operate. We are being pushed off our old maps into what for many of us is uncharted territory.

The old maps, the old ways of doing business, will not work in today's new territories. Simply improving an existing process will not solve a problem. This is the failure of the "R-words"—reshaping, reengineering, reinventing, and reposturing. *Doing the same thing you have always done—no matter how much you improve it—will get you only what you had before.* The old ways lead to the same old failures.

These last years of the twentieth century are a transitional period when old structures are falling away and new ones, some viable and some transitory, are emerging and competing for survival. The world is moving from the Industrial Age into the Information Age.[2] Alvin and Heidi Toffler call the emerging world the "Third Wave," contrasting it with the Agrarian Age (the First Wave) and the Industrial Age (the Second Wave). MIT's Nicholas Negroponte argues that we are already in a Postinformation Age, an age of extreme specialization.[3] "Technology," says futurist John Petersen, "is transforming our lives and shaping our futures at rates unprecedented in history, with profound implications that we can't even begin to see or understand."[4] All this hyperbole is useful because it helps us put ourselves into the right mind-set. Peter Drucker, the preeminent guru of Industrial Age management science, says, "The one thing we can be sure of is that the world that will emerge from the present rearrangement of values, beliefs, social and economic structures, of political concepts and systems, indeed, of world views, will be different from anything anyone today imagines."[5]

The defining characteristic of Information Age society is the ability to *apply and integrate* rapid technological change. The application and integration of information-based technologies create greater knowledge, enable us to act and behave differently, and are driving structural change in our organizations. But more technologically advanced society will exist side by side with less technologically advanced society for many years to come. The asymmetries themselves create opportunities. For example, for many people in the world, the first telephone they will ever use or own will be a wireless one. Older technologies will simply be bypassed.

But such gross asymmetries are relatively easy to understand compared to the more subtle asymmetries created when an agrarian society reaches up and "borrows" bits and pieces of the Information Age. When we brought the troops home from Somalia, for example, we moved them from Mogadishu to Mombasa, Kenya, on a cruise ship and then flew them home from Mombasa on jumbo jets. The troops loved it: the sea journey gave them a couple of days to clean up and relax before the long flight home. Our concern was the welfare of the troops, but in a completely different sense than seemed obvious at the time: we were concerned that there might be some shoulder-fired air defense missiles in the hands of the Somali warlords—agrarian people with Information Age weapons—and we did not want to take the risk that they would use them against a troop aircraft.

In February 1995, *Newsweek* published a photograph of a Masai warrior carrying a spear and a cellular phone. The image is profound. The Masai are not an Information Age society, but they can reach into the Information Age and pull out various technological applications. Such asymmetries vastly complicate our understanding of the dynamics of human interaction. They present untold opportunities, but they are also fraught with risks and are more complicated than they appear at first glance. To find opportunity in the midst of these significant technological, economic, and cultural discontinuities, we must transform our organizations.

The Power of Information: Atlantic Resolve

Since the time of Frederick the Great, autumn has been the season for military maneuvers in Europe. Since the 1950s, NATO has held annual fall maneuvers involving hundreds of thousands of troops, putting soldiers and their equipment out into the countryside after the harvest and before the snows. Today, complex political issues and missions make that kind of training more critical than ever, but new technologies now make it possible to practice the most difficult tasks and relationships without putting tanks and howitzers into the countryside—and to do it better at higher levels, where the payoff is greatest.

In 1994, a multinational force of more than 400,000 soldiers, sailors, airmen, and marines assembled to deploy to the mythical nation of Atlantis in a border crisis somewhere in the European theater—but with almost no actual troops involved. During this exercise, called "Atlantic Resolve," senior leaders from six nations joined to work through the difficult issues of strategic deployment and operational employment in the complex NATO-U.N. environment of a crisis today. The exercise was made possible by networking simulations from war-gaming centers all over the world and downlinking them into real-world command posts. Never before had there been a large-scale simulation of such high fidelity.

What we saw in Atlantic Resolve was a new way of exercising at a very high level. In a seeming paradox, with almost no troops on the ground, the realism of the political, strategic, and operational issues could actually be made much greater. Moreover, in a Germany grown less and less tolerant of field training since the end of the Cold War, a live exercise would have been constrained by a host of complicated restrictions. The simulation was not.

Equally important, linking powerful simulations directly to command and control systems broke down the "stovepipes" that persist when individual pieces (for example, the air defense battle) are exercised in isolation and spliced in artificially to keep the overall situation moving. It was possible, for example, to link air, air defense, and ground events directly so that, instead of our people carrying out procedures by rote, they could actually make process improvements along the way. At an even higher level, simulation enabled forces in NATO's Central Region to break out of the mold of Cold War plans and to think and learn about the issues associated with contingency operations, such as ad hoc command arrangements, deployment, sustainment over long lines of communication, and so forth. The scenario was purely fictional, but the issues were fundamental, so that in them we could see learning that became applicable when, less than two years later, some of these same forces were on the ground in Bosnia under NATO command.

Atlantic Resolve, the brainchild of U.S. Army Europe's General David Maddox, raised the bar not only for the Army but also for many of our friends and allies.[6]

THE DUAL NATURE OF CHANGE

Change can be characterized as both a *condition* and a *process*. Change as a condition describes what is happening in our environment; change as a process describes the leadership and managerial actions we take to transform our organizations. Change as a condition may influence us profoundly, but it takes place externally; change as a process is what we foster internally. Change as a condition is part of the reality we must accept; change as a process is ours to influence.[7]

This distinction is useful, because when we accept change as a condition in our lives and in the lives of our organizations, we are better able to see it in terms of opportunity and less likely to see only "problems." Change as a condition is like the sun coming up—it *will* happen! The working hypothesis can *never* be the status quo. Because the environment is *always* changing, the working hypothesis must *always* be that the organization must change. To lead effectively, to provide real direction, requires coming to grips with both of these dimensions of change, using change as a process to create opportunity in the changing environment.

It is also useful to think about change in terms of velocity, mass, and complexity.[8] The *velocity* of change is the rate at which change takes place. In most environments, velocity is increasing—that is, change is taking place faster and faster. The *mass* of change is a measure of how widespread it is. Change is taking place in virtually all aspects of our lives and the lives of our organizations. The *complexity* of change refers to the fact that in today's world there is no such thing as change in isolation. Each change affects others in often misunderstood and unanticipated ways that lead to unintended second- and third-order effects that can be advantageous or disastrous. By all three measures, change is more pervasive today than at any time in our lifetimes.

CHANGE VERSUS TRANSFORMATION

Change can be evolutionary or revolutionary; that is, it can take place gradually, within an existing paradigm; or it can come in the form of a more dramatic shift to a whole new paradigm. Both are legitimate strategic choices. If your environment is fairly stable, gradual change may be your best course. More likely, your strategy to create the future will involve both transformation and gradual change. Recall that, in the case of the Army, we made only gradual changes in the critical process of recruiting and retaining quality soldiers and in the process of leader development. The Army has made and is making transformations in other critical processes. The defining characteristic of a transformation is that it results in the creation of a different organization; hence you can legitimately transform your organization without having to transform every single process.

As Figure 9-2 suggests, the process of transformation involves bridging a discontinuity brought about by change in the environment. For the Army, there were two primary discontinuities: missions and technology. Because armies do not operate in a free market, our new missions were thrust upon us; we did not go out and find or develop them. In the case of technology, the discontinuities we faced were much like the problems faced by many other organizations.

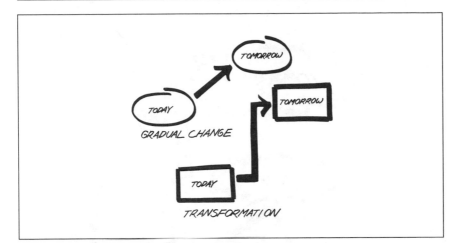

Figure 9-2—Gradual Change and Transformation

THE CHALLENGE OF TRANSFORMATION

The challenge of transformation is to bridge discontinuity while continuing to operate today. The main effort, illustrated in Figure 9-3 by the darkened arrowhead, involves getting the organization into tomorrow but doing it by creating a whole new context for tomorrow, as opposed to going head to head with today.

The intent of transformation is not simply to accommodate discontinuities or to "keep up" with changes in process or changes benchmarked by others; it is, rather, to move into the future and create a new standard. It is to be like Dick Fosbury, or Toyota redefining how automobiles are made, or Apple redefining the purpose of the computer, or Motorola exploding the potential of cellular communications, or McDonald's creating the fast-food industry. Transformation is about becoming something fundamentally different—something better.

Being able to do this is more art than science. A leader will be plagued with the same uncertainties that face the organization as a whole. He or she will always want more data, better analysis, better options. But the more you apply existing methods to study a prob-

Figure 9-3—The Challenge of Transformation

lem, the more you tend to settle for marginal improvements to existing solutions. An adage from the battlefield seems to apply: A good plan, arrived at quickly and pursued vigorously, is better than a perfect plan, arrived at late or executed poorly. Today's environment demands prompt, vigorous action focused on the critical point, and perfected in the execution. It is art, not science.

SUCCESSIVE TRANSFORMATIONS

One of the immutable facts about transformation is that you must start with today's reality. When you visualize the future, you are dealing with intellectual constraints; but when you *build* the future, you must accept physical constraints. The realities of today—your environment, resources, people, technology, and so forth—are your only means. You must blend a dose of pragmatism into your campaign; one way of doing so is by building the future in stages, from point to point, or, in the language we used for the vision, building the "next," then the "after next" (see Figure 9-4).

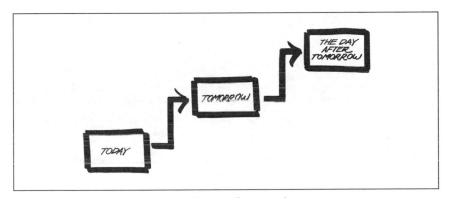

Figure 9-4—Successive Transformation

In the case of the Army, it was impossible to move directly to some manifestation of Force XXI, as it would take time to develop both the doctrine and the fieldable technology. But it was possible to move away from the Cold War and create a "Power Projection Army" that was more capable of meeting the challenges of the emerging world by using means readily at hand. The tools for doing this were deployment doctrine, reserve equipment prepositioned aboard ships, modernized airlift, training for contingency operations, more flexible reserve call-up policies, flexible deployment planning, digital communications equipment with a true global reach, and even such things as standby logistics packages containing food, prefabricated shelters, and other supplies. Those tools were within today's means; they involved reconfiguration, process improvement, and marginal investment. As still more means become available, the transformation to a still more capable, more versatile force can be effected. The Power Projection Army is not an end state—nor will Force XXI be an end state—but building it was a way of making significant progress by growing from point to point.

RULE EIGHT: BETTER IS BETTER

Winning organizations understand that "better" is not necessarily defined in terms of today's rubrics. Better is not about improved quality, reduced costs, faster cycle time, flatter structure, empowerment, or shared information. Better may include all those things and more, but those are the dimensions of gradual change. Better is about establishing and sustaining an edge in tomorrow's world. Better is becoming something different. Better is winning.

EIGHT MINUTES TO THREE MINUTES: ORGANIZING AROUND INFORMATION

Engaging an unseen target with a mortar has always been a complex, difficult process. It involves an observer, a fire direction center, the unit command post or tactical operations center, the mortar itself with its crew and ammunition, and the communications network. For years, the time standard for this task was eight minutes from the time the target was observed until it was engaged and destroyed. In experiments at the National Training Center at Fort Irwin, California, in 1994, a tank crew was able to identify a target and determine its exact azimuth and distance with a laser range finder. An onboard global positioning system indicated the precise location of the tank, so that the tank commander could compute the precise location of the target with the press of a button. All this information was broadcast digitally directly to the mortar crew, who computed the firing data using small onboard computers. At the same time, the task force database was automatically checked for friendly locations to make sure the target was really an enemy. All of this done, the crew set the correct explosive charge, armed the fuse, and fired the rounds, hitting in less than three minutes (including the sixty-second flight time of the rounds)—with fewer steps, faster communications, and less error.

Speed and accuracy—in other words, effectiveness—were achieved by giving the mortar crew and tank crew the tools to act as a semi-independent, ad hoc team brought together by a common understanding of the concept and intent and enabled by the power of information technology. This was a genuine breakthrough in the effectiveness of people, leveraged by technology.

"Eight minutes to three minutes" is an example of what it means to be organized around information. In the eight-minute organization, the tanks and mortars were organized into their own stovepipes and integrated by human interfaces—a forward observer assigned to the tanks; a fire direction center to compute and check the data; command posts to check databases to ensure, as best they could, that no friendly forces were in the target area; and command posts to establish communications channels and coordinate all these actions. The three-minute organization was formed around information—information the tank crew had that the mortar crew needed, which could unleash a capability the mortar crew had that the tank crew needed. It could exist because of technology—a global positioning system, laser ranging devices, digital communications, on-board computers, and so on—that greatly reduces human error. But it all came together because of the organizational concept. And with success achieved, the team ceased to exist as quickly as it had formed.

In retailing today, we see numerous equally dramatic examples of organizing around information. In casual fashions, stores such as the Gap link point-of-sale terminals directly to real-time production and distribution decisions. This reduces and focuses inventory at the retail level while at the same time minimizing losses on overstocked, slow-moving merchandise.[9] In an industry where the old ways meant four- to six-month cycles, the Gap and retailers like it can influence what is on the shelf in as little as two weeks.

Organizing around information gives organizations the ability to

carry out both *simultaneous* and *synchronized* operations. These are
two very important concepts that are related but different.

Simultaneity simply means doing many things at once. The Information Age organization has both a greater capacity for doing many
different things at once and a whole new capacity for performing
multiple phases of an operation simultaneously. To explain that, let's
go back to some theories of military operations. Contemplating the
nature of future warfare, Richard Simpkin, in his classic *Race to the
Swift*,[10] demonstrated that armies must operate and plan simultaneously. This important foundation thought underlies the concept of
cycle time in organizations. Whatever the cycle being considered, it
ultimately must be collapsed so that all cycles are running concurrently. To Simpkin's ideas about simultaneous operation and planning, we add recovery. The Information Age organization has the
ability to conduct an operation, plan the follow-on operation, and re-
cover from the previous operation, all at the same time. Given
today's short product life cycles and the rate and volume of change
as a condition, such capabilities are now essential to success. The
same environment that has created the need for faster cycle times
has also given us new organizational forms, organized around information, to exploit new opportunity.

Information Age organizations are also vastly more capable of
synchronizing operations, getting things to come together at a point
in time to achieve a decisive effect. *Synchronizing* operations can be
thought of as getting the functional pieces coordinated so that they
are focused on the customer at the same moment. A great promo-
tional rollout is of little value if the product is not ready on time! Organizing around information creates horizontal links that facilitate
synchronization.

Organizing around information also enables operations to be *distributed*—that is, spread geographically but combined in effect.
Everything does not have to be under one roof, either literally or
figuratively, at any phase of an operation. The Industrial Age model
led us to self-contained units. Information Age units can be virtual,
coming together with only what is needed where it is needed and
when it is needed, thus creating both greater economy and greater
flexibility.

Information Age organizations are evolving around a number of important shared characteristics:

• They are organized around information, rather than around traditional business functional areas.

• They are able to synthesize and focus knowledge rapidly, learning and adapting almost organically.

• They take risks and make mistakes, but they do not gamble and they can outrun their mistakes.

• They are inherently more versatile at every level; connectivity is more important than boundaries.

• They recognize that many of their processes, even some critical ones, extend beyond the traditional organizational boundaries

• They are developing a capacity for simultaneity in thought and execution.

• They share an awareness of their global situation.

• Distributed operations, including many that are outsourced, are routine.

As can be seen, organizing around information tends to decentralize the decision-making process—an obstacle that is often difficult to overcome. Once it is overcome, however, senior leaders are actually liberated to focus on the longer-term decisions. The old ways of doing business, with precise checks and balances in multiple organizational areas, only add time and induce error.

Finally, to organize around information, we can put quality and speed into perspective. There has been a genuine quality revolution both in America and in other countries. Increasingly, high quality is the cost of entry into the marketplace, but it cannot be a vision, process, or strategy because, by itself, it does not relate very well to purpose. However, when we consider speed as a second ingredient of sustained vitality in the Information Age organization, we can see both in their proper perspective; they combine to form a base from which learning and growth can evolve. Quality and speed are the new basics; they are the blocking and tackling of the Information Age organization.

TRANSFORMATION AS HUMAN DRAMA

The nature of transformation is such that organizations will constantly have to face the challenge of reassuring their employees—creating positive feelings about the future. This is especially so in the 1990s, when change has generally been accompanied by layoffs, closures, and downsizing. People find meaning in their jobs, and making major changes in their jobs affects not only their economic well-being but also their sense of self-worth. It is a critically important leadership task to establish an atmosphere of growth so that change can be seen in a positive light by the people involved. How can this be done?

First, a leader must lead the human dimension of change. It is not enough to be the good idea guy who works only the positive actions. You have to personally work *all* the people dimensions, both good and bad. In the Army, we used all the means of communication we could to show the most senior leaders actively leading the Army the way to the future. We used videos, newspaper and magazine articles, conferences and meetings, speeches, and even letters. We made sure our successes were publicized, but we also let people know about bad news, setbacks, downsizing, and necessary retrenchments as early as possible. We formalized a process of chain teaching, so that every leader, down the chain, got both the good and the bad news from his or her superior and passed it on using factual teaching materials. We quickly found out that if they did not hear the good *and* the bad news from their leaders, they would pick it up in the trade papers and from the grapevine—sources that generally put the most negative spin possible on whatever is being reported.

The fact that we had to downsize made leading the human dimension much more difficult. One of our biggest challenges in establishing the defense budget was the constant negotiations about the "end state," the magic number for the future strength of the Army that would balance the programmers' books. In an operational sense, this was a meaningless concept; we could predict that technology would lead us to change our organizational designs in as yet unpredictable ways. But emotionally, without an end state in which they could have confidence, the troops saw us as being in free fall, which badly undermined our efforts to provide them with a sense of security.

Another challenge was deciding when to announce unit inactivations and how long to keep them in readiness once we had decided to inactivate them. We were often criticized for having no plan, when in fact we had made a conscious decision to withhold the plan for the health of the organization. We were not always able to tell everybody everything, but we told people as much as possible as soon as possible because inevitably bad news known was easier for the organization to deal with than worse news imagined.

Whether you are letting people go, moving them to New Mexico, or simply reassigning them to new jobs in the same plant or headquarters, you must treat them with dignity and respect. That is a principle to be adhered to in the best of times, but it is absolutely critical during times of uncertainty and stressful change. Otherwise, your people will look at your actions, no matter how fine your words, and withdraw their loyalty. If you treat the people who are moving or leaving in a summary fashion, you cannot expect those who are staying to have confidence that when the chips are down you will treat them any better. The best will be tempted to leave, and everyone will spend too much energy worrying about the future—energy that should be used to *create* the future. People should be given as much notice as is feasible, their service should be recognized, and they should be assisted in their transition as much as possible. You should do these things not only because you owe it to those who have been a part of your organization but also for those who are staying—they will respect you more for having taken care of their friends and coworkers.

We have seen most organizations grow, or try to grow, through successive approximation, by going from solution to solution, only occasionally making real breakthroughs. In tomorrow's world, winners will be characterized by their ability to handle continuous transformation; they will have made transformation—not process improvement—a part of their culture. It is only by a process of transformation—*continuous* transformation—that organizations that are competitive today can change and be competitive tomorrow.

Overthrowing Success

Demonstrating the Future

Professor Roger Spiller, resident historian at the Army's Staff College, wrote me a letter early in my tenure in which he said, "When a people can only define their times by reference to what has gone before, it is a sure sign of ambivalence about the present and anxiety about the future. We have not yet been able to make sense about the times in which we now live, and this failure makes us nervous when we expected that, on the contrary, we would feel calm and confident in the future when the Cold War was finally over." Roger spends his days with midcareer officers, and his thoughts often reflect their concerns. He was telling me, with greater clarity than I could muster, that the Army was in a kind of "Age of Anxiety," and that, lacking a clear focus on its future, it was focusing instead on its recent past.

After the Persian Gulf War, there were some who

wanted to "fix" the "problems" they had encountered by creating armored divisions one third larger than the Desert Storm design. Their experience led them to believe that a division should be more self-contained, optimized for what they had experienced in the Gulf and would likely experience again under similar circumstances.

This behavior was logical and not at all surprising. It had been fifty years since armored battles on anything approaching the scale of Desert Storm had been fought, and the Army was relating to its most recent successful battlefield experience. However, we could not optimize ourselves to fight only one kind of war. The challenge we all faced was to break out of this mold—to look ahead, not backward. The world we faced demanded flexibility, smaller units we could mix and match not only for another Desert Storm but also for other, very different contingencies as well. We needed a flexible solution, not a perfect one. Had we rebuilt the Army to "fix" all the lessons of Desert Storm, we would have been like a man who can afford only one suit—and buys a tuxedo. He is well prepared for New Year's Eve but is caught short the rest of the year.

Most of us have a difficult time appreciating the practical application of the ideas of visionaries; we have to touch something real. In my speeches, I talked about Keats's poem "Ode on a Grecian Urn." You can read that poem a hundred times, and it will say many things to you, but to really understand a Grecian urn, you have to hold it in your hands, touch it, feel its texture and shape. To get beyond the words of the visionaries and really begin to understand the future, we had to touch it. I challenged the Army to produce a "Grecian urn," a manifestation of the future that we could touch. To do that, we created "forcing functions," activities or events that would force people to grapple with the technological and organizational issues of tomorrow—not by trying to make yesterday perfect but by building on what we were learning about the future. My vehicle for doing that was the creation of a focal point for purposeful thought, experimentation, and action.

In 1991, the Center for Military History had just published a study of the Louisiana Maneuvers, a series of large-scale field exercises that George Marshall had used to forge the Army that would fight World War II.[1] I was compelled by the power of Marshall's idea and by his intent to conduct experiments that would be the basis for designing new units and new battlefield processes. To that end, we created the Louisiana Maneuvers Task Force. Borrowing Marshall's title was a signal that business as usual was not good enough, that I was fostering innovation and growth in extraordinary ways, but that the outcome would not be completely foreign or threatening to the Army. I made it part of my office to signal that I—not merely my staff—was going to be personally involved.

Because the Louisiana Maneuvers were an adjunct to the formal organization, there was tension between the task force and the formal organization, notably the headquarters staff and the commands normally charged with future developments. To them, the Louisiana Maneuvers represented a loss of control and a threat to existing processes. My intent was not to establish competition, but I did feel that a certain amount of tension would be good— that it would accelerate positive action and help motivate the keepers of the traditional processes to break their old molds.

The Louisiana Maneuvers Task Force was charged with integrating, and in some cases jump-starting, the experimental processes and then bringing the results back to the senior generals. These were ambitious experiments. Normally, in troop tests, the Army attempts to establish a controlled environment in which one variable at a time can be studied. However, because we were dealing with potentially whole new ways of operating, it was necessary to cope with large numbers of variables at one time. This was not about which new gadget to buy or where to mount the latest widget; it was about prying open a window onto a whole new world. By experimenting with digitization, advanced simulations, new structures, and new kinds of operations, I was trying to cut short the cumbersome, bureaucratic test and evaluation processes that we had developed during the Cold War, processes best suited to gradual, marginal change and not to breakthrough discovery. The details could come later; we needed to find a direction, quickly, and get on with the job.

In addition to the experiments, we were able to use our periodic commanders' conferences, symposia, and other meetings to showcase demonstrations. For example, at the 1994 annual meeting of the Association of the United States Army[2] in Washington, D.C., the Louisiana Maneuvers Task Force demonstrated the linkage of different kinds of simulations, networked from different locations around the world, into a common environment on the floor of the exhibit hall. More than 25,000 people, in and out of uniform, saw that demonstration. To pull it off, the Louisiana Maneuvers Task Force had been forced to solve data transfer and synthesis problems that had never been solved before, putting soldiers in Alabama and Kentucky in flight simulators and armored-vehicle simulators linked to a major training event in California and related to larger-scale computer war games in Kansas—and there were more pieces than that—all fused into a common experience in a conference hall in Washington, D.C. Forcing people to do that—to link virtual, live, and constructive simulations of battle—helped us create new capabilities, and demonstrating those capabilities to thousands of people helped them begin to understand the power of this new age and encouraged them to become disciples.

These activities all took resources—time, energy, talented people, and scarce dollars—and there was tension because of that. But in the process, people began to be excited about the future. Some began to see and experience what I had been talking about when I spoke about growth.

In this process, we gained momentum. We grew a critical mass of change agents, at every level and in a number of different parts of the Army. Over time, they came to see the success of the organization as dependent on growing into the future and not simply as accommodating change or perfecting the processes they had been part of all their lives.

—GRS

★ ★ ★ ★

EVERY ORGANIZATION HAS A SINE CURVE

As we contemplated the need to transform the Army, we knew that failure was a real possibility. Armies do not fail the same way corporations do. Bankrupt armies continue to exist, but they become inept. It takes a Korean War kind of event to expose decay and unreadiness. That thought was, and continues to be, an enormously heavy burden on everyone involved in reshaping the Army. We had to keep the force ready to fight.

After World War I, World War II, Korea, and Vietnam, readiness had fallen dramatically while the Army demobilized. After World War II, things had gotten so bad that in July 1950 the North Koreans had nearly pushed us off the Korean Peninsula. The most powerful nation on earth, whose Army had been without equal only five years before, was able to hang on only by the extraordinary heroism of a handful of men neither trained nor equipped to defeat the North Koreans.[3] Nearly forty years later, as the Cold War ended, we knew that the bias in America would be to repeat that cycle, to put the Army onto the shelf, to let it demobilize and atrophy, thus setting the stage for another near-disastrous Korea somewhere in our future.[4]

The historic problem of an unready Army is not simply a problem of politics and budgets. In the past, the Army bureaucracy was slow to adapt to changing conditions. In 1939, the year Germany invaded

Poland and with Japan already at war on the mainland of Asia, the U.S. Army was still worried about how to transport machine guns by horse and the latest innovations in coast artillery. The history of America's first battles is a costly history of failure—of being unready for war. It is a history of failure to stay ready, failure to adapt, failure to prepare.[5]

This led us to think about our history in terms of an effectiveness cycle that we called a "sine curve" (see Figure 10-1). In building the World War II Army, we had come off the bottom. George Marshall recognized that fact in 1939, when he said, "When we had time, we had no money and now that we have money, we have no time."[6] The same was true when we built the Cold War Army during the Korean War and rebuilt it after Vietnam. Each case involved transformation off the bottom. In the first two cases, a sense of crisis had focused the organization and made resources available. After Vietnam, there was more ambiguity and the amount of resources available was initially variable, but the Army had support for what it was doing and a clear sense of internal crisis. The question in 1991 was how to make a *transformation off the top*. This is a very different problem.

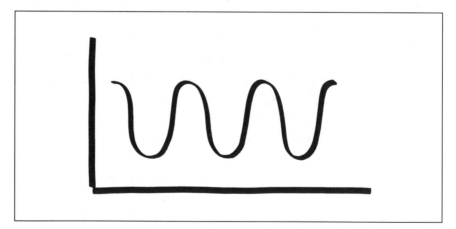

Figure 10-1—The Sine Curve

Other organizations have wrestled with the same issue. If we look at the U.S. automobile industry, for example, each of the Big Three automakers has had to come off the bottom; the most recent, still in transformation, is General Motors. Most of the dramatic cases have been transformations off the bottom by companies such as Xerox, British Airways, and Ford. There have been successful transformations off the top—General Electric is a premier example—but the Paradox of Action suggests that these are much more difficult. When they do occur, they are less visible than crisis-driven turnarounds, because from the outside they look like continuous growth.

The challenge in transforming off the top is, as Arie de Geus, the legendary planner at Royal Dutch Shell, has said, "to recognize and react to environmental change before the pain of a crisis."[7] But that is very difficult. Without a perceptible crisis to galvanize people to action, there is enormous resistance to change, resistance that does not show up until later in the process if you are starting from the bottom.

THINK . . . DO . . . BE

Knowing we were at the top and believing that there was nowhere to go but down unless the Army could be led to embrace fundamental change, we had to overthrow a successful organization. We found two important tools with which to begin the task: *communication* and *demonstration*.

We come back to our belief that high-performing organizations communicate aggressively to share information. Making transformation a reality requires communication up, down, and laterally, both inside and outside of the organizational boundary. A leader fosters this communication by using conferences, speeches, newsletters, posters, computer bulletin boards—the entire communications spectrum—to create an awareness of the transformation and to nurture faith in the leadership. Communicating the need to grow is crucial.

Once the strategic architecture (the thinking) has begun to be put into place, the leader can direct the campaign by a series of demonstrations. "Doing," or executing a series of carefully chosen demonstrations of the future, creates believers and builds momentum for the actual physical processes of transformation. As this momentum grows, the organization slowly becomes something else—it transforms. The sequence is "Think, Do, Be" (see Figure 10-2).

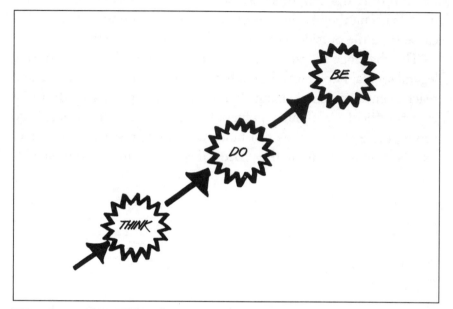

Figure 10-2—"Think, Do, Be"

Benchmarking the Future

The "Do" of "Think, Do, Be" is a process of benchmarking the future by actually demonstrating the new theory. Initially, the Army set out to do that with a series of experiments and exercises that were focused primarily on benchmarking the capabilities of emerging information technology. We quickly found, however, that carrying out some of our new missions provided important benchmarks as well.

Desert Hammer

In 1992, the United States Army Armor Center, under the leadership of then Major General Paul Funk, began a series of experiments to create a digital battlefield. Funk's vision, shared by General Fred Franks at the Training and Doctrine Command and others, was digital connectivity throughout a mobile armored unit. This would link all the elements of the force—tanks, infantry, artillery, helicopters—across all the battlefield systems—intelligence, fire support, logistics, and so forth. Funk's vision was that by using high-speed digital communications and onboard microprocessors, he could get everybody in the fight operating off of the same high-quality information. By integrating the rapidly emerging capabilities of global positioning systems, laser range finders, unmanned aerial reconnaissance, digital photography and video, and the like, he could take much of the ambiguity and time delay out of traditional man-in-the-loop voice and analogue systems and make it possible for commanders to assess the situation, issue orders, and move decisively with lightning-fast speed and accuracy.

The first experiments were very simple: there was a platoon of four tanks, then a company of fourteen, then Funk and his people began integrating infantry, artillery, and other battlefield systems. It was a long step from theory to practice, especially with the then-available systems and a shoestring budget. In some cases the troops were literally lashing the laptops into the tanks with duct tape, but the prototypes were good enough for us to see the potential for raising land warfare to a new level.

From these early experiments, the Army went to the National Training Center at Fort Irwin, California—a Rhode Island–sized stretch of desert just south of Death Valley—where, in the spring of 1994, a battalion-sized task force was formed to operate with "digital connectivity" in an exercise against the Army's best-trained opposing force. This experiment, called Desert Hammer, had a lot of rough edges. The Army had brought together forty-four different agencies to make it happen, and some of the software was still being tuned up when the exercise started. But overall, the digital task force was able to move faster and more confidently, achieving better results and suf-

fering fewer casualties than a similar force in a standard configuration.[8]

From that demonstration, support grew. We created an Army Digitization Office and designated the 4th Infantry Division at Fort
Hood, Texas, to experiment at an ever-higher level of organization,
integrating ever-more-capable equipment into larger and larger units
in a process that was both transformation and continuous process
improvement. At the same time, what the Army was learning was
being fed directly into the operational units. For example, a man-
portable, day-night digital video camera, broadcasting intelligence directly into the command post from miles away, went through three
generations of development in the course of the experiments and
was fielded on a prototype basis with forces in Haiti.

Operation Support Hope

Operation Support Hope, conducted to provide humanitarian support to the refugee operations in central Africa in the summer of
1994, is an example of an actual operation that gave a benchmark
for the future. The lessons of Somalia and the Kurdish refugee problem after Desert Storm had taught us that such operations would
be conducted with ad hoc units operating within joint-service
task forces and networked to United Nations agencies and nongovernmental relief organizations from many nations. When the Army
went into central Africa, it created the organizational structure
needed as it deployed. Starting with an airborne task force gar-
risoned in Italy, units and capabilities were added and deleted to give
the commander on the ground the kinds of engineering, transportation, medical, logistics, communications, and other support he
needed to achieve a decisive victory. No existing unit type could have
accomplished that mission, and simply amalgamating existing units
would have created a force too large, too cumbersome, and with too
much excess capacity. What was needed was a well-tailored force
that could be adjusted as the operation went through its several
phases.

The Support Hope benchmark for the Army was two-dimensional. First, it was one more compelling example of our new mis-

sions. For those who opposed using the Army for humanitarian assistance and other similar missions, it was an important practical lesson in the role of America's Army in today's world. From a second perspective, it illustrated not only that we did need units with greater versatility and flexibility but that we had a substantial capability already in hand if we could learn how to better exploit it.

THIN THREADS

We called these experiments and real-world operations "thin threads." The notion comes from the idea of transformation as a discontinuity. In Figure 10-3, we suggest that new ways supplant old ways in a bold and coherent *fait accompli*. The implication is that you somehow step from the present into tomorrow in one move.

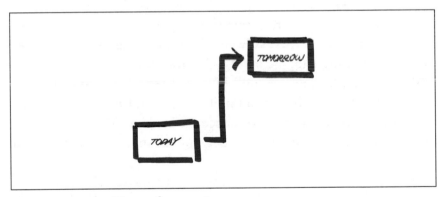

Figure 10-3—Transformation

The real world is not so simple. Our organizations are very complex, and getting across the discontinuity involves changing hundreds or even thousands of individual processes. *A thin thread changes a single process or small group of processes to bridge the discontinuity in a demonstrable way, establishing a foothold in the future.* As the first thin thread is joined by others, they are woven into a stronger and stronger web until, at some point, there is a sufficient pattern of change that the whole organization begins to cross over, aligning with the new paradigm and rejecting the old (see Figure 10-4).

Figure 10-4—Thin Threads

A thin thread is an end-to-end prototype that represents an important part of the larger transformation. Its demonstration of success reinforces the necessity for the transformation, thereby attracting increasing support for it.[9] The thin thread must in and of itself be a significant accomplishment. Desert Hammer, for example, was a major achievement in its own right. Operation Support Hope was a magnificent performance on its own. In demonstrating the potential to go beyond those beginnings, they became true thin threads.

You can also see the other important characteristics of thin threads in these examples. A thin thread must be achievable. You have to stretch, but in designing thin threads it is important not to stretch too far, not to be unrealistic. You must structure for success but you cannot stack the deck, or your results will be discounted as trivial. A thin thread must not appear to be unique; it represents what can be done across a range of applications. That Desert Hammer was done with an operational unit, in a recognized training center, across many disciplines made it much more representative than if it had been done under laboratory conditions or with only a specialized segment of the force.

Thin threads must have the support of the leadership. By means of the Louisiana Maneuvers, the senior generals took ownership of this process. That made it more likely that any given experiment would succeed or fail on its own merits, not because of organizational biases. The senior-level sponsorship also helped ensure that people were paying attention to what was happening. In sponsoring the experiment, the senior leaders were saying "This is the direction we think we need to take, and we are willing to take a lot of risks to learn more about it."

Finally, a thin thread should not be completely independent. The event itself may stand alone, but the processes with which it deals should have deep-rooted networks so that the thin thread will pull other things along. A good thin thread acts like a magnet, creating the kind of "aha"s that inspire people to take ownership of new ideas and begin translating them into other areas.

Peacekeeping Training

Recognizing the complexity of our new missions, we knew we had to legitimize them within the Army culture and learn to perform them well. We were able to do both by conducting peacekeeping training exercises at our training centers. One such exercise, at the Joint Readiness Operations Training Center at Fort Polk, Louisiana, brings together diverse Army units with Air Force, Marine, Navy, and Special Operations forces to practice peacekeeping operations. The troops are employed on a "battlefield" containing both friendly and unfriendly civilians and paramilitary forces. Participating in the training are representatives from other U.S. government organizations, the United Nations, various nongovernmental organizations, and television and print media. The places of some are filled by role players, but as many as possible are actual representatives of these organizations. This is the world as it is, a world in which those same organizations will be operating side by side, a world they and the Army will be better prepared to face because of their experience training together. Not only do these exercises better prepare soldiers to execute their tasks in peacekeeping operations, they also break down cultural barriers within and between the organizations involved.

These types of training exercises have been held at each of the Army's training centers and thus have created a standard that units copy at their home garrisons. The power of the thin thread is that it helps you establish a new benchmark. In this case, the benchmark was telling the Army to take an expanded view of tasks and conditions in its training environment.

In-Transit Visibility

Desert Storm had taught the Army that our depot-based logistics systems were badly out of date. The Army lacked an in-transit visibility system, including such basic elements as the means of electronically identifying the contents of shipping containers and the locations of critical parts in the supply pipeline. This was a case where benchmarking outside the Army gave us the thin thread to effect fundamental change within the Army. Under the leadership of General Jimmy Ross, the Army Material Command went to the Department of Transportation's Volpe Center, Penn State University, and elsewhere and began a process of bringing in best practices from the civilian sector.

Ross's people brought in bar coding and a Federal Express–type tracking system that could be accessed by both the requester and the shipper. By the time the Army deployed to Somalia, soldiers in Mogadishu could track a shipment of repair parts on laptop computers from the time the requisition was received at the depot in the United States until the shipment arrived in country. By the time the 25th Infantry Division deployed from Hawaii to Haiti, the Army's pencil-and-paper shipping documentation had been transformed. It was possible to track every container throughout its journey and to know what was inside. Ultimately, this is leading to expanded information-based logistics, a major paradigm shift for an organization that, in the nineteenth century, pioneered inventory-based logistics.

Own the Night

Since the 1960s, the Army has been a leader in the development of night vision technologies. By the 1990s, we had a range of aerial and ground devices, including tank gunsights, binocular-type devices for the individual soldier, aircraft sights, sensors for intelligence gathering, and so forth. We spoke of "owning the night" and had made great progress in our night-fighting capability, especially in the mechanized force and in aviation. Reflecting on a recently published account of the Panama operation[10] that seemed to emphasize the importance of this issue, in February 1992[11] the Chief of Staff asked a simple question of the commander of the Training and Doctrine Command: "What do we mean when we say we own the night?"

This became the initial research question posed to the Dismounted Battlespace Battle Laboratory, located at the Infantry School at Fort Benning, Georgia. From the Battle Lab, the inquiry grew to the establishment of a much larger integrated team, the 2d Generation Forward Looking Infrared (2d Gen FLIR) Task Force, which in turn put out tendrils throughout the research-and-development and acquisition community. Because virtually all the Army's many communities had some interest in night operations, the network became very broad.

Out of this effort came a reengineered approach to developing and fielding the new systems: breaking down functional barriers so that a tank gunsight, a helicopter gunsight, individual viewing devices, and so forth can be built from common components and modules. What is more, they are being manufactured to be backward compatible with existing hardware, so that fielding can be immediate and continuous. Much of this might have happened anyway, because people were headed in this direction. But this simple question, "What do we mean when we say . . .?" brought people together horizontally, accelerated the development and fielding of new capabilities, saved money and effort, and fundamentally changed how we viewed the development, acquisition, and assimilation of emerging technologies. The 2d Gen FLIR Task Force was a thin thread.

Overcoming Resistance to Change

No matter how clear and convincing demonstrations may be, to effect a transformation leaders must overcome people's resistance to change. This is a particular problem in the military. George Patton observed in 1931 that we in the military "tend to consider the most recent past war as the last word, the sealed future pattern of all contests. . . . First, we realize, none better, that in the last war it was necessary to make many improvisations and to ply our trade with ill-assorted tools. . . . In our efforts to provide for the avoidance, in future, of the mistakes which we personally have encountered . . . we proceed to enunciate rules." [12] Patton argued that this is futile, that it is not rules that lead to success in war but the indomitable spirit of the leader and his ability to motivate and inspire superhuman performance.

In "The Paradox of Action" we suggested that the turnover in the *Fortune* 500 is testimony to the tendency to look back, to make rules based on past successes (or failures). It is not a habit to which the military has sole claim. This bias to see the future through yesterday's eyes leads to resistance to change and is characteristic of all of our organizations. It arises naturally from today competing with tomorrow, from the unintended consequences of our actions, and from aversion to personal risk. A leader overcomes resistance by taking cognizance of it, by accommodating people's needs to a reasonable degree, and by helping them understand their roles. Overcoming resistance is a big step and will influence the rate at which transformation can take place as much as any other factor will.

The Breech-loading Musket

By the beginning of the Civil War, the standard infantry weapon was the muzzle-loading rifle, normally .58 caliber (that is, the barrel was .58 inch in inside diameter). It fired a hollow-based, pointed lead bullet called a "Minic ball." A soldier carried paper cartridges holding a measure of black powder and one Minie ball. To fire his rifle, he would bite through the cartridge, grasping the Minie ball in his teeth, pour the black powder down the length of the barrel, stuff the paper cartridge into the barrel on top of the black powder, then drop in the Minie ball and ram it all tight with a metal ramrod carried in the rifle stock under the barrel. Doing all this required a soldier to be standing up, with the shoulder stock resting on the ground. Once the musket was loaded, he would pick it up and put a percussion cap over a tiny hole in the breech. When struck by the hammer, the percussion cap produced the spark necessary to ignite the black powder and propel the Minie ball its lethal distance of two to four hundred yards. A well-trained soldier could manage four rounds per minute with this kind of rifle, although the black powder and paper residue tended to build up and slow him down as he progressed through a battle.

By 1861, advancing metallurgy and manufacturing techniques had produced a number of alternatives. The simplest designs adapted existing muzzle loaders by means of a simple breech block that could be opened and loaded with a single round. Most notable was the Marsh rifle, which used the standard paper cartridge and percussion cap. The more complex included the Spencer and Henry repeating rifles, both of which used copper cartridges, and a revolving rifle by Colt that used paper cartridges.

Although breechloaders were used extensively for cavalry and some special regiments of sharpshooters and volunteers, in spite of a constant stream of recommendations from field commanders and even the support of President Lincoln, they were not adopted for wide use by infantry troops until the war was over. The records of the War Department provide a rich dialogue on the resistance to this change.

- The principal objection from the Ordnance Department was based on complexity: introducing breechloaders, it said, would increase the number of types of weapons and ammunition required.

- The second principal objection was also made on the basis of logistics. Using a simple, single-shot breechloader, an infantryman could easily increase his maximum rate of fire from three or four rounds per minute to twelve, a minimum 300 percent increase. Even allowing for the greater effectiveness of a higher volume of fire, breechloaders would more than double the requirement for ammunition, and it was by no means clear that twice as much ammunition could be manufactured or delivered to the front lines.

• Logisticians were not alone in voicing concern, however, as regular officers feared that the soldiers would take less care with each shot and many bullets would be wasted. That was a particularly ironic criticism given the tactics of the day, which relied on volley fire aimed not so much at individuals as at the mass of enemy troops.

• In battle, soldiers stood shoulder to shoulder, firing into the ranks of the enemy. Some field officers opposed the breechloader as an infantry weapon because it would not be conducive to such tactics. With the new rifle, the soldiers could easily lie down and shoot, making it more difficult to control formations. Some even suggested that once they had learned to shoot lying down, "We'll never get them up again." At the very least, most agreed that the Army's training system would have to be revamped to accommodate this radically new technology.

• Finally, critics made the point that the "new technology" was generally untested, unproved, and more fragile and prone to break down on the battlefield.

While it seems clear that the benefits would have far outweighed the costs and that the criticisms of fragility and unprovenness were spurious, most of these criticisms had standing. It would have been more difficult to supply an Army of breechloaders because licensing and standardization in manufacturing capability did not yet exist on a large scale, and ammunition requirements would have more than doubled. That would have put enormous pressures on the distribution system, still dependent on the horse once the forward railhead was passed. It would have been necessary to retrain soldiers and to develop new ways to fight. But as Carl Davis suggests in his *Arming the Union*, less resistance to innovation could have led to a very different kind of army.[13]

There is an ironic postscript to this story: In the 1960s, the Army adopted an automatic rifle as the standard weapon, replacing a very good, modern semiautomatic rifle. The resulting debate in the infantry community had an all-too-familiar ring: there would be a need to retrain the troops, soldiers would shoot too much ammunition, it would degrade marksmanship skills, the new rifle was not durable enough, what might work in Vietnam would not work in Europe, and so on. Seeing tomorrow through yesterday's eyes is a normal, albeit frustrating, part of the life of every organization.

BUY-IN AND CRITICAL MASS

We were able to use stories like that of the Civil War musket as one way of breaking down resistance to change. Another tool was wide publicity of the results of experiments, constantly emphasizing our concept and intent. Once we had created the umbrella concept for Force XXI, it seemed to give people more confidence. Inevitably, however, there were some who "just didn't get it," and that was problematic.

An organization's culture can be thought of as its collective "personality," which defines and constrains its behavior very strongly. Transformation means changing those ingrained and valued behaviors and convincing people that your ideas are substantive, not just the latest fad. It takes time and momentum to break down resistance, and there are no easy solutions.

As we watched the Army grow through its transformation, four stages of growth appeared.

Stage One, Avoid Change. In the first stage, in 1991, resistance was the most intense. There was a bias toward making yesterday perfect, fixing the lessons of the Gulf War, enduring the downsizing, and getting on with things the way they had been for a decade. There was a feeling shared by many that if we got the story right, the Army would be left alone to sort itself out. In this stage, many people were focusing on how substantive change could be avoided.

Stage Two, Endure Change. As the Army came to grips with the necessity to change, it focused on the negative aspects of change: downsizing, moving, redefinition of responsibilities, being forced to perform missions that many saw as "nonmilitary." This was normal, even healthy, given the turmoil of letting 600,000 people go; but it was not a healthy focus for the long term. This was the stage in which people were focusing on change as a condition, change to be accommodated with as little disturbance as possible to the status quo, either for them personally or for the Army.

Stage Three, Accept Change. As the experiments began to mature and as people came to grips with the positive aspects of new missions, the collective focus shifted to the more positive aspects of change. People were now more focused on change as a process, demonstrating concern about what changes were taking place, how they were being effected, and how they related to them and the organization.

Stage Four, Embrace Change. In this last stage, the fact that we were truly transforming began to be accepted and people began to see the change process as a tool for them to use to become something different. In this stage, people were focusing on what they and the Army were becoming. It was only after several years that we began to see a critical mass of the leaders beginning to think like this.

These stages were not as progressive as we have made them look. Often it seemed as if we were in two or three at once; indeed, different parts of the Army were in different stages at any given time. Our experience is anecdotal, but the logic of the progression through the stages seems reasonable: avoidance; acceptance of change as a condition; acceptance of change as a process; and finally, exploitation of change to effect real transformation.

RULE NINE: FOCUS ON THE FUTURE

A leader today does not have the luxury of waiting until the organization perceives a crisis. A leader must focus on the future from wherever the organization is on the sine curve and thereby nurture a positive, creative culture, one marked by optimism. By sponsoring specific activities and events designed to illustrate and test the new paradigm, a leader encourages similar behavior in others, causing them to look beyond today and participate in creating the new organization.

A MARK ON THE WALL

As we rolled out our concepts for Force XXI, not simply as a pie-in-the-sky future force but as a process of experimentation and discovery to begin right away, we tried to focus on the future. We could predict that Force XXI would feature flexible, mix-and-match units, probably smaller but more capable, organized around information. This concept pulled our programs together and helped people get to the point of embracing change. It put a mark on the wall that people could look at and say, "Okay, *now* I understand."

Growing the Learning Organization

Disagreement Is Not Disrespect

British military historian Sir Michael Howard wrote, "I am tempted to say that whatever doctrine the armed forces are working on now, they have got it wrong. I am also tempted to declare that it does not matter. . . . What does matter is their ability to get it right quickly, when the moment arrives."[1] Howard was exactly right. As we, the leaders, deal with tomorrow, our task is not to try to make perfect plans. It is not possible to make perfect plans, but we will not be held to a standard of clairvoyance. Our task is to create organizations that are sufficiently flexible and versatile that they can take our imperfect plans and make them work in execution. That is the essential character of the learning organization.

The Army began its journey to becoming a learning organization in the 1970s. In 1973, Chief of Staff General Creighton Abrams created the Training and Doctrine Command (TRADOC) to pull together the Army's school system, training centers, and development activities—to put individual training and education and the responsibility for modernization[2] under a single organization. The first TRADOC commander was General William E. DuPuy.

As a captain just four years out of the Reserve Officers' Training Corps (ROTC) at South Dakota State University, Bill DuPuy had landed in France with the 90th Infantry Division on June 8, 1944 (D-Day plus 2), and participated in some of the toughest fighting breaking out of Normandy. The 90th Division had not been trained for the kind of fighting it had to do and was not well led. Ultimately, with new leadership and hard training, it distinguished itself; but it was the hard reality of having to learn the basics under fire that molded DuPuy's personality. He became one of the Army's most outspoken disciples of tough, realistic small-unit training as the cornerstone of a sound, effective Army. Thus, in 1973, he was the perfect choice for the new Training and Doctrine Command. He devoted himself to restoring discipline to the Army training system based upon the fundamental precept that the Army's training program must be uncompromising in preparing the Army to fight and win the nation's wars.[3]

DuPuy set out in two principal directions. First, he undertook to rewrite the basic war-fighting doctrine of the Army as a "key integrating medium for an increasingly complex military bureaucracy."[4] In other words, he recognized that change in how the Army thought about war must come first, to give the Army an intellectual context within which it could create a coherent and rational future.

At the same time, DuPuy's experience had taught him that Army training needed to be focused on the performance of well-defined tasks directly related to performance in combat, especially for the individual soldier and small-unit leader. Improvement of that process did not need to wait for a doctrinal revolution; all it lacked was a disciplined approach. DuPuy and those who followed him created such a training system. The most important element was standards, without which quality performance is meaningless. The Army had had such standards for many years for things such as road marching and rifle marksmanship; DuPuy's inspiration was to broaden that approach to virtually every task taught in the training centers, in the schools, and eventually in the units.

For example, an infantry battalion task force must be able to *defend;* that is its task. (The tasks derive from doctrine and are very specific.) Conditions can vary; in my example, the condition might be doing so *at night.* The standard can also vary; in this case it might be defeating the enemy *forward of the main defensive position.* That is not a task that can or should be performed with the precision of eighteenth-century drill. Every combination of units, terrain, equipment, weather, and so on will result in a different outcome. So performance, beyond some gross metrics, cannot be understood and evaluated by simple means. Thus, the next step was to create a structured way of facilitating learning from complex experiences that are often very ambiguous.

The answer came in what is called an After Action Review. An AAR takes place after every training event. Its purposes are simple: learning, improving, doing better the next time. The participants sit down with a facilitator called an "observer-controller" who has been with them throughout the event, and they discuss what happened. To do this effectively requires several things. First, there must be a fairly good basis for understanding what actually happened. In the training centers, electronic data collection enables high-fidelity recording and playback of events. It is like looking at football game films on Monday morning; you may think you know where you were at such-and-such a time, but in an environment where one hilltop can look pretty much like the next, you may or may not be correct. Thanks to unobtrusive sensors, the database can pinpoint exactly where you were and what you were doing. Soldiers call this "ground truth." Combined with ground truth, there must be a fairly unambiguous understanding of what should have happened, and that comes from having standards derived from doctrine.

Given those elements, it is possible to talk about an event in a way that focuses on improving team performance without getting caught up in individual performance, rank, position, or personality. By asking questions such as "What did you think I wanted you to do?" (as opposed to questions such as "How did you screw that up?"), one can get to the roots of both success and failure. This is not an easy process, and it generally takes a lot of time, maybe two to three hours to "AAR" a major event. The cost in time alone is heavy, but the outcome is a much more in-depth understanding of what happened. The return on investment, measured by improved performance, is very high.

The most difficult challenge is developing a culture that values this kind of learning. A colleague in industry once described an attempt to initiate a similar program in his company. He told me of a dialogue with a loading dock foreman who, in great frustration, finally said to him, "Look, I can either ship product or talk about it. Which do you want me to do?" The answer can only be "Both," but it is hard to make that answer a reality. It took a decade for the AAR process to become respected in the Army, for us to learn that you can do both—ship product and talk—and that carefully structured talking leads to more effective shipping or whatever. It is an investment that no one can afford not to make.

Over the decade it has taken for the AAR process to become imbedded in the Army's culture, its value has been accepted and it has spread to activities other than training. In the Gulf War, commanders conducted AARs after each rehearsal and each battle. Today AARs take place in garrisons, on staffs, and in headquarters—everywhere soldiers gather to perform some task. My personal staff would hold AARs for me after a major event in which I had participated. I did not especially enjoy discussing the gaps in my own performance—especially when I felt pretty good about what I had done—but these AARs helped me improve, and they helped my staff learn to support me better.

For America's Army, the AAR was the key to turning the corner and institutionalizing organizational learning. You probably never become a learning organization in any absolute sense; it can only be something you aspire to, always "becoming," never truly "being." But, in the Army, the AAR has ingrained a respect for organizational learning, fostering an expectation that decisions and consequent actions will be reviewed in a way that will benefit both the participants and the organization, no matter how painful it may be at the time. The only real failure is the failure to learn.

—GRS

★ ★ ★ ★

The Learning Organization

Peter Senge, director of the Systems Thinking and Organizational Learning Program at the Massachusetts Institute of Technology, defines a learning organization as "an organization that is continually expanding its capacity to create its future. For such an organization, it is not enough merely to survive. 'Survival learning' or what is more often termed 'adaptive learning' is important—indeed it is necessary. But for a learning organization, 'adaptive learning' must be joined by 'generative learning,' learning that enhances our capacity to create."[5] Generative learning is not about amassing a body of knowledge so much as it is about amassing a body of experience, interpreting that experience, and changing behavior as a result. Thin threads give an organization a way of learning by sponsoring and executing specific, very focused experiments about the future. In a larger sense, becoming a learning organization involves learning from *everything* you do, not just thin threads. Achieving and sustaining this kind of learning requires communicating openly, sharing information, and developing a culture in which team members share the responsibility for team performance and growth.

A structured, open process of sharing information about events is the basis for this kind of learning. In the Army, the After Action Review was the key step. Initially, creating this kind of feedback results in what Senge terms adaptive learning, but over time it does much more than that. An effective feedback process fosters trust throughout a team. Once an organization grows comfortable with dialoguing about performance *after* an event, it is a small step to dialogue more effectively about plans and preparations *before* an event. This fosters greater innovation and risk taking, which in turn lead to greater sharing of information—hence, continuous generative learning and better performance. Creating and participating in a structured feedback

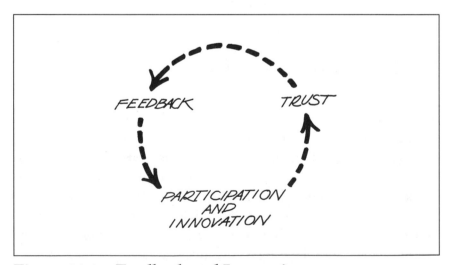

Figure 11-1—Feedback and Innovation

and innovation process (see Figure 11-1) is an effective first step toward growing a learning organization.

Developing the After Action Review

To be successful, the feedback process must be structured. It cannot simply be a group of people talking about what they "think" happened and what they "feel" should be done next. The process of writing doctrine had enabled the Army to define the complexity of ground combat in terms of tasks, conditions, and standards that, while undoubtedly imperfect, were universally accepted. Feedback could therefore be structured around identifiable events and against measurable standards. "Performance last quarter" is not an identifiable event; it is too vague, too complex. "Delivery to such-and-such an account last quarter" or "Opening the new plant in India" is an identifiable event.

After Action Review Questions

- What happened?

- Why did it happen?

- What should we do about it?

Next, there must be a common understanding of what was supposed to have happened. In the Army, this is accomplished by reviewing the higher headquarters' orders and the unit commander's orders. All the commanders involved participate; these normally include those on at least three levels: the commander of the unit being exercised (the principal), the commander of the parent unit (the principal's boss), and the commanders of the subordinate units. Because it is essential that everyone who contributed to the outcome participate, the leaders of supporting units will normally be there as well. Thus we have at least three levels of direct reports and the principal's counterparts from adjacent "stovepipes."

In a dialogue, these leaders discuss their various understandings of what was supposed to happen, reinforcing their effective communications patterns and identifying misunderstandings and weak communications patterns. This dialogue is facilitated by an especially competent officer whose experience normally makes him slightly senior to the commander of the unit being exercised. This facilitator is called an "observer-controller"; he or she has been with the commander of the unit being exercised throughout the entire exercise. His or her observations, while supported by data collected by other observer-controllers and by electronic means, are thus firsthand observations. His credibility derives from his experience, his access to information, and his skill as a facilitator.

The third key element in the AAR is knowing what actually happened: the "ground truth." The observer-controller team is able to replay the exercise with a high degree of accuracy. Having reviewed the intent of the plans and orders and knowing the standards for each task, the participants can now evaluate their performance, discussing each action to discover why things happened the way they did.

As we look at the three AAR questions, it is in asking "Why" that opportunities for learning—for reinforcing successful behaviors and for improving unsuccessful behaviors—are discovered. And while it is not true that we learn only from our mistakes, our shortcomings, highlighted in such a process, give us the most fruitful basis for improvement. Mistakes made in this environment are not to dwell on but to learn from.

The AAR is not a critique. A critique is merely an assessment of success or failure. *In the AAR process, the establishment of success or failure, sometimes in a very precise (and painful) way, is only a tool with which to learn.* Nor is the AAR intended to fix blame; it is a process designed to improve performance. It will not work if the leader lets it become a scorecard or a basis for public executions. Sparky Anderson, the legendary manager of the Detroit Tigers, said it this way: "I love to make mistakes. How are you going to become a ballplayer unless you make mistakes? I've made more mistakes than I've done things right. But then they're gone. Over."[6]

The final element that must be in place for an AAR to be successful is a learning culture. Each team member must be doing his or her best to contribute to the team's success. The environment must be nonthreatening on a personal level, and team members must be willing to take risks both individually and collectively, to learn, and to improve their performance.

Elements of the After Action Review

- Identifiable event, with associated standards

- Identifiable players

- Knowledge of what happened (ground truth)

- Nonthreatening environment

- Willingness to take personal risks in order for the team to learn and grow

Seeking Insights

Let's join an AAR in progress to see how it works

Imagine yourself at the Army's National Training Center, deep in the Mojave Desert between Las Vegas and Los Angeles. Our unit, an infantry task force, has been "in the box" exercising for about a week. We are part of a contingency operation, participating, with real or assumed forces from other nations, in the defense of a friendly third-world nation that has been invaded by a neighbor. Things have been going pretty well for us overall, but we have had some bad days. We are tired but not exhausted; we feel good about our successes and concerned about our shortcomings. In the engagement that ended about four hours ago, we were defending a position and were attacked by a much larger force. It was a tough fight; we lost a lot of people, but so did the enemy. In our minds, it was less than a win, especially in Team Charlie's sector, where the enemy made its main attack and some of the bad guys got through. We have been talking about it for about an hour and are getting down to the real meat of the dialogue.

OBSERVER-CONTROLLER (OC) TO THE TASK FORCE COMMANDER (CDR): "Let's go over your concept for this part of the battle one more time."

CDR: "I expected that the attack would be in the northern part of our sector, against Team Bravo. The terrain seemed to indicate that, and so did our intelligence. So that's where I put our main effort—the strongest minefield, the heaviest artillery fires, and the greatest preparation. That's where I was prepared to commit the reserve. But I knew he [the enemy] might come south [toward Team Charlie] or even do something unexpected, so it was important that I not move too quickly—we were prepared to go either way."

OC: "How were you going to decide?"

CDR: "When he came through the gap in the mountains to our east [pointing to map] he would have to commit north or south. At that point, he was still nearly twenty kilometers out, but he would be beginning to move fast. Once he committed, I could begin to take him out with long-range fires at the same time that we were adjusting back here. The scouts were out there to tell me which way he turned."

OC TO SCOUT: "What happened?"

SCOUT: "We got off to a late start because I had one element with some battle damage from the fight two days ago. We finally got into position—two positions really, one in the gap and one overlooking the gap—by midnight but we found his [enemy] people already up there. My team on the high ground spent the night fighting his infantry, and by morning my people up there were dead. The team in the gap ran into a mine and lost their communications capability."

OPERATIONS OFFICER (S3): "I didn't know any of that. How come we didn't know you still had battle damage?"

SCOUT: "I thought it would be operational. It seemed like no big deal yesterday morning, but we never got the right repair parts."

INTELLIGENCE OFFICER (S2): "I stopped getting scout reports about 0200 [2 A.M.], but I figured you would come back on the net at dawn."

OC: "Let's talk about that. What could you have done?"

SCOUT: "I had people still alive in the gap. We just couldn't talk back. I should have had another radio or even a flare."

S2: "I should have realized that you might be in trouble when you did not check in. I could have gotten something else working to back you up. We should have talked this over before you went out."

CDR: "Damn, guys, we've been through some of this before. My plan depended on early warning. Next time, I want to review this more carefully myself and talk to the scouts before they go out. Deuce [intelligence officer, S2], you need to get your whole team wired more tightly into my head and with the Three [operations officer, S3]. XO [executive officer], the staff needs to give me some ideas about redundancy in a situation like this—look, we all lost the bubble, okay?"

OC: "Good, but now let's move on. What happened next? Let's review the tapes" [ground truth].

The OC now displays a series of computer-generated images of the battlefield on which the players can see the enemy force coming at Team Charlie. The enemy is unimpeded by fire because the task force was slow to realize that they were through the gap and even slower to realize that they had taken the unexpected route south to Team Charlie's sector. On the large video screen, the nearly twenty kilometers between the enemy and the outer limits of Team Charlie's fires are quickly filled by advancing enemy.

CDR: "By this time, I was hearing from the aerial scout and I could see that they were going to hit Team Charlie hard, so I ordered things into action—artillery, shifting the reserve, getting the gunships on target—but we had not slowed them down because I was unsure of where they were. I had expected to have twenty to thirty minutes and that we would have taken out twenty percent or more of his elements with the artillery. Suddenly, I had five minutes and he was at full strength with lots of momentum."

OC: "In fact [plays audiotape time-synchronized to the large screen], at the time you were giving your orders, the enemy advance element was already beginning to breech Team Charlie's minefields. It was Team Charlie's forward observer who was beginning to engage them."

FORWARD OBSERVER: "From my vantage point, I could see their lead elements as they came in, and so I knew where they were. Our plan was to reinforce our barriers with scatterable mines at the enemy's breach site, and I had a quick fire channel open to shoot that as an emergency mission—we had talked about it and rehearsed it. Even then there was some delay, because the guns were still set up and waiting for the mission to fire deep; but they came on target pretty quickly."

OC: "Just in time, in fact [plays computer-generated battle map], to begin stacking them up. That was the first time they slowed down. Charlie's fire mission also helped to create a good target mass for the helicopter gunships the task force commander was bringing into battle position."

And so it goes, for about another hour. The high level of detail enables people to discover their own roles: what they did right, what they did wrong, but, most important, how working together more effectively as a team leads to success. In this vignette, one team (the scouts and the intelligence officer) failed because they had prepared poorly, failed to develop options, and lost their focus at a critical time. One team (the forward observer and the howitzer batteries) succeeded because they had rehearsed, had a high level of trust, and were very focused. Both teams were small teams well down in the organization, but at the critical moment their actions were decisive.

The Army's AAR guide suggests that the time spent in the AAR be divided 25-25-50 in answering the three questions: 25 percent reviewing what happened, 25 percent reviewing why it happened, 50 percent dialoguing about what to do to improve. That division of time is a good rule of thumb, but, as we saw in the vignette, the questions are not discrete; rather, they tend to run together in a stream of consciousness. The role of the observer-controller is very important; he or she guides the dialogue to the most important and most generalizable lessons.

The long-term legacy of the AAR is that the Army learned how to apply it beyond the training center, where the requirements for a good AAR can be carefully controlled. Conducting an AAR where there are only imprecise standards, where there is no thorough understanding of "ground truth," or where there are no highly skilled observer-controllers is possible in a mature team, so long as everyone keeps in mind the weaknesses incurred by relaxing the framework. The leader may act as the facilitator, or someone else may perform that role. The objective or goal of the project or event may be taken as a standard. The participants can decide, as they conduct their review, whether or not they are comfortable with the level of information available. In this relaxed format, the AAR can be the basis for robust generative learning.

Desert Storm—A Look Back

It was this kind of less rigorous process that was involved in March 1992, when the Army's division, corps, and major logistical unit commanders gathered to conduct an AAR of the ground operations in Operation Desert Storm. This meeting, a group of senior generals, had two objectives. The first was to look at the current systems and processes and to affirm those that had been satisfactory while identifying those that needed to be changed. The second objective was to try to look into the future to see how land warfare was changing. It was a complex AAR involving both learning how to improve the current paradigm and attempting to learn about the next.

Out of that meeting came a series of recommendations that formed the basis for immediate improvements to the force. As a result the 1st Armored Division that went into Bosnia was slightly different from and more effective than the 1st Armored Division that had fought in the Persian Gulf. Out of that meeting also came important insights for the Army's new field manuals (writing new doctrine); for reengineering the process of developing new equipment and tactics (creating the Battle Laboratories); and for what became the Force XXI experiments (creating a more flexible Information Age force). That meeting also made a powerful statement to the participants and to the Army as a whole. In the words of General Fred Franks, who hosted the meeting, it said emphatically that "We were not going to stand still."[7]

Such a complex AAR was possible because this was a team that had long ago bought into the process. Because they were comfortable with the process and with one another, they could have an effective AAR even though many of the normal aspects of the AAR structure were not in place.

Any team that has a clear task can use the AAR process to improve its performance. You must be able to focus on some discrete event (or at least be able to isolate the event). You must also be able to identify fairly clearly what was supposed to happen (intent and concept; task and standard) and what did happen (ground truth). It is normally helpful to have a facilitator of some kind, although a mature team can accomplish a good AAR without much help.

The process will not come automatically; you must structure your own learning for success. The following hints may be helpful.

1. Do not start your AAR experience with an enormous, complex task; build the skills with simple but not inconsequential tasks.

2. Make sure you have as much information as possible about what really happened, and make sure every participant has access to that information as you go through the process.

3. Ensure that the leader endorses the ground rules.

4. Finally, set aside enough time to really get into things. If you are reviewing a major project at a critical milestone, with twenty or thirty team members, it could easily take an afternoon to work through the most important issues. If you don't allow enough time, you will be unlikely to get beyond the "measurables" and into the "unmeasurables," where the most significant learning can take place.

The ultimate result of this kind of process, whatever you call it and however it is structured, is that people not only learn but become more engaged as leaders, sharing the responsibility for a team's success. Formal leadership does not change hands, but the organization comes to see the leading roles of its members in a better perspective. It is a common experience at the training centers for plans to break down because some small element failed—a gap in a minefield was not closed properly, a scouting report did not get back to the commander, a resupply operation was not accomplished on time, or a unit got lost. The AAR process allows such shortcomings to be uncovered in a way that is as nonthreatening as possible, discovering the cause so that it can be corrected—fixing the *problem*, not the *blame*. One outcome is that the organization comes to understand the leadership role of *all* the team members; the responsibility of each leader to make sure that his or her task is accomplished is highlighted, and the critical path to success becomes more clear.

In *Flight of the Buffalo*, authors James Belasco and Ralph Stayer suggest that the new leadership paradigm should be a flock of geese. They write,

> *What I really wanted in the organization was a group of responsible, interdependent workers, similar to a flock of geese. . . . I could see the geese flying in their "V" formation, the leadership changing frequently, with different geese taking the lead. I saw every goose being responsible for getting itself to wherever the gaggle was going, changing roles whenever necessary, alternating as a leader, a follower, or a scout. And when the task changed, the geese would be responsible for changing the structure of the group to accommodate, similar to the geese that fly in a "V" but land in waves. I could see each goose become a leader.[8]*

The metaphor is powerful—leadership distributed among the team members, rotating as necessary so that the best-qualified leader makes the right things happen at the crucial moment, when his or her skill as a leader is most needed.

LESSONS LEARNED:
A STRUCTURE FOR ORGANIZATIONAL LEARNING[9]

Organizational learning, in a broader sense, can occur only when an organization as a whole is communicating and adopting what is being learned in its various parts. Learning begins in isolation; one individual or one team learns something of value. Turning that into organizational learning requires a mechanism for sharing. Given the success of the AAR, could the entire Army benefit from what was taking place one event at a time in the training centers?

The answer lay in the rebirth of the Army's *lessons learned* process. During World War II, Marshall had initiated "lessons learned," under the direction of the chief of military history, to gather up what was being learned in the far-flung operational theaters and cycle it back into the training base and to other units. The system did not survive the war, but the idea behind it did, enabling it to be revived in both Korea and Vietnam. As the system matured, mechanisms were developed to feed these battlefield lessons into the development of new tactics, procedures, organization, and equipment. With that institutional background, it was a natural step, in 1985, to establish a formal Center for Army Lessons Learned (CALL) at Fort Leavenworth, Kansas, for the express purpose of capturing the learning taking place at the training centers and disseminating it throughout the Army. Since its inception, CALL has expanded its charter to include capturing lessons from actual operations. Furthermore, thanks to the capabilities of information technology to report and disseminate using on-line databases, experience can now be disseminated almost as rapidly as it is collected.

From Somalia to Haiti

The soldiers who went into Haiti in September 1994 were from the same 10th Mountain Division that had gone into Somalia in December 1992, but they were better prepared. Each soldier had a handbook that covered the current situation in Haiti, common phrases in Creole, preventive medicine for the tropics, and tactics and small-unit procedures for the kind of operation they were facing. Their predeployment training had been carefully tailored to include crowd control techniques, dealing with local officials, operating in urban areas, dealing with the media, and other unique challenges posed by the operation.

All that was made possible by a team from the Center for Army Lessons Learned that had been studying the Somalia operation and other, similar operations and had been developing contingency plans in the face of the deteriorating refugee situation in the Caribbean. Once the 10th Mountain was alerted, the CALL team deployed to Fort Drum, New York, the division's home base, and began working with commanders and unit leaders to transfer all the knowledge at their disposal to the troops who would be on the ground in Haiti.

Other teams, drawing on the same information base, were working around the clock to bring the troops the latest equipment to assist them—still and video digital cameras, life-finder sensors to sense body heat in dark alleys, and laptop computers to downlink all available intelligence. The effort enabled the Army to increase the effectiveness of the division significantly.

CALL's role did not end there. CALL teams deployed to Haiti alongside the troops of the 10th Mountain and began a collection-and-analysis effort to capture the knowledge that was being gained every day. When the troops who would rotate in behind the 10th Mountain—the 2d Cavalry Regiment and the 25th Infantry Division from Hawaii—were alerted, CALL dispatched teams to those units to deliver knowledge packages directly to deploying units—"real-world" maps, rules of engagement, intelligence, and direct feedback from the troops that had gone in ahead of them. Additionally, on their way to Haiti, these units cycled through the training center at Fort Polk, Louisiana, where the observer-controller teams, also working with CALL, created a training environment in which the troops could rehearse operational tasks under Haiti-like conditions.[10]

THE LEARNING CHALLENGE

Earlier we argued that, as we face our external environment, "We don't know what we don't know." As we face our internal environment, it seems that the opposite is too often true: "We don't know what we *do* know."[11] As an important organizational asset, knowledge is usable only if it can be identified and disseminated so as to contribute value. The challenge is to discover what is known in any part of the organization and, if it is valuable, make it known to all. Success in helping units prepare for Haiti was made possible by the establishment of a learning culture and by the expansive CALL knowledge base that makes the experience of one unit, anywhere in the world, quickly available to all. Thus there are three key elements: the right culture, the knowledge itself, and access to the knowledge.

The Process

The CALL experience also suggests a six-step process: targeting opportunity, collecting data, creating knowledge, distributing knowledge, short-term applications, and long-term applications.

Targeting Opportunity. Deciding what to learn from is the first and most critical step in the process. There will be some easy targets. If you are moving your business into a new part of the world or undertaking a new kind of operation, they will present prime opportunities for learning. If you have a successful process improvement or quality program in some part of the organization, it will present prime opportunities for learning. Other high-payoff learning opportunities may be less obvious. Look for things you do repetitively, where a lesson that seems minor in itself may have a high payoff when replicated many times.

Collecting Data. Collecting data involves observing a targeted event or process and recording what happens—but it is not easy. As much as possible, data collection should target factual events that can be measured against a clear standard or at least an intended outcome.

Observations should be as unambiguous as possible to minimize bias by the collectors, even the best of whom will tend to impose personal judgments as they observe events.

Creating Knowledge. Some of the data will have meaning by itself and can be disseminated with relatively little analysis—especially for quick-fix applications. More often, judgments about the quality of the data and interpretations about its meaning will be needed to realize its full value. This requires expertise, maturity, and a degree of isolation from the organizational hierarchy to preclude filtering, especially of bad news.

Distributing Knowledge. Distribution can be by any number of means but should include both push and pull strategies. In a *pull strategy*, knowledge is available to planners and students in a central, easily accessible knowledge base. Think of it as a library. In a *push system*, knowledge teams go on site to assist leaders preparing for similar operations, bringing selections from the library with them.

Short-Term Applications. Short-term applications are quick fixes, things that are relatively simple to diagnose and correct. They have the greatest value to whoever will be doing something similar next. Key short-term issues include failed planning assumptions, clarification of unknowns, invented procedures, identification of unanticipated problems, and on-the-spot fixes of unanticipated problems.

Long-Term Applications. Long-term applications address systemic issues that are identified through repeated observations and that often require interpretation. Long-term applications feed back into basic policies, organizational concepts, the formulation of strategy, and long-range plans.

BUILDING A KNOWLEDGE NETWORK

The Army's CALL experience provides some other important lessons for anyone attempting to build a knowledge network.

Developing Competent Collection Teams. Collection team members need both data collection skills and subject matter expertise. Multidisciplinary teams can often illuminate greater complexity. Try forming ad hoc collection teams that combine people expert at the lessons learned process with people drawn into the process on a project basis to provide subject matter depth. Collection teams need to be trained to be as objective and nonjudgmental as possible.

Maintaining a Customer Focus. The process of developing lessons learned must be focused on the needs of the organization, and resources should be concentrated on those issues with the potential of adding the most value. This helps structure the process for success and garners support for expending the resources involved.

Exploiting Technology. The CALL experience produced little of enduring value during its first several years of operation because the data coming out of the training centers overwhelmed our pencil-and-paper system. Analysts received thousands of units of written, audio, digital, and video data and attempted to distill them into bulletins and booklets. CALL found that units often made similar mistakes and provided some insights into how to train to overcome those mistakes, but the results obtained tended to aggregate at such a high level that they were not always useful.

Putting CALL on-line, so that the CALL database was available to any user Army-wide, greatly improved the interpretive process, especially for quick-fix lessons. Quick storage and retrieval with great specificity at a very low level were now possible. In the pencil-and-paper system, for example, a logistics planner might have found "Depending on the light conditions, the unit will need an adequate supply of chemical illumination markers"—helpful but not much more than a reminder. On-line, he can get into specific data points, things like "We thought we would need about 6,000 chemical illumination markers over the two-week period, but because we were there during the new moon, we needed nearly twice that many to be able to manage traffic in the rear area."

Perhaps even more important, an on-line system enables users to access the knowledge base when *they* need something. This turned out to be much more effective than a paper-based system, whose lessons were too often not available at the time and place they were needed.

Protecting the Messenger. Some of the most important lessons will involve poor performance; exposing and identifying bad news raises tough issues in any organization. Sometimes lessons can be neutered so that poor performance is not easily identifiable with specific units; but most of the time, simply identifying an event will be tantamount to identifying its participants. Rapid dissemination makes interference or filtering more difficult. But in the final analysis, the data collectors and the lessons learned organization must be protected from editorial heavyhandedness. Over time, protection will flow naturally from a learning culture: people will value the process for its goodness. Initially, however, there is no substitute for high-level sponsorship.

Avoiding Reinventing the Wheel. Avoid targeting events for which the outcomes, whether plus or minus, will be predictable and unremarkable. Much of the challenge in distilling lessons learned is in separating poor performance at tasks the organization knows how (or should know how) to do from new tasks or new methods for doing familiar tasks. Careful targeting of high-payoff issues and selection of mature, experienced collectors and analysts will help you avoid this problem.

Keeping It Simple. Developing a simple system, particularly in the early stages, keeps expectations within bounds and facilitates early success—both of which are important to long-term success.

> ### Rule Ten: Learn from Doing
>
> Learning from doing and sharing the knowledge gained are
> the essence of organizational learning. By listening to the orga-
> nization and fostering a dialogue about performance, the
> leader opens the door to learning, sharing lessons learned, and
> reducing risk. By stretching the organization to act differently,
> to do new things in a learning atmosphere, the leader fosters
> an entrepreneurial spirit of innovation and growth.

More than anything else, learning involves listening and a willingness to change for the sake of growth and improvement. Many
lessons have already actually been learned; they simply have not been
captured or disseminated. Our organizations are already full of
lessons learned, but these are of little value if they are not part of the
knowledge asset or we fail to exploit them. Remember, McDonald's
Big Mac, fried apple pie, large fries, McDLT, and Egg McMuffin all
came up from the bottom, not from McDonald's large corporate machinery.[12] To be useful, they had to be identified and shared.

A structured program of organizational learning not only helps
disseminate best practices and new knowledge, it also reduces risk.
The more people and teams know, the more effectively they perform
and the less likely they are to fail.

Investing in People: Leadership Training

Those Whose Lives We Touch

Fort Leavenworth, Kansas, is home to the Army's most important complex of schools, including the Command and General Staff College, where the Army educates officers for midlevel leadership positions and refreshes the skills of those newly selected for battalion and brigade command before they assume their new responsibilities. Fort Leavenworth is the jewel in the crown of the Army's school system and the main repository of our professional knowledge and research.

The men and women attending the Pre-Command Course there will be responsible for leading anywhere from five hundred to five thousand soldiers in peace or war, for planning and conducting their training, and for maintaining their equipment and real property, the value of which can run into hundreds of millions of dollars. These men and women are relatively few in number, and all have been carefully selected by a board of senior officers on the basis of both their performance and their potential.

In addition to providing these new commanders with an update on the latest training innovations, personnel policies, doctrine, and other current issues, the Pre-Command Course is a window through which the senior leadership, by its personal participation, can see and influence the Army down to its lowest level. By design, the program enables these young leaders to exchange experiences and views with very senior people. There is a constant flow of senior generals who conduct key seminars, exchanging views, ideas, and concerns and instilling values. Everyone, including the generals, learns, and the institution is strengthened. This dialogue made the Pre-Command Course one of the most important innovations during the rebuilding after Vietnam because it strengthened our standards, our sense of purpose, and our shared values. The men and women who attend this course, over the course of time, rise to lead the Army. They, like those who came before them, will also talk to each new commander, handing down, in a rich oral tradition, the essence of the Army.

Like previous chiefs, I went to Fort Leavenworth nearly every month. I spent more time flying back and forth to Leavenworth and talking to the students out there than I did performing any other single task as chief. I did it to help them understand what we were trying to accomplish and to help them learn by hearing my thoughts and concerns. Very few of us, whether in government or in industry, remain in office long enough to accomplish every goal personally. Thus our effectiveness as leaders is sometimes not so much in what we do as in what we influence others to do. I believe my time was well spent.

If I were to reduce my guidance to those new brigade and battalion commanders to a few words, I would say this: You must be men and women of your time, living in the world as it is and as it is becoming, not as it was for your mentors. You must take charge of your organization and be responsible for moving it into the future in a way that will enable those who follow you to succeed.

Our job is to grow the people who will lead the organization when we are gone, and we begin that by instilling the kind of values that we want our organizations to reflect in the future.

—GRS

★ ★ ★ ★

DEVELOPING LEADERS

Developing subordinates to distribute leadership throughout the organization is the essence of empowerment. Empowerment is an unfortunate word, because leadership is not about power or authority. A senior manager in a large firm told us, "Our people are empowered. We have given them everything they need to do their jobs." But that is only the beginning. Empowerment is not simply about having the tools to do your job. Empowerment is about responsibility—both responsibility delegated and responsibility accepted. Empowered subordinates accept responsibility for themselves, for their team, and for their contributions to the organization. From that sense of shared responsibility come self-confidence, motivation, and commitment. Leader development—investing in people—is about creating that kind of empowerment.

Times of great change create an enduring need to do more leader development, more often. Learning must truly become lifelong, not merely episodic. Leaders must practice something we call leadership legacy behavior: growing their successors. Developing leaders strengthens the ability of the organization to win today and tomor-row. Developing leaders is bottom-line behavior.

To attack this issue and realize the potential of their people, top-performing organizations are making a renewed commitment to leader development, understanding that the enormous changes going on around us demand continual renewal of our human resources. However, this is not an easy concept to put into practice: management systems tend to be about control and rewards, and it is hard to measure the return on your investment in leader development. Senior leaders tend to understand its value, but in many cases it is hard to provide the resources, both time and dollars, to actually make the investment. Dr. Mark Otto suggests, "Leadership is tough hard work because it challenges our traditional view of people as liabilities versus people as assets."[1] People are assets, and like other assets they can be developed for a higher return or depleted to yield less and less.

The Army model for leader development is based on three elements: education and training, on-the-job experience, and self-development[2] (see Figure 12-1). This has proved to be a useful way of keeping leader development in a broad perspective—it is more complex than simply providing schooling.

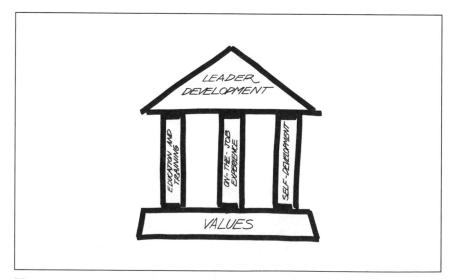

Figure 12-1—Leader Development Model

Education and Training. This is the formal element. In the Army we called it "institutional training" because it takes place in our schools, in universities, or in other formal courses. The essential character of this element is time dedicated to structured and focused learning facilitated by professional teachers. This kind of learning is especially efficient for updating skills, establishing a theoretical grounding in a subject area, introducing new skills, and facilitating the transition to a new job. This is an organization's most powerful leader development message because it so obviously reflects investment.

On-the-Job Experience. The experiential element reflects the value of learning on the job. Every job experience is a learning experience, and those experiences can be either relatively random or structured. Most organizations attempt to identify high-potential leaders early in their careers and may go so far as to manage their job progression and institutional training carefully, grooming them for ever-greater responsibility. In some organizations there is a division that has a special cachet, or perhaps there is a stint in corporate headquarters that is considered essential. We believe that structured career progression is important to *every* leader and that desirable patterns of experience—balancing the difficulties and expense of moving and the negative impacts of turnover with the advantages of being exposed to a structured array of experiences—are an essential element of leader development that must not be left entirely to an individual or to the seemingly random requirements of a personnel department.

Self-Development. Leader development is a responsibility shared by the organization and the individual. Self-development may be as simple as a structured reading program, it may include taking courses to qualify for a new skill or educational level, it could encompass private research and writing for publication, or it could take any number of other directions. The common threads are that it is self-initiated and directed and that it is focused toward some tangible developmental goal.

To make on-the-job experience and self-development as effective as possible, every leader must play a role in developing his or her subordinates. By counseling, coaching, and mentoring, a leader helps guide a subordinate by providing feedback, suggesting goals, defining expectations—giving structure to these two elements, especially self-development. As a rule of thumb, you should be involved two levels down, with most of your emphasis one level down.

RULE ELEVEN: GROW PEOPLE

The potential to build organizations that can thrive in tomorrow's environment lies in our people. The challenge is not to be the most creative boss or to have the most creative headquarters staff; it is to have the most creative organization, limited only by the collective imagination of all its constituents.

THE LEARNING LEADER

The kinds of leaders we want to develop are *learning leaders*.

For many years, we have used the metaphor of the orchestra conductor to describe the perfect manager, one who could handle enormous complexity with creativity and harmony. In the Army as well as in industry, we used the word "orchestrate" to describe managing complexity. There was a period after Vietnam when you could pick up the major Army journals and find articles about how to "orchestrate" the complexity of the battlefield, and we went to great lengths to develop precise techniques to do just that.

Certainly, managing complexity is no less important in today's world, but the kinds of leaders we need today are more like great jazz musicians, thoroughly schooled in the fundamentals and absolutely technically competent but able to improvise on a theme.[3] It is this ability to improvise, to develop events as they unfold, that is so critical. For much of what a leader is asked to do today there is no score, only a theme around which he or she must work, improvising.

The jazz metaphor is a rich one that leads us to think about leadership in new ways. Consider, for example, the careers of jazzman Dave Brubeck and General Matthew Ridgway, a legendary combat commander in World War II and Korea. There is a remarkable similarity between the two men. Both were thoroughly grounded in the fundamentals of their profession—one as a soldier, the other as a classical musician. Both demonstrated the discipline so common to champions. Both were great team builders: Brubeck of his several bands, most notably the great Dave Brubeck Quartet, which played for sixteen years beginning in 1951, and Ridgway of his command teams, most notably the fledgling airborne corps of World War II and the Eighth U.S. Army in Korea. Both were great innovators: Ridgway the creative force behind the airborne, the peacemaker in Korea; Brubeck the great jazzman whose virtuosity has been applauded for five decades. Both had a passion for the success of their teams that was matched only by a compassion for their people. Ridgway's teams were much larger, but the two men shared the same humility: giving, not taking, credit. What both men teach us is that it is not the instrument but the musician that produces the music that counts. It is the leader and his or her ability to engage, improvising on a theme and moving decisively to a crescendo, that makes the difference.

The Jazzman

- Grounded in fundamentals

- Disciplined

- Team builder

- Innovator

- Passionate

- Compassionate

To be an organizational jazzman, an effective leader must continuously improvise and learn. He or she must live through the Leadership Action Cycle, sensing, reflecting, deciding, acting, and—most important—learning so that their actions can be continually shaped and reshaped. For the organization, this learning behavior includes *defining, teaching*, and *shaping*.

Defining. Leaders give meaning to the future by defining it in understandable terms. They clarify current events, separating the important from the unimportant, and create a context for the future; they dream dreams and create a shared vision. They personally lead the process of redefining the purpose and scope of the organization and of clarifying its essence. Learning leaders keep the organization in balance, taking those actions necessary for near-term success and stability while focusing intellectual and physical investment on the future. They keep the organization doing the right things by their personal sponsorship and support.

Teaching. Learning leaders understand that commitment to change requires face-to-face communication, constant repetition, and demonstrated value. The learning leader understands that sometimes explaining can be more important than directing and that listening can be of more value than talking. Even in disagreement, the learning leader will find new insights as well as the means of breaking through resistance and building support for innovation and growth.

Shaping. Leaders use the past to shape the future by reinforcing values, drawing on a sense of history, and establishing continuity between change and traditional organizational strengths. More important, the leader demonstrates the way ahead by means of carefully selected and structured projects, reinforcing success at every level. Leaders make constant adjustments to the course of change as they update their sense of the environment. These are not wild swings in emphasis or direction but adjustments driven by shared information and feedback. Leaders must be prepared to moderate pace, to shift investment priorities, to acknowledge failure, and to exploit success.

A learning leader is able to gain and sustain initiative. Having the initiative means setting the conditions for competition and growth, not constantly reacting. A passive leader will try to accommodate change, reacting to the environment, but change is happening so fast that reaction—accommodation—is not good enough. We remember the Charles Lindberghs, not the Bert Hinklers. Bert Hinkler was the second pilot to solo across the Atlantic. He did it faster than Lindbergh did it, and by all accounts he was a better pilot. But he was second in a world that appreciates firsts. Gaining and maintaining the initiative are the essence of growing an organization.

Twenty-first-Century Leaders

As we come to understand the future, we see that leadership for the twenty-first century is about intervention and change; to be successful, leaders must have the skills, confidence, and intuition to create a degree of stability out of apparent chaos. Understanding that leadership must rest on such a foundation, and understanding the shortcomings of characterizing leadership qualities by a list of traits or mannerisms, we believe that we can describe some of the characteristics that future leaders should possess.[4] We think this list provides some insight about how we should develop leaders by describing the kinds of skills our subordinates and our successors will need to win. In the twenty-first century, our organizations will need:

> • *Leaders who can* scan *and* focus—*who can maintain a broad personal outlook but who can relate what they are seeing and learning in a purposeful way.* Change places unprecedented demands on leaders to sense their environments and to respond in increasingly compressed time cycles. Leaders gather information in numerous ways: from their staffs, subordinates, external information providers, and other sources. They also

collect their own information, often cutting across conventional sources in unconventional ways. Successful future leaders will not be mere information sponges, however. The more challenging, more important dimension is that of analysis and synthesis, translating sensory data into information and knowledge to be acted on.

• *Leaders who can create strategic architecture based on the cornerstones of values and vision.* Frances Hasselbein of the Drucker Foundation said it this way: "Leadership is not a basket of tricks or skills. It is the quality and character and courage of the person who is the leader. It's a matter of ethics and moral compass, the willingness to remain highly vulnerable."[5] The leader's personal values must be consistent with the organization's shared values in order for the power of shared values to be realized.

• *Leaders who can see* patterns *where others cannot and have the* courage *to decide and act quickly*. In the fog that is the future, there are as yet indecipherable patterns. In the Information Age, an age of compressed time when the opportunity for success may be fleeting, a leader must have the personal capacity to act decisively with alacrity. This requires decision making under much greater ambiguity, with less time for staff work and analysis than in the past. Future leaders will develop personal information systems to give them an edge, to try to bring the future into focus a little more sharply or a little more quickly than their competitors do, but they themselves must be prepared to follow through with their team as each situation develops. Leaders must take decisive action.

• *Leaders who can lead in a* learning *organization, networking, influencing, and inspiring*. Learning organizations are ambiguous leadership environments when compared to traditional, top-down bureaucracies. Learning involves taking risks, and it also involves both success and failure. There is no such thing as "freedom to fail"; but there must be freedom to learn.

That is, leaders must be accountable for their actions, including their failures; but the organization must be able to learn from both success and failure. Learning organizations also tend to be flat, with networked relationships that are themselves ambiguous. In these circumstances, leaders influence more than they control. The net result can be liberating and powerful, but a learning organization requires a leader who can embody and foster a determination to innovate, to take risks, to work through setbacks, and to work effectively in teams.

• *Leaders who are personally empowered by* technology. Information technology is providing new ways of learning, communicating, and searching the environment. Electronic mail, bulletin boards, websites, and all the other dimensions of cyberspace threaten to overwhelm us with an avalanche of data. This is part of the everyday reality of our young leaders, who, more and more, have grown up "on-line." To lead effectively in this environment, leaders must understand and be a part of this new technology, using it to enhance their productivity, their ability to monitor and influence, and their ability to lead.

• *Leaders who can* teach *and* develop *subordinates*. Each leader must be committed to leader development in both its formal and informal sense. Formally, he or she must be both a participant, growing personally and setting an example, and a sponsor, making sure his or her people have a range of leader development opportunities and are rewarded for pursuing them. Informally, leaders must be coaches and mentors. This is hard, one-on-one work—hard because it brings us face to face with subordinates, giving and accepting feedback that is not always positive. But this kind of informal learning and development is one of the best ways for leaders to align their vision, strengthen organizational values, and create a common understanding of the concept and intent—all of which contribute greatly to strategic alacrity and empowerment.

• *Leaders who can make the* human dimension *central to their organizations.* No matter how the Information Age changes the role of people in organizations, we can safely predict that people and their ideas will remain at the heart of our organizations. In less rigid organizational structures, where influence and teamwork replace control and structure, we can surmise that the human dimension of leadership will be still more important than it is now. Treating people with dignity and respect is the keystone of effective team building, leader development, and empowerment.

Observations About Leading

As we conclude our thoughts about developing leaders, we return to leaders themselves, what they believe and how they behave. Here are some observations born of our experience.

• *There are no universal truths.* Each person you work with is unique. Each organization is unique. Each situation is unique. The leader, today and tomorrow, must be aware of that and must continually tailor his or her behavior to the situation at hand within a consistent framework of values.

• *Leading means understanding that "we" are "they."* This is the beginning of accepting responsibility for your own actions and for the team.

• *Be yourself!* The best leaders act out of their own set of values and their own intellectual construct, and with their own style.

• *Leaders respect people.* The hardest decisions involve people—people who have families and friends affected by the things that happen to them. Treating people with dignity and respect is the only acceptable framework in which to make the hard decisions.

• *Good leaders have a sense of humor*, a healthy respect for the lighter side of life. The best leaders are unambiguous about what they are serious about, but they do not try to be serious about everything.

• *Good leaders make time for themselves*, family, and other interests. You need to sustain a broad focus, keep the personal needs of your team members in perspective, and sustain your own personal renewal.

• *Successful leaders know their team members*. They know their needs, their unique talents, their goals, and their strengths and weaknesses. By knowing their team members, leaders make more effective assignments, develop team members more fully, and better balance the needs of their people and the needs of the organization.

• *Leaders generate enthusiasm*. They are able to align organizational goals with personal goals for themselves and their team members in a way that motivates and inspires others. They cultivate a climate in which their team members feel good about what they are doing.

• *Leaders take personal responsibility for their actions*, especially when things go wrong. They get involved and fix things when they do go wrong—fix the problem, not the blame. In any event they learn, searching for systemic solutions so that a problem does not occur again.

• *Successful leaders give credit*. Teams can accomplish more when it does not matter who gets personal credit. A good leader will bask in the reflected light of organizational success without turning a spotlight on himself.

• *Successful leaders establish expectations*. They make sure people understand goals and objectives, personal roles, individual responsibilities, and rewards, and they establish expectations about feedback and other communication.

• *Successful leaders take charge.* Their followers, their teams, expect them to take charge. Just as the leader establishes expectations for the team, so does the team have expectations for the leader. The team expects the leader to lead it to a win.

The legacy of the Industrial Age and "scientific management," as it was given to us by Frederick Taylor and generations of like-minded thinkers and leaders, is highly bureaucratic organizations designed to force people to conform, to stifle initiative and idiosyncratic behavior. In many organizations (including the Army) we still "requisition" people as if they were interchangeable parts. When we look back at the Industrial Age, it is easy to understand why Grant did not want a lot of creative thinking on the battle line, any more than Henry Ford wanted a lot of original thought on his production line. But those kinds of organizations cannot function effectively in today's world. The challenge today is not to be the most creative boss or to have the most creative headquarters staff. The challenge is to have the most creative organization, limited only by the collective imagination of all of its constituents. Winning organizations pivot on the collective imagination of *all* their people.

CHAPTER 13

Hope Is Not a Method

★ ★ ★ ★

Moving Forward

Like the leader of any large organization, I was often confronted with bad news. At times like that—when our plans did not seem to be working, when some seemingly isolated event had diverted our attention, when we were under pressure to move faster to some ill-defined end state, or when it seemed we might not get the resources or political support we needed—I would go back to basics, back to my interpretation of the essence of the Army and what we were trying to do. In thinking about those issues, I used sketch books in which I attempted to translate my thoughts into pictures—pictures with sentences or phrases related to events. This helped me understand the relationship between the events of the moment and the more fundamental strategic issues and keep our campaigns on track. Looking back, I find three pictures that came into my mind repeatedly. In these sketches, I can see how I was wrestling with good news and bad, and I can see continuity and growth in my thoughts.

First, I drew a symbol for maintaining readiness while we were downsizing. It was a simple curve with little boxes drawn on it (see Figure 13-1). It grew out of our work in reshaping the force in the years immediately before and after the opening of the Berlin Wall. It reflected our most basic approach to downsizing: maintaining the integrity of the Army at each step in the journey, balancing force structure and readiness. The little boxes represented integrity at each point on the curve. Downsizing was a tricky problem: we had to maintain an army large enough and sufficiently diverse to defend America's interests, and we had to keep the pace of downsizing under control so that our tactical units did not become hollow, as they had in the early 1970s. But we could not succumb to the temptation to keep the force bigger than we could adequately pay, train, and equip.

Those little boxes reminded me that, at each step in the downsizing process, the Army had to maintain balance. It had always to be ready to do whatever America asked it to do. Since we could not predict our future, our job was to be able to deal with a variety of futures. I drew little arrows from the boxes to remind myself of that.

As I leaf further through my sketchpads, again and again I find a sine curve reflecting the historical reality of the Army's readiness roller coaster—the fact that the effectiveness of America's Army had declined after every war. The history of America's Army is a history of being unprepared for war.

Once again, take a look at the sine curve (Figure 13-2). The vertical axis of the figure is effectiveness. I never made any attempt to describe a precise scale—it was merely a symbol. I drew a small triangle, a "delta," beside the top of the last hump of the curve that I thought of as a "readiness delta." I was trying to describe, graphically, the necessity of reversing the long-term strategic trend. When I spoke of

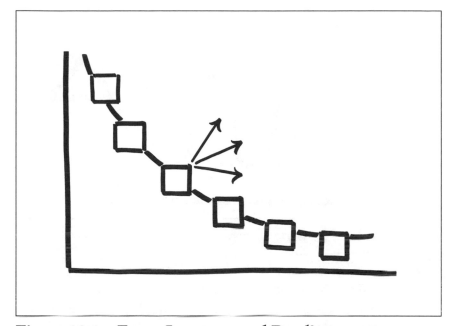

Figure 13-1—Force Structure and Readiness

growth, I was thinking not in terms of size but rather in terms of capability—that the Army would have to continue to grow the capabilities demanded by the realities of the world in which we were living. It was essential that we resist the temptation to shrink into a smaller version of our Cold War self; we had to become something different, an organization uniquely American that could meet and satisfy the mission requirements of today and tomorrow.

The sine curve helped us explain the historical reality of the Army's unpreparedness between wars to others, especially to the Congress, which provides the resources and which ultimately decides whether or not the investment profile will be adequate. Equally important, it was a reminder to me that I would have to foster innovation and growth within the organization—that, during my brief time as chief, I would have to take action to keep the Army focused not only on today but on tomorrow as well.

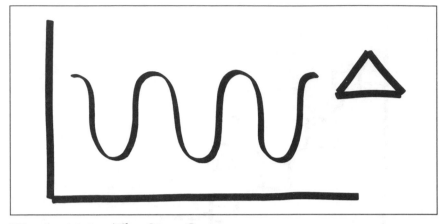

Figure 13-2—The Sine Curve

As I thought about that challenge, my thoughts often went back to the star representing the Six Imperatives (see Figure 13-3), the critical processes by which we sustain the Army. The star demonstrated that the processes were connected; if any one of them failed, it would influence all the others in a downward spiral. Each of our transformation campaigns was connected; each would influence the outcome. Breaking the long-term historic trend would require us to sustain the vitality of each of those processes. Growing meant that we would have to grow along all six dimensions.

As I contemplated these challenges, using my sketches to assist me in keeping current events in focus, I reflected, "Focus, Sully, focus."

What was really important? As it turned out, it was seldom the issue of the hour—whatever it was that had gotten us up at the crack of dawn, who was saying what in *The Washington Post* or *The New York Times* or whatever. By going back to my basics, I put tactical issues into a strategic context so that I could explain to myself what was happening and what was not happening. This helped me explain events to others, to the Army, in a functional way as we attempted to keep our heads in the future, aligned with the vision. It was difficult.

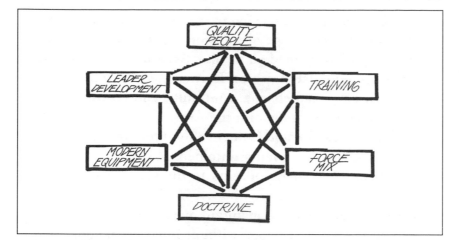

Figure 13-3—The Six Imperatives

In reflecting, I would talk to the other Army leaders, my vice chiefs (the first, Denny Reimer,[1] then Binnie Peay,[2] and finally John Tilelli[3]), and especially Sergeant Major of the Army Richard Kidd, the Army's senior enlisted soldier, to get their sense of what I did not already know. They were a strong team, each a leader and each a team player. Each championed a different dimension of the future, and they kept things on an even keel day by day. There were others: the secretaries of the Army, Mike Stone and Togo West; my friend Carl Vuono; the commanders in the field; the Army Staff; Mike Harper and the other members of my personal staff; and friends of many years, military and civilian. This circle of friends was important to me as I reflected on the tasks that confronted the Army.

And I would think about what we could do, how we could act. Lying in bed worrying an issue to death was not the answer. Hoping that when I woke up things would be better was not the answer. Hope is not a method. As the leader, I had to act. I had to make things happen that would guide us into the future, and I had to do my best to keep bad things from happening, things that would have a negative effect on some future battlefield.

Much of this is clearer to me now than it was at the

time; but even then it seemed to me that the best way of approaching the challenge of transforming the Army was the same way I had trained all my life. Accordingly, within the bounds of our shared values, I articulated a vision; a concept that embraced change, continuity, and growth; and a strategic intent to transform the Army. I stayed personally involved so that I could influence the process—taking deliberate actions—as events unfolded. It was my job to relate seemingly disparate events to the vision. My biggest challenge was that of creating an intellectual framework that would enable us to maintain our standing as the best army in the world. Change without intellectual substance would have been dysfunctional.

Finally, I knew that whatever picture we had of the future, it was imperfect. My intent was simply to provide a framework within which future leaders could make rational, coherent decisions that would lead the Army on its journey. I knew that my tenure was transitory, that those who followed me would have different challenges. My challenge was to operate, change, and open the door to a future in which America's Army would be capable of performing the tasks and missions required of it. My challenge was to build a foundation on which others could build a sound future.

—GRS

★ ★ ★ ★

STRATEGIC ARCHITECTURE FOR CHANGE

Strategic leadership is the process of creating a future for our organizations. It is a human process, involving first and foremost the leader and the people who make up the organization, working as a team. The central thesis of this book is that it is possible to transform any organization so that creative, adaptive behavior becomes imbedded in its culture, so that it can be successful in a future that cannot be predicted. This process of creating the future is anchored in a strategic architecture for change based on values and vision, unified by strategy, directed by purposeful action, and continually evolving through a process of organizational learning.

The exercise of strategic leadership establishes the *context* of the future organization. This context forms the basis of a leadership environment in which a leader's skills can be brought to bear to actively transform the organization—to deal with the future in a positive way. Without a strategic context, an organization will be merely reacting to environmental change, leadership actions will be disjointed, and growth will be much more difficult to achieve.

A common theme in contemporary management literature is that a strategic leader must have a narrow focus. We disagree. A leader must have a broad outlook but, when appropriate, must be able to narrow to a laserlike focus. That can be effected only by a coherent strategic architecture that is diffused and embedded throughout the organization.

As we've seen, the next step in creating a future is imagining it—creating a vision. A vision is empowering because it liberates people to act by giving them an understanding of the organization's long-term focus and purpose. It provides an intellectual bridge to the future by accommodating today and tomorrow. The vision enables people to see where they are going without losing sight of where they are and feeling cast adrift. The vision enables the leader to transform "change" into "growth."

Your shared values are your foundation. They are what you will take with you into the future. As you begin your transformation, you must clarify and strengthen them.

Strategy is a concept for action that relates means to ends. Understanding your substance—your values, your vision, and the critical processes that make you what you are—gives you the basis on which to develop an effective strategy for action. The set of concepts that make up the strategy derives from the critical processes that define the organization. Only by clarifying, changing, and growing its critical processes can an organization make fundamental and enduring change.

Having done the front-end work of formulating values, vision,

and strategy, the leader must act to grow and change the organization. Now the leader sponsors deliberate activities—thin threads—to
demonstrate and engage support for the vision, forcing people to
begin to experience the new state. This is the essence of *Hope Is Not
a Method*. It is not enough simply to create an architecture for
change; the leader must act to make the future a reality. Demonstrating the future by means of thin threads creates a groundswell for
change in the organization, but it is a difficult, time-consuming
process. It is hard for people in an organization to accept a different
view of its future, and resistance to change will be the most intense
as the leader goes from theory to practice—from talking to doing.
But as the momentum for transformation builds, the leader's role
can shift from one of pulling to one of encouraging and guiding.

In a successful transformation, an organization evolves to become
one that is constantly seeking opportunity, that adjusts to changing
conditions in a way that looks almost spontaneous. The learning organization accepts and values feedback, evaluating itself and making
adjustments on a continuous basis. A continuous process of feedback fosters trust, which, in turn, broadens the basis for participation. Teams at every level emerge and participate in the leadership of
change and growth. When an organization reaches this stage, the
strategic leadership function no longer rests solely with the leader
but has truly become *distributed*. In a learning organization, the creative force for change and growth wells up from the organization
itself as its members become more and more empowered and self-
confident.

SUCCEEDING IN THE WORLD AS IT IS

The people who make up our organizations, all of the stakeholders,
look to the leaders for success. When an organization is facing a crisis, people expect their leaders to pull them through. *If you are the
leader, your people expect you to create their future. They look into your
eyes, and they expect to see strength and vision*. To be successful, you

must inspire and motivate those who are following you. *When they look into your eyes, they must see that you are with them*.

Several times we have talked about General Ulysses S. Grant. It is easy, from the perspective of 1996, to be critical of Grant. Many feel he was a disappointment as president; many criticize his generalship and the bloody battles he fought. But Grant has taught us two important things.

First: You have to live in the world as it is and not as you wish it to be. The coming of the Industrial Age swept away the theory of war that had been built up since the beginning of modern times. In Wellington's time, beating Napoleon at Waterloo was tantamount to beating France; war could be thought of in terms of single campaigns culminating in decisive battles. Grant's task was at once more complex and yet brutally simple: to enable Lincoln to preserve the Union, the capacity of the South to make war had to be destroyed before political support for the war eroded in the North. Beating Lee, Joe Johnston, and the others was never the endgame for Grant; he understood the necessity of defeating the Confederate field armies, but he also saw beyond that.

Second: When faced with ambiguity and change, a leader must go forward. Grant forged the first Industrial Age army. While others were holding slavishly to early-nineteenth-century ideas about battle, Grant harnessed the emerging power of industrial processes—steam transportation, rapid communications, processed food, mass-produced goods—and acted in new ways. In so doing, Grant led the Union Army into a new age. His tenacity teaches us that you cannot wait for the perfect plan, better information, or exactly the right resource mix—opportunity belongs to the leader who can grasp it and engage with whatever he or she can muster.

Grant was a remarkably practical man. Another Grant story illustrates how this great leader could also be very pragmatic as he forged new concepts into reality.

In the spring of 1864, as he prepared to renew the fight throughout the Southeast, Grant made his headquarters with Meade's Army of the Potomac, personally supervising the critical campaign against Lee in Virginia. Grant needed more infantry to replace battle losses and to fill the gaps left by expiring enlistments. Throughout the war, horses had been in short supply. The Union Army could rely on rail transport as far as its forward depots, but attacking overland required huge numbers of horses and mules to pull the wagons and field artillery. Pulling a single six-gun field artillery battery required more than one hundred horses. In 1864, Grant's army in the Wilderness was supported by more than 50,000 horses and mules.[4] As he surveyed his situation, Grant discovered that there were thousands of cavalrymen in depots in the East waiting for horses—horses that simply did not exist. Noting that these replacements were consuming rations at the same rate as his infantry was, Grant requested that they be turned over to him as replacements or sent home. Grant's request, as well as one that he be allowed to take troops from the defenses of Washington, was not initially well received in Washington, but he prevailed and mustered the needed replacements for the Army of the Potomac as it marched south.

Apprised of all this, Lincoln remarked:

Now when Grant took hold, I was waiting to see what his pet impossibility would be, and I reckoned it would be cavalry, of course, for we hadn't enough horses to mount what we had. There were fifteen thousand or thereabouts up near Harpers Ferry with no horses to put them on. Well, the other day, Grant sends to me about those very men just as I had expected; but what he wanted to know was, whether he could make infantry of them or disband them. He doesn't ask impossibilities of me and he's the first general I have had that didn't.[5]

Lincoln knew he had found his general. Grant took what he had and acted decisively. That is why Lincoln selected him over any number of other officers who might have appeared better qualified.

Grant's people, especially the Army of the Potomac, with which he rode during the last year of the war, understood that he was leading them to victory. They understood his tenacity and determination and that he was massing all his resources to achieve victory as quickly as possible. After the battle in the Wilderness, his first on Virginia soil, he moved south. Behind Hancock's corps, in the burning forest, he came to a crossroad surrounded by soldiers who had withstood some of the hardest fighting of the battle. Grant paused, then by-passed the turnoff to Washington and personally led his staff south, deeper into Virginia. First-person accounts record that the battle-weary soldiers came to their feet and cheered. In Grant, they had their first leader who did not turn tail at the first encounter with Lee. In Grant, they had the man who would "fight it out on this line if it takes all summer."[6] His men looked into his eyes, red from the smoke of gunpowder and burning timber, tired from lack of sleep, saddened by the losses of battle, and in those eyes they saw a leader who would take them to victory.

The people who make up our organizations are looking for that kind of leadership. They have every right to expect it. They expect you to have a vision and a strategic plan for taking them to a new success—a plan for leading them out of their Wilderness.

- To be such a leader, you must dream great dreams. You must imagine the future and then bring it back to your organization in such a way that people can understand it.

- Like Grant, you must be pragmatic—balancing today and tomorrow, using all the means at your disposal, and stretching yourself, your team, and your organization.

- You must learn to thrive in ambiguity and uncertainty, find-ing opportunity where others find only frustration.

- You must be able to draw strength from the fact that others have succeeded where you must succeed. You are where you are because of the success of others, and you, in turn, must de-velop your successors.

- You must write things down and work through your ideas. If they do not make sense to you, they will not make sense to anybody else, and certainly not to your organization. Your hardest job will be communicating your concept, intent, and objectives.

To be such a leader, you must be the guardian of your organization's substance, intellectual, moral, and physical. All are important. The intellectual substance is your sense of purpose and direction. The physical substance is your value added—what you accomplish as an organization. The moral substance is what you value, what you stand for. These are not balance sheet categories; they are unmeasurables. But in the long run, they are more important than the things you can easily measure. Your intellectual, physical, and moral substance is your essence today and tomorrow.

There are no absolutes in doing all of this. Strategic leadership is both art and science; there is no truth with a capital "T." We have, however, found some guidelines that we call rules (with a small "r") that can help the leader develop and lead campaigns to create the future.

RULES (WITH A SMALL "R") FOR GUIDING CHANGE

Rule One: Change Is Hard Work

Leading change means doing two jobs at once—getting the organization through today and getting the organization into tomorrow. Most people will be slow to understand the need for change, preferring the future to look like today, thus displacing their lives and sense of reality as little as possible. Transformational leadership requires a personal and very hands-on approach, taking and directing action, building the confidence necessary for people to let go of today's paradigm and move into the future.

Rule Two: Leadership Begins with Values

Shared values express the essence of an organization. They bind expectations, provide alignment, and provide a foundation for transformation and growth. By emphasizing values, the leader signals what will not change, providing an anchor for people drifting in a sea of uncertainty and a strategic context for decisions and actions that will grow the organization. Leadership begins with values.

Rule Three: Intellectual Leads Physical

The most important phase of the exercise of strategic leadership is the front-end work—the in-depth, serious thinking by a leader and his or her team—that results in the creation of an intellectual framework for the future. Imaging the future first takes place in the mind of the leader and then must be communicated throughout the organization. This intellectual change guides the physical changes—in process, structure, and output—that manifest the transformation. Without the tough up front work of intellectual change, physical change will be unfocused, random, and unlikely to succeed.

Rule Four: Real Change Takes Real Change!

Your critical processes provide the link between thinking about change and actually effecting change, because by changing the critical processes—not simply making adjustments at the margin—the leader creates a pattern, a structure, for doing things differently at the most basic level of the organization. Only by making change at this fundamental level is it possible to effect substantive and enduring transformation.

Rule Five: Leadership Is a Team Sport

Effective leaders forge alliances and build teams. They break down walls, floors, and ceilings, distributing leadership throughout the extended organization. Team building empowers people with a sense of responsibility so that the momentum for growth and transformation originates throughout the organization, not just from the top. Effective leadership is not about controlling from the top; it is about unleashing the power of people.

Rule Six: Expect to Be Surprised

The paradox in creating the future is that you cannot predict the future. Success will come from being able to accommodate the unexpected, exploiting opportunity and working through setbacks. A leader must build flexibility and resilience into the organization, conditioning it *not to be surprised to be surprised* so that, when the unexpected occurs, response is prompt, action is deliberate, and the organization stays on course. The organization that is successful is the one that can best deal with surprise.

Rule Seven: Today Competes with Tomorrow

An organization has only so much energy, so many resources, so many bright people capable of leading. Most of that organizational energy must be focused on today's requirements—meeting the needs of the market in real time. A certain amount of resistance to any change campaign is not disagreement so much as exhaustion. But the leader knows that some of the resources—time, energy, the best people—*must* be directed toward the future and that he or she must find a balance between today and tomorrow.

Rule Eight: Better Is Better

Winning organizations understand that "better" is not necessarily defined in terms of today's rubrics. Better is not about improved quality, reduced costs, faster cycle time, flatter structure, empowerment, or shared information. Better may include all those things and more, but those are the dimensions of gradual change. Better is about establishing and sustaining an edge in tomorrow's world. Better is becoming something different. Better is winning.

Rule Nine: Focus on the Future

A leader today does not have the luxury of waiting until the organization perceives a crisis. A leader must focus on the future from wherever the organization is on the sine curve and thereby nurture a positive, creative culture, one marked by optimism. By sponsoring specific activities and events designed to illustrate and test the new paradigm, a leader encourages similar behavior in others, causing them to look beyond today and participate in creating the new organization.

Rule Ten: Learn from Doing

Learning from doing and sharing the knowledge gained are the essence of organizational learning. By listening to the organization and fostering a dialogue about performance, the leader opens the door to learning, sharing lessons learned and reducing risk. By stretching the organization to act differently, to do new things in a learning atmosphere, the leader fosters an entrepreneurial spirit of innovation and growth.

Rule Eleven: Grow People

The potential to build organizations that can thrive in tomorrow's environment lies in our people. The challenge is not to be the most creative boss or to have the most creative headquarters staff; it is to have the most creative organization, limited only by the collective imagination of all its constituents.

And Reflect

The most important tool a leader uses is not a list of rules but a mind sharpened by a habit of reflection. We use three questions: What is happening? What is not happening? How can I influence the situation? Taking time to reflect is one of the hardest habits to cultivate. "When you are up to your neck in alligators, it is hard to remember that your task is to drain the swamp." But even if you are at the bottom of your sine curve, the most important imperative is that you take time to reflect, to put events into perspective.

It All Comes Back to People

When we look at organizations that are being successful in making the transition to the new age, we see some common ideals:

• A genuine passion for what they do

• A sense of becoming and never of merely being, accompanied by a healthy sense of urgency

• An openness of vision that accommodates risk taking—daring to succeed—grounded in values and linked to the future by a strategic architecture that people believe in

• A zest for learning from everything they do

• And a deep, abiding belief in people, without whom all the words and good intentions are meaningless

In the final analysis, everything comes back to people. People are not *in* the organization, they *are* the organization. The bricks and mortar, machines and computers are there only to leverage the power of those people. Be they soldiers on some outpost far from home, high school teachers, sales associates in a department store, flight attendants, software engineers, machine operators, whatever—it is the people in your organization that make the difference.

When we think of what it means to value and respect people, our thoughts go to one of Grant's commanders, Joshua Chamberlain. He was a citizen soldier, a college professor who was awarded the Medal of Honor, wounded six times, and repeatedly breveted for gallantry. He would later become a four-term governor of Maine. It was Chamberlain's intuition, good sense, and personal valor that enabled the Union to hold the Little Round Top at Gettysburg and it is for his actions that day that history generally remembers him. We remember him not for that day but for a day nearly two years later.

As a tribute to its heroism, Grant selected Chamberlain's division to formally accept the Confederate surrender at Appomattox, forming a line in front of which Gordon's II Corps surrendered their arms and battle flags as they marched off the field at Appomattox. John B. Gordon was a thirty-two-year-old Georgian, also a citizen soldier who would continue a life of service after the war. His entire corps could muster only a few thousand men, scarcely as large as its brigades had been when "Stonewall" Jackson had been their commander at Chancellorsville, when Dick Ewell had led them at Gettysburg, or when Jubal Early had led them in the Wilderness. Jackson was dead. Ewell, one leg lost at Second Manassas, had been captured in the retreat from Petersburg. Early had finally been worn out by Phil Sheridan in the Shenandoah Valley.

Gordon recorded what happened that day at Appomattox:

We were ragged and had no shoes. The banners our Army had borne to the heights of Gettysburg were bloody and in shreds. . . . We were only the shadow of an army, the ghost of an army, and as we marched in tattered, hungry columns between those magnificent straight lines of well-fed men, faultlessly armed and perfectly equipped, most of us wished, as our great chief did, that we might have numbered with the fallen in the last battle. . . . Suddenly I heard a sharp order down that blue line, and on that instant I saw the whole brigade present arms to us—to us, the survivors of the Army of Northern Virginia. It was a Maine brigade, comrades, and I confess to you that . . . I never hear the name of that state but that I feel a certain swelling pride as I reflect that there was an army good enough to deserve that salute—and another magnanimous enough to give it.

Chamberlain and Gordon, two of America's citizen soldiers, understood the most basic truth: leadership always comes back to people.

The Army Today

The Army's process of rebuilding, begun under such difficult circumstances twenty-five years ago, continues today. This transformation created the volunteer army from the draft army that fought in Vietnam and forged it into a superb professional force. It created the force that made such an important contribution to our victory in the Cold War and that won so decisively in the Persian Gulf War. It then transformed that Cold War force into the force at work in countless places around the world today, places unimaginable four or five years ago.

We have not tried to write the history of those decades of change, nor is it within our ability to adequately acknowledge the many leaders who made the transformation a reality—men and women who lived their professional lives believing that "Hope is not a method" and who acted to make a difference for the Army. The nation owes them a great debt.

Six years after the Berlin Wall came down, the Army is smaller by one third. The difficult, traumatic process of downsizing the Army is nearly complete. The Army, taking a lesson from the most successful examples of corporate downsizing, released people with dignity and respect. The Congress, two administrations, and the American people supported rational downsizing, providing both incentives and assistance to those leaving. Army leaders were able to focus on those remaining, recruiting and keeping the best and making every move with an eye to future personnel requirements so that we would have the right mix of experience and skills in the force at every step in the process. Today's young soldiers, both officers and enlisted personnel, are as good as or better than ever, and their opportunities for advancement and responsibility are also as good as or better than before the drawdown began.

The troops have come home from overseas in great numbers. Today, the U.S. Army has as many troops in the Pacific basin as in Europe, reflecting the shifting balances in the world. The Army has brought home more than a quarter-million soldiers and family members and hundreds of thousands of tons of ammunition and equipment, including all the Army's nuclear and chemical weapons. All of that was accomplished without degrading readiness unacceptably.

Nevertheless, there remains the question of size—of both the active and reserve establishment. Today, the uniformed force stands at about 1.1 million active and reserve, with about 500,000 in the active force organized into ten divisions and other units. Today the Army is spending less, as a percentage of GNP, than at any time since the late 1940s. It is smaller in proportion to the population than at any time since the Great Depression and, depending on who is doing the counting, is about eighth or ninth in size in the world.

In a free society, there will always be many opinions about the appropriate size of military forces and about defense spending. Our opinion is that the Army now needs to level out in strength and to begin to infuse resources into a program to recapitalize major equipment and infrastructure.

We must not be beguiled into thinking that we can win our wars and defend our interests without putting our young men and women on the ground. Numbers do count. As long as people take up arms, that will remain an immutable fact. Given the demands being placed on America's Army today, it is perilously close to being too small.

Throughout this difficult transition, hard work, adherence to quality standards, concern for families, and good training have kept recruiting and retention at record levels. By all quality measures, today's is the best Army America has ever fielded. It is a drug-free, equal opportunity environment, and America's soldiers are virtually all high school graduates with above-average test scores. They are fit, disciplined, and highly motivated. Whether they stay for an enlistment or for a career, they return to civilian society enriched by their experiences in uniform and by an ethic of service.

The Army's transformation has also had a major impact on its infrastructure. Reengineering has been a remarkable success. New and changed processes have made the Army a true power projection force that is capable of going anywhere in the world to do, it seems, almost anything.

But the real reengineering story is not in the fighting part of the Army so much as in the sustaining base, the more bureaucratic and industrial part of the Army. It is in the Army Material Command, the Medical Command, the Training and Doctrine Command, and the other major commands that we find the unsung heroes of the Army's transformation. These are the men and women who give us the capability to raise, train, and equip the United States Army. Transforming that infrastructure in the difficult political environment of base closures and federal jobs has been very difficult, but significant progress has been made. Progress has also been made in reengineering basic processes such as those for developing and fielding new equipment. Logistics processes have been completely reengineered since the Persian Gulf War. The Medical Command is making enormous strides in telemedicine and other advanced information-sharing techniques that have already proven their utility on the Army's battlefields and that have enormous potential for civilian applications.

Much remains to be done, but when we look back over the last decade, we see that progress has been made in virtually all the sustaining functions, large and small. The measure of success has been in maintaining a level of readiness that supports today's increasing operational commitments. Today, readiness, as measured by the Joint Chiefs, is as good as or better than it was the day Saddam Hussein moved into Kuwait. The number of soldiers deployed operationally has increased threefold in the six years since the Berlin Wall came down, and they are literally going all over the world: to Macedonia, the Sinai, Ukraine, Russia, Poland, Mongolia, central Africa—some places that were not even places during the Cold War. On a typical day, soldiers are deployed on operations and training missions in seventy to eighty countries, sometimes more than one hundred different countries. Three times they have returned to Kuwait to deter aggression, and they still stand guard in Korea. As we write this, they are in Bosnia. It is impossible to predict the success or failure of every aspect of that extremely difficult mission, but America has never sent better-prepared or better-led soldiers into harm's way. They will do their part. Their sacrifice and heroism speak for itself. The nation has awarded soldiers more than seven hundred Purple Heart medals, the decoration for wounds received in action, since November 9, 1989, and two soldiers, Master Sergeant Gary I. Gordon and Sergeant First Class Randall D. Shughart, were posthumously awarded the Congressional Medal of Honor for their heroism in Somalia.

In today's world, America's Army is America's strategic force.

We don't know what lies ahead, but today's Army is focused on the future. Experiments going on now and continuing into the remaining years of the decade are enabling the Army to continue its move into the Information Age, to achieve an unprecedented level of effectiveness across a wider spectrum of missions than ever before.

But there are no silver bullets. The business of America's Army has always been about sending America's sons and daughters into harm's way when compelled by the national interest. Nothing will ever replace that human dimension. In the end, service to nation is not about good management or technology, it is about putting our young men and women into the mud and leading them to victory. America's soldiers will accomplish their mission as long as they have the resources and the support, as long as we sustain their training, leader development, and modernization, and as long as we continue to recruit and retain men and women of the quality we have today.

APPENDICES

★ ★ ★ ★

APPENDIX I

ARMY PERSONNEL STRENGTH, FISCAL YEARS 1989–1995*

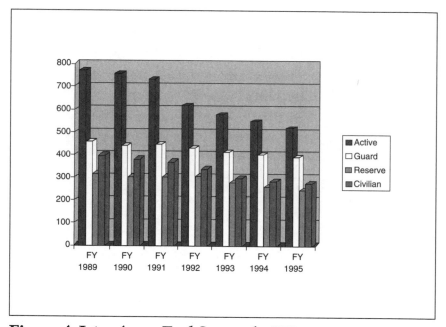

Figure A-I-1—Army End Strength, FY 1989–1995, Year-End, in Thousands

* Official Army data provided by the director, Program Analysis and Review, project officer Lieutenant Colonel Edward G. Koucheravy, January 23, 1995.

Table A-I-1

Total Army End Strength, FY 1989–1995, Year-End, in Thousands

	FY 1989	FY 1990	FY 1991	FY 1992	FY 1993	FY 1994	FY 1995*
Active Army†	770	751	725	611	572	541	510
Army Guard	457	437	441	426	410	397	387
Army Reserve	319	299	300	303	276	260	242
Army civilian‡	403	380	365	334	294	280	270
Total Army	1,949	1,867	1,831	1,674	1,552	1,478	1,409

* Figures for FY 1995 are budgeted year-end end strength. All others are actual year-end end strength to the nearest 1,000.

† Cold War active end strength was maintained at approximately 780,000 throughout the 1980s and began to drop with the implementation of the Intermediate-range Nuclear Forces (INF) Treaty in FY 1988.

‡ Department of the Army civilian employee end strength peaked in FY 1987 at about 413,000. Contractor employees are not reflected in these numbers.

APPENDIX II

ARMY BUDGET, FISCAL YEARS 1989–1995*

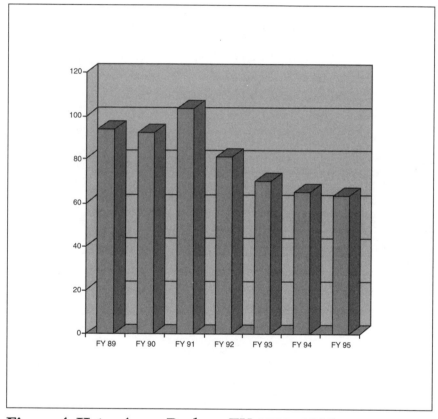

**Figure A-II-1—Army Budget, FY 1989–1995,
FY 1995 Dollars, in Billions**

---

* Official Army data provided by the director, Program Analysis
and Review, project officer Lieutenant Colonel Edward G.
Koucheravy, January 23, 1995.

TABLE A-II-1

Army Budget, FY 1989–1995,* Dollars, in Billions

	FY 1989	FY 1990	FY 1991†	FY 1992	FY 1993	FY 1994	FY 1995
Current dollars	78.6	79.1	92.3	74.8	66.7	63.1	63.0
FY 1995 dollars	93.6	91.6	102.5	80.7	69.5	65.0	63.0

* In FY 1995 dollars, the Army Cold War budget peaked at $100 billion in FY 1985, dropping to $98 billion in FY 1986, $97 billion in FY 1987, and $95 billion in FY 1988.
† FY 1991 numbers include Desert Storm supplemental appropriations.

TABLE A-II-2

Army Budget, FY 1989–1995 by Major Appropriation
FY 1995 Dollars in Billions

	FY 1989	FY 1990	FY 1991	FY 1992	FY 1993	FY 1994	FY 1995
Operations and maintenance	31.1	31.7	43.8	27.3	23.5	21.8	22.3
Military personnel	35.1	34.8	36.6	34.1	29.6	27.7	26.2
Procurement	17.2	15.8	12.2	9.3	7.7	7.1	6.9
Research, development, test, and evaluation	6.2	6.1	6.2	6.8	6.3	5.6	5.5
Military construction, Army	1.7	1.3	1.4	1.3	0.7	1.3	0.9
Army family housing	1.9	1.7	1.7	1.7	1.6	1.3	1.2
Total*	93.2	91.4	101.9	80.5	69.5	65.0	63.0

* Differences are due to rounding.

APPENDIX III

PRINCIPAL ARMY OPERATIONS,* 1989–1995

1989

JTF Bravo (Honduras)

Multinational Force and Observer Mission (Sinai)

Panama coup attempt (Operation Nimrod Dancer)

Hurricane Hugo (U.S. Virgin Islands)

Loma Prieta (California) earthquake

Panama invasion (Operation Just Cause)

1990

JTF Bravo (Honduras)

Multinational Force and Observer Mission (Sinai)

---

* On a routine day, Army forces may be involved in operations or training in as many as eighty countries. There have been times in these recent years when that number has gone to more than one hundred countries. We have not applied a strict definition to "principal operations" in determining what should be listed here; however, they have generally involved large numbers of soldiers (well over 1,000 in every case) or were of long and important duration (such as the Macedonian border operation or JTF Bravo in Honduras). The data are from personal records; information provided by the Army Operations Center, the Pentagon; and information provided by the chief of military history, project officer Steven Gammons.

Restoration of Panama (Operation Promote Liberty)

Defense of Saudi Arabia (Operation Desert Shield)

California-Oregon forest fires

1991

JTF Bravo (Honduras)

Multinational Force and Observer Mission (Sinai)

Liberation of Kuwait (Operation Desert Storm)

Restoration of Panama (Operation Promote Liberty)

Support for Kurdish refugees (Operation Provide Comfort)

1992

JTF Bravo (Honduras)

Multinational Force and Observer Mission (Sinai)

Support for Kurdish refugees (Operation Provide Comfort)

Reinforcement of Kuwait

Los Angeles civil disturbances

Guantanamo I (Haitian refugees)

Western United States forest fires

Hurricane Andrew (Florida and Louisiana)

Hurricane Iniki (Hawaii)

Typhoon Omar

Support for operations in the former Yugoslavia (Zagreb)

Somalia (Operation Restore Hope)

1993

JTF Bravo (Honduras)

Multinational Force and Observer Mission (Sinai)

Support for Kurdish refugees (Operation Provide Comfort)

Somalia (Operation Restore Hope)

Midwestern United States floods

Reinforcement of Kuwait

Support for operations in the former Yugoslavia

Macedonian border operations

1994

JTF Bravo (Honduras)

Multinational Force and Observer Mission (Sinai)

Northridge earthquake (Los Angeles)

Support for operations in the former Yugoslavia

Macedonian border operations

Partnership for Peace operations

Reinforcement of Korea

Support for Kurdish refugees (Operation Provide Comfort)

Southeastern United States floods

Western United States forest fires

Reinforcement of Kuwait (Operation Intrinsic Action)

Guantanamo II (Cuban and Haitian migrants, operations in Cuba and Panama)

Rwanda (Operation Provide Hope)

Reinforcement of Kuwait (Operation Vigilant Warrior)

Haiti (Operation Uphold Democracy)

1995

JTF Bravo (Honduras)

Multinational Force and Observer Mission (Sinai)

Support for Kurdish refugees (Operation Provide Comfort)

Support to United Nations operations in Haiti

Guantanamo II (Cuban and Haitian migrants)

Partnership for Peace operations

Safe Border operations (South America)

Support for operations in the former Yugoslavia

Macedonian border operations

Bosnian peacekeeping

Throughout this period, the Army also conducted the return of forces from European operations, redeploying all chemical weapons, all nuclear weapons, approximately 150,000 soldiers and their families, and more than one-half million tons of war material.

ACKNOWLEDGMENTS

★ ★ ★ ★

In the spirit of the learning organization, this book is our "After Action Review," an assessment of what happened in America's Army from which we endeavor to learn. With the benefit of hindsight, we have asked ourselves "What happened?" "What could we [the Army] have done—what did we [the Army] learn?" In doing this, we appreciate the problems of the personal pronoun. This is not a book about the two of us or our small role in making change in the Army, and it would be presumptuous for us to suggest that we represent the views of all those who, over two decades, made change possible. In a very real sense, we are merely two who were privileged to have a unique perspective on the organization at a critical time. The "we" in this book certainly refers to us when we draw conclusions or offer new lessons. But we appreciate that there are other views on some of the issues we have written about, and we take responsibility for our interpretations.

We acknowledge that in many respects our views are drawn from the experiences of others. If there is any power in this book beyond our thoughts about leadership, it will come from the realization that men and women, proud to be called American soldiers, gave of themselves to fight and die in Vietnam, created an army capable of doing its part in the Cold War, and now are growing into a new world, serving America. We especially acknowledge those who led the rebuilding after Vietnam; their story has yet to be told, but it is a proud, honorable story of selfless service. It is in this sense that the real "we" of this book is the American soldier, and we are their spokesmen, two soldiers attempting to tell the story written by thou-

sands of others. For the lessons we have tried to glean from their experience we are greatly in their debt.

There were many without whom this book would not have been
written, and to them we owe a deep sense of gratitude. It is simply
not possible to acknowledge all of them, but we would be remiss if
we did not express our appreciation to as many as we can.

There was first the leadership team that did, and is still doing, the
work of transforming the Army. Chief among them are the late
Michael P. W. Stone, Secretary of the Army under President George
Bush, and Togo D. West, Jr., the Secretary under President Bill Clinton, both men of great character and substance. On our list also
must be General Carl E. Vuono, who as Army Chief of Staff from
1987 to 1991 not only set the course but was the Army's leader during both the Panama campaign and Desert Storm; and General Dennis J. Reimer, the present chief, who was an integral part of the
Army's senior leadership team from 1990 onward and who is now
shouldering the burden of leadership with indomitable spirit. There
were many others, far too many to enumerate, ranging from very senior to very junior people both in and out of uniform; but we must
especially note the commanders of the Training and Doctrine Command, Generals Frederick M. Franks and William W. Hartzog, who
contributed so much to intellectual change in the Army; the commanders of the Army Material Command, Generals Jimmy D. Ross
and Leon E. Salomon, who transformed the Army's $16 billion in-
dustrial operations; and Sergeant Major of the Army Richard A.
Kidd, who more than anyone kept his finger on the pulse of the force
during this difficult time.

Between us we have spent more than sixty years in uniform and
during that time our thoughts about leadership have been influenced
by many—teachers, former commanders, close friends, sergeants,
soldiers, and mentors—literally hundreds of people. Our memories
are filled with the faces of people whose lives have touched ours in
many ways. Unfortunately, we cannot acknowledge all those who influenced our views about leadership and whose thoughts are manifest in this book. They know who they are, and we thank them.

To the extent that this is our own personal After Action Review,
we are indebted to the work and the sacrifices of the Army Staff,

dedicated officers laboring faithfully with little credit or recognition. We also acknowledge the CSA Staff Group, outstanding young officers who, during the period from 1991 to 1995, contributed immeasurably to the process of transforming the Army and to our thoughts about leadership. Many will go on to lead the Army on the course they helped chart, and we wish them all well.

Our appreciation of history is especially influenced by Major General William A. Stofft and Brigadier General Harold W. Nelson, both former Chiefs of Military History. We especially thank Hal for his many hours spent reading the manuscript and assisting in our interpretations of past events.

The idea for the book came slowly, over many hours of discussion. In the end, our decision to write was prompted by our belief that in the Army's story are lessons for leaders from all walks of life. When we wavered in our commitment, we were bolstered by the encouragement of many who believed strongly in the importance of the story we have tried to tell. Thanks especially to Doctor Roger Spiller, Colonel Ed Guthrie, Major Angela Manos, Professor Lloyd Baird, and others who convinced us we could do it.

Our title was first used by Gordon Sullivan for a 1978 student paper at the Army War College in which he examined the strengths and weaknesses of the NATO defensive posture. More recently, it was used by Roger Spiller as the title of a December 1993 *American Heritage* interview of Gordon Sullivan. We appreciate the generosity of the editor of *American Heritage,* Mr. Richard F. Snow, in permitting us to use it for our book.

We acknowledge and thank the great publishing team at the Times Business division of Random House, especially our mentor, Sam Vaughan; our editor, Karl Weber; and the others who played crucial roles, including Benjamin Dreyer, Lynn Anderson, Mary Beth Roche, Carie Friemuth, Eleanor Wickland, and publisher Peter Osnos. They had faith in the project and patience during the hard days of polishing the work; their professional insight and hard work resulted in a far more readable story than would otherwise have been possible.

We are both proud to have been American soldiers. We thank the American people for that privilege.

Finally, we thank our families, especially our wives, Gay and Leigh, who have put up with us as we have stolen the time from them to complete this task. Their love has been a great strength in this project and in so many other ways.

Gordon R. Sullivan   Michael V. Harper

NOTES

★ ★ ★ ★

All sources referred to by short titles will be found in the References.

1. Remaking America's Army

1. Donnelly, Roth, and Baker, *Operation Just Cause*.

2. General Carl E. Vuono, "On the Fiscal Year 1991 Department of the Army Budget," Statement before the Subcommittee on Defense, Committee on Appropriations, United States House of Representatives, February 21, 1990.

3. General Barry McCaffrey, commander of the 24th Infantry Division in the Gulf War, said it best when he told the Senate, "The war didn't take 100 hours to win. It took fifteen years." General Barry McCaffrey in testimony before the Senate Armed Services Committee, May 9, 1991.

4. A careful study of the Army's publications will show that the vision actually appeared in different forms at different times. Originally, it included the phrase "Total Force" to emphasize the role of the National Guard and Army Reserve. As the term "America's Army" came to be accepted as a more robust synonym for "Total Force," the term itself was dropped. The other principal change, made in 1993, was to add the phrase "into the 21st Century" at the end to complement the explosive growth that was being made in the development of a technologically superior, information-based force.

5. This historic meeting was held September 19, 1991, at Fort Belvoir, Virginia. The principals were General Gordon Sullivan, chief of staff;

General Dennis Reimer, vice chief of staff; General George Joulwan, commander in chief, U.S. Southern Command; General Robert RisCassi, commander in chief, United Nations Command, Korea; General Edwin Burba, commanding general, U.S. Army Forces Command; General Carl Steiner, commander in chief, U.S. Special Operations Command; General Fred Franks, commanding general, Training and Doctrine Command; General Jimmy Ross, commanding general, U.S. Army Material Command; Lieutenant General Johnnie Corns, commanding general, U.S. Army, Pacific; and Lieutenant General J. H. Binford Peay III, deputy chief of staff for Operations and Plans. The only two serving Army four-star generals absent were General Colin Powell, chairman of the Joint Chiefs of Staff, and General John Galvin, the Supreme Allied Commander, Europe. The chairman typically did not attend such meetings; General Galvin's duties precluded his attending this particular meeting.

6. The new doctrine was formally published as Field Manual FM 100-5, "Operations," in June 1993, followed a year later by FM 100-1, "The Army," and, ultimately, a complete rewrite of the Army's "100 Series" field manuals, from which all other doctrine flows. This effort included completely new works entitled "Peacekeeping Operations," "Mobilization, Deployment, Redeployment, and Demobilization," and "Domestic Support Operations." This process also led to the publication of TRADOC Pamphlet 525-5, "Force XXI Operations," as a precursor to a still more advanced FM 100-5.

7. The concept of the three states we owe to Major General Bill Stofft, a former commandant of the Army War College.

2. The Paradox of Action

1. John P. Newport, Jr., "A New Era of Rapid Rise and Ruin," *Fortune*, April 24, 1989, pp. 77–88; Arie P. de Geus, "Planning as Learning," *Harvard Business Review*, March–April 1988, pp. 70–74.

2. Pascale, *Managing on the Edge*, pp. 16–17.

3. See Insight Team of the London *Sunday Times*, *The Yom Kippur War* (Garden City, N.Y.: Doubleday, 1974).

4. Ibid.

5. Alex Taylor III, "GM's $11,000,000,000 Turnaround," *Fortune*, Octo-

ber 17, 1994, pp. 54–74. See also Womack, Jones, and Roos, *The Machine That Changed the World*.

6. Taylor, p. 56.

7. Shelby Foote, *The Civil War: Fort Sumter to Perryville* (New York: Vintage, 1986), p. 700.

8. Doughty, *Seeds of Disaster*, p. 3. The authors are indebted to Colonel Doughty for this excellent case study; see especially pp. 1–13, 178–190, and chap. 4, "The Legacy of the Past."

9. Of the volumes that have been written about General Electric, probably the best concise, analytic review of its long history is "Transformation Without Crisis: General Electric," in Pascale, *Managing on the Edge*, pp. 174–219. The quote (p. 201) is from an interview by Pascale of William E. Rothschild, a former member of the GE Strategic Planning Staff.

10. Ibid., p. 197.

11. Sentell, *Fast, Focused, and Flexible*, pp. 59–62.

12. Pascale, *Managing on the Edge*, pp. 18–21.

13. "Fad surfing" is a wonderful phrase used to describe a leader or an organization that moves aimlessly from management fad to management fad. It appears to have been coined by Mark Otto in his book *I'm Always Right* (Cincinnati, Ohio: Profit Consultants Group, 1995).

14. Hammer and Champy, *Reengineering the Corporation*.

15. Hamel and Prahalad, *Competing for the Future*, p. 11.

16. See, e.g., Bernard Wysocki, Jr., "Some Companies Cut Costs Too Far, Suffer 'Corporate Anorexia,' " *The Wall Street Journal*, July 5, 1995, p. 1. See also Patricia M. Norman, quoted in Jay Matthews, "Odd Jobs," *The Washington Post*, August 21, 1995: "Practitioners must be cautious of turning to downsizing before considering other alternatives. Growing evidence suggests downsizing rarely results in increased performance" (p. H5).

3. Leadership for a Changing World

1. Stephen Madden, "So You Want to Be an Olympic Athlete," p. 131.

2. Daniel J. Boorstin, "The Fertile Verge," from *Hidden History*, republished in *The Daniel J. Boorstin Reader* (New York: Modern Library, 1995), p. 837.

3. Wheatley, *Leadership and the New Science*, p. 27.

4. See, e.g., Senge, *The Fifth Discipline*.

5. Interview with Lieutenant General (Ret.) Hal Moore and Joe Galloway. Moore, who went on to complete a distinguished career in the Army, was the battalion commander in the fight; Galloway, presently a correspondent for *Newsweek*, was on the ground with him covering the war. Their book, *We Were Soldiers Once . . . and Young*, is an extraordinary account of soldiers in battle and of leadership.

6. "The Fertile Verge," from *Hidden History* in *The Daniel J. Boorstin Reader*, p. 847.

7. Dee Hock, unpublished speech, "Institutions in the Age of Mindcrafting," p. 8.

8. To our knowledge, this model was actually first used for fighter pilots.

9. This model owes its origins to Professor K. Hugh Macdonald's "RADAR" model, the elements of which are reconnaissance, analysis, decision, action, and review. The mnemonic may be helpful but is of little importance by itself. The distinction of this model compared to the OODA loop is the implicit integration of feedback and learning.

10. The full text of the letter can be found as "Letter to the Army's General Officers on 'Chancellorsville,' " in Gordon R. Sullivan, *Collected Works* (Washington, D.C.: U.S. Army Center for Military History, 1996).

11. The full text of the speech can be found as "Address to the USMA History Department Dining-In" in ibid.

4. Values: The Leverage of Change

1. Sorley, *Thunderbolt*, pp. 350–368.

2. The Gulf War peak in active strength was 744,240 plus 147,388 mobilized reservists. By September 1992, the active strength stood at 611,000, and all reservists had been mobilized.

3. Gordon R. Sullivan, "Address at the Eisenhower Luncheon," Annual Meeting of the Association of the United States Army, Washington, D.C., October 15, 1991.

4. Collins and Porras, *Built to Last*, p. 55.

5. Grant's account, including his strategic thinking, is recorded in his memoirs; see Ulysses S. Grant, *Memoirs and Selected Letters* (New York: Library of America, 1990), pp. 283–356.

6. William T. Sherman, *Memoirs of General W. T. Sherman* (New York: Library of America, 1990), p. 428.

7. Wheatley, *Leadership and the New Science*, p. 32.

5. Seeing the Elephant

1. General Vuono's papers and speeches from 1990 and 1991 make repeated reference to the impact of change in the world and the need for a fundamental restructuring of the defense establishment. See, e.g., "Desert Storm and the Future of Conventional Forces," *Foreign Affairs*, Spring 1991, pp. 49–63; and "National Strategy and the Army of the 1990s," *Parameters*, United States Army War College, June 1991; pp. 2–12.

2. Noel Tichy and Ram Charan, "Speed, Simplicity, and Self-Confidence," *Harvard Business Review*, September–October 1989, pp. 112–120.

3. General Frederick Franks in *America's Army, Focusing on the Future*, a video production of the Louisiana Maneuvers Task Force, Department of the Army, 1994.

4. Alison Corke, *British Airways*.

5. Dee Hock, unpublished speech, "Institutions in the Age of Mindcrafting," and a series of interviews with the authors.

6. Hock, p. 5.

7. Ibid., p. 7.

8. Ibid., p. 8.

9. Spector and McCarthy, *The Nordstrom Way*, p. 117.

10. Our thoughts on vision and buy-in have been influenced by the excellent work of the 1994–1995 CSA Fellows at the Army War College: Colonels Ulrich H. Keller, Elizabeth L. Gibson, Herbert F. Harback, and Gordon R. Burke, Jr.

11. Hanson W. Baldwin, "The Sho Plan—The Battle for Leyte Gulf," in *Sea Fights and Shipwrecks: True Tales of the Seven Seas* (London: Curtis Brown, 1955), p. 134.

12. Samuel Eliot Morison, "The Battle of Cape Engano," *History of United States Naval Operations in World War II* vol. 12, chap. 14 (Boston: Little, Brown 1958), p. 319 (further attributed by Morison to Ozawa's after-action report).

6. Creating a Strategic Architecture

1. See Carl E. Vuono, white paper: "The United States Army: A Strategic Force for the 1990s and Beyond," in *Collected Works*, pp. 404–412.

2. Grant, partly to avoid the entanglements of Washington and partly to be able to personally sense the most critical action, located his headquarters with the most important of these attacking armies, Meade's Army of the Potomac, attacking toward Richmond against Lee's Army of Northern Virginia.

3. Grant would have had Banks advance on Mobile. This is the only significant time he was overruled by his political superiors, who were anxious to secure the rest of Louisiana, capture what they believed were large stores of cotton, and be in a position to defend against an opportunistic move from Mexico, then under the influence of the French emperor Napoleon III.

4. General George A. Joulwan, U.S. Army, is the NATO Supreme Allied Commander, Europe, and the U.S. commander in chief, Europe. Before assuming his role in Europe, he was the commander in chief, U.S. Southern Command.

5. Christopher A. Bartlett and Sumantra Ghoshal, "Changing the Role of Top Management: Beyond Strategy to Purpose," *Harvard Business Review,* November–December 1994, pp. 79–88.

6. Ibid., p. 80.

7. DuPuy, p. 40.

8. British Airways has been the subject of numerous case studies and articles. The definitive study of the turnaround remains Corke's *British Airways*. James Leahey and John Kotter's Harvard Business School case study, "Changing the Culture at British Airways" (#9-491-009, rev. September 13, 1993), is the definitive case study.

9. Corke, foreword.

10. King, quoted in Corke, pp. 100–101.

11. "From Bloody Awful to Bloody Awesome," *Business Week*, October 9, 1989, p. 87.

7. Building the Team

1. Lewis Carley, *Thunderbolt*, p. 81.

2. General Colin L. Powell, Message from the Chairman, in JCS Pub. 1;

Joint Warfare of the US Armed Forces (Washington, D.C.: National Defense University Press, 1991).

3. General Bernard J. Rogers served as chief of staff from October 1976 until June 1979, departing after an unusually short tenure as chief to become the Supreme Allied Commander, Europe, a position in which he served with distinction for eight years.

4. Colonel Dandridge M. Malone, "X = H," an undated, unpublished Task Force Delta Concept Paper prepared for the U.S. Army Training and Doctrine Command.

5. "Battle Labs: Defining the Future" (Fort Monroe, Va.: United States Army Training and Doctrine Command, May 1995); "Battle Labs: Maintaining the Edge" (Fort Monroe, Va.: United States Army Training and Doctrine Command, May 1994).

6. Lieutenant General Julius Becton commanded VII Corps when Sullivan was the corps operations officer in 1978–1980. Major General (later Lieutenant General) Walter Ulmer was commanding general, 3d Armored Division, when Sullivan commanded 1st Brigade, 3d Armored Division, from 1980 to 1983.

7. "The Nagutsky Story," *Journey*, The Magazine of the Coca-Cola Company, vol. 9, no. 1, January 1996, p. 24.

8. Campaigning

1. Donald, *Lincoln*, p. 15.

2. FM 100-5, "Operations," Washington, D.C.: U.S. Army, 1993, pp. 6–7.

3. Pascale, *Managing on the Edge*, p. 146.

4. Letter from Lee to Colonel J. Gorgas, chief of ordnance, Richmond, Virginia, in *The War of the Rebellion: A Compilation of the Official Records of the Union and Confederate Armies*, ser. 1, vol. 21 (Washington, D.C.: United States War Department, 1899), p. 1047.

5. Kearns and Nadler, *Prophets in the Dark*, pp. 160–185.

9. Transforming the Organization

1. This literal interpretation of raising the bar was given to us by General Leon E. Salomon, commander, U.S. Army Material Command, who, with his predecessor General Jimmy D. Ross, led the transforma-

tion of the Army's major logistics operations and in-house industrial capability.

2. The concept of the Information Age began to be introduced about 1980 in various books and articles. Alvin and Heidi Toffler, in *The Third Wave* (New York: Bantam Books, 1980), and John Naisbitt, in *Megatrends* (New York: Warner Books, 1982), were especially important to the early development of the idea that change in the world today is the result of some profound, discontinuous shift propelled by information technologies.

3. Negroponte, *Being Digital*, p. 163.

4. Petersen, *The Road to 2015*, p. 27.

5. Peter Drucker, *Post-Capitalist Society* (New York: HarperCollins, 1993), p. 5.

6. General David Maddox was commander in chief, U.S. Army Europe, and commander of NATO's Central Army Group from 1992 to 1994. Atlantic Resolve involved linked participants from all over the world in the first multiservice, large-scale linking of constructive, virtual, and live simulations. Participant nations included the United States, the United Kingdom, France, Germany, and the Netherlands.

7. Our thoughts about change as a condition and change as a process were developed by Lieutenant Colonel Anthony M. Coroalles and published in "Seeing the Elephant: Leading America's Army into the Twenty-first Century," by Gordon R. Sullivan and Anthony M. Coroalles, National Security Paper 18, Institute for Foreign Policy Analysis, Washington, D.C., 1995.

8. Sullivan and Coroalles, *Seeing the Elephant*, p. 7; see also Conner, *Managing at the Speed of Change*, pp. 37–41.

9. Russell Mitchell, "The Gap Dolls Itself Up," *Business Week*, March 21, 1994, p. 46.

10. Simpkin, *Race to the Swift*.

10. Overthrowing Success

1. Gabel, *The U.S. Army GHQ Maneuvers of 1941*.

2. The Association of the United States Army is a private association of more than 135,000 individual and corporate members whose common interest is land warfare and the United States Army.

3. T. R. Feherenbach, *This Kind of War* (Washington D.C.: Brassey's, 1994); see especially pp. 95–107.

4. General Vuono felt this pressure so strongly that in the spring of 1991 he wrote in *Foreign Affairs*, "Some commentators go so far as to assert that the world is on the threshold of a new era in which military power will no longer be of central importance." General Carl E. Vuono, *Foreign Affairs*, Spring 1991, p. 49.

5. John Shy, "First Battles in Retrospect," in Stofft and Heller, *America's First Battles*, p. 339.

6. General George C. Marshall, *Annual Report to the Congress*, 1939.

7. Arie P. de Geus, "Planning as Learning," *Harvard Business Review*, March–April 1988, p. 71.

8. "Force XXI: Meeting the 21st Century Challenge," Department of the Army, Washington, D.C., Office of the Chief of Staff, Louisiana Maneuvers Task Force, January 15, 1995, p. 20; see also "The Digital Difference," Center for Army Lessons Learned, Fort Leavenworth, Kans., undated.

9. The notion of thin threads was first formalized by Colonel Edward R. Guthrie, USA (Ret.), then working as technical advisor to the Army chief of staff. Additional robustness was given to the concept by Professor K. Hugh Macdonald of the University of Bath, England. This section draws heavily on the work of both men.

10. Donnelly, Roth, and Baker, *Operation Just Cause*.

11. "Battle Labs: Defining the Future" (Fort Monroe, Va.: United States Army Training and Doctrine Command, May 1995), p. 27.

12. George S. Patton, Jr., "Success in War," *Infantry Journal*, January 1931, p. 27.

13. See Carl L. Davis, *Arming the Union: Small Arms in the Civil War* (Port Washington, N.Y.: National University Publications, 1973); *War of the Rebellion: A Compilation of the Official Records of the Union and Confederate Armies*, ser. 3, vol. 1 (Washington, D.C.: United States War Department, 1899), p. 264; and *Ordnance Reports and Other Important Papers*, vol. 4 (Washington, D.C.: Ordnance Department, 1890), pp. 850–853.

11. Growing the Learning Organization

1. Michael Howard, "Military Science in an Age of Peace," Chesney Memorial Gold Medal Lecture given on October 3, 1973, and published in *RUSI Quarterly*, vol. 119, no. 1 (March 1974), p. 7.

2. TRADOC, absorbing the Combat Developments Command, assumed the responsibility for developing future concepts and requirements, which are the first step in the modernization process. See "Changing an Army, an Oral History of General William E. DuPuy, USA, Retired," by Lieutenant Colonel Romie L. Brownlee and Lieutenant Colonel William J. Mullen III, United States Military History Institute, Carlisle Barracks, Pa., undated, pp. 175–184. See also General Paul F. Gorman, USA (Ret.) "The Secret of Future Victories," IDA Paper P-2653 (Washington, D.C.: Institute for Defense Analysis, 1992), pp. III-1 to III-4.

3. Brownlee and Mullen, ibid.

4. Herbert, *Deciding What Has to Be Done,* p. 1.

5. Senge, *The Fifth Discipline*, p. 14.

6. Willy Stern and Elias Levenson, "Secrets of the Survivors," *Business Week*, October 9, 1995, p. 84.

7. Interview with General (Ret.) Frederick Franks, January 16, 1996. General Franks was the Desert Storm commander of VII Corps and subsequently the commander of the Army's Training and Doctrine Command. As such, he was the host of the March 1992 meeting and the man responsible for making many of the changes that came out of it.

8. Belasco and Stayer, *Flight of the Buffalo*, p. 18.

9. In our assessment and interpretation of organizational learning and the Center for Army Lessons Learned, we acknowledge the study "Maximizing the Power of Learning: From Organization Learning to Exploiting Expertise; An Analysis of the Center for Army Lessons Learned (CALL)," prepared for the Boston University School of Management, Executive Development Roundtable and Systems Research Center, and directed by Stephanis Watts, John Henderson, and Lloyd Baird with the support of Colonel Orin Nagel, director of the Center for Army Lessons Learned, and the members of the CALL staff.

10. This summary is based on an essay by Major Chris Hughes, CALL, first prepared for the Boston University study.

11. This inside-out approach to what we know and don't know was suggested to us by Margaret Wheatley.

12. Mingo, *How the Cadillac Got Its Fins*, pp. 35–36.

12. Investing in People: Leadership Training

1. Mark E. Otto, "More About That 'Leadership Thing' " (Cincinnati, Ohio: Profit Consultants Group, 1992), p. 1.

2. This leader development model is based on the Army's 1987 Leader Development Study, directed by then Major General Gordon R. Sullivan, deputy commandant, U.S. Army Command and General Staff College.

3. The "jazz metaphor" has been used by many leaders and teachers in recent years. We attribute our exposure to it to Max DePree, the legendary chairman of Herman Miller, but Gordon Sullivan's lifelong affinity for jazz made him a natural disciple. His article (prepared with the assistance of Lieutenant Colonel Daniel Bolger) "Leadership, Versatility, and All That Jazz," appearing in the August 1994 *Military Review*, was the first place he formally introduced the Brubeck-Ridgway comparison, though reference to the model appears in numerous speeches beginning much earlier.

4. Our work on future leaders is indebted to the work of the 1994–1995 CSA Fellows at the Army War College: Colonels Ulrich H. Keller, Elizabeth L. Gibson, Herbert F. Harback, and Gordon R. Burke, Jr. From their excellent beginnings, the War College is continuing this important research as it develops its curriculum for the twenty-first century.

5. Frances Hasselbein, "The Drucker Foundation," *Fortune*, November 27, 1995, p. 96.

13. Hope Is Not a Method

1. Now Chief of Staff of the Army General Dennis J. Reimer.

2. Now Commander in Chief, United States Central Command, General J. H. Binford Peay III.

3. Now Commanding General, United States Forces Command, General John H. Tilelli, Jr.

4. Wilderness and Spotsylvania Staff Ride "Briefing Book" (Washing-

ton, D.C.: United States Army Center for Military History, undated),
pp. 61–71.

5. Attributed to Murat Halstead in William C. Church, *Ulysses S. Grant and the Period of National Preservation and Reconstruction* (New York, Putnam's, 1897).

6. Grant to Lincoln after Wilderness-Spotsylvania in Donald, *Lincoln*, p. 501.

REFERENCES

★ ★ ★ ★

Baird, Lloyd S., and Alan L. Frohman. *Directing Strategy*. Englewood Cliffs, N.J.: Prentice-Hall, 1993.

Belasco, James A., and Ralph C. Stayer. *Flight of the Buffalo: Soaring to Excellence, Learning to Let Employees Lead*. New York: Warner, 1993.

Berry, F. Clifton, Jr. *Inventing the Future: How Science and Technology Transform Our World*. Washington, D.C.: Brassey's, 1993.

Block, Peter. *Stewardship*. San Francisco: Berrett-Kochler, 1993.

Brownlee, Romie L., and William J. Mullen III. *Changing an Army*. Carlisle Barracks, Pa.: U.S. Army Military History Institute, undated.

Buzan, Tony, and Barry Buzan. *The Mind Map Book*. London: BBC Books, 1993.

Champy, James. *Reengineering Management*. New York: HarperBusiness, 1995.

Clausewitz, Carl von. *On War*. Edited and translated by Michael Howard and Peter Paret. Princeton, N.J.: Princeton University Press, 1984.

Collins, James C., and Jerry I. Porras. *Built to Last: Successful Habits of Visionary Companies*. New York: HarperBusiness, 1994.

Conner, Daryl R. *Managing at the Speed of Change*. New York: Villard Books, 1993.

Corke, Alison. *British Airways: The Path to Profitability*. London: Pan Books, 1986.

Covey, Stephen R. *The 7 Habits of Highly Effective People*. New York: Fireside, 1990.

Davidow, William H., and Michael S. Malone. *The Virtual Corporation*. New York: HarperCollins, 1993.

DePree, Max. *Leadership Is an Art*. New York: Dell, 1989.

————. *Leadership Jazz*. New York: Dell, 1992.

Dewar, James A., et al. *Assumption-based Planning*. Santa Monica: Rand Corporation, 1993.

Donald, David Herbert. *Lincoln*. New York: Simon & Schuster, 1995.

Donnelly, Thomas, Margaret Roth, and Caleb Baker. *Operation Just Cause: The Storming of Panama*. New York: Lexington Books, 1991.

Doughty, Robert Allan. *The Seeds of Disaster: The Development of French Army Doctrine 1919–1939*. Hamden, Conn.: Archon, 1985.

Drucker, Peter F. *Managing in a Time of Great Change*. New York: Truman Talley/Dutton, 1995.

DuPuy, William E. "Concepts of Operation: The Heart of Command, the Tool of Doctrine." *Army* (August 1988): 26–40.

FM 100-5, "Operations." Washington, D.C.: Department of the Army, 1993.

Freedman, David H. *Brainmakers*. New York: Simon & Schuster, 1994.

Fuller, J. F. C. *Generalship: Its Diseases and Their Cures*. Harrisburg, Pa: Military Service Publishing, 1936.

Gabel, Christopher R. *The U.S. Army GHQ Maneuvers of 1941*. Washington, D.C.: Center for Military History, United States Army, 1991.

Gardner, Howard. *Leading Minds*. New York: HarperCollins, 1995.

Gates, Bill. *The Road Ahead*. New York: Viking, 1995.

Gell-Mann, Murray. *The Quark and the Jaguar*. New York: W. H. Freeman, 1994.

Gorman, Paul. *The Secret of Future Victories*. Fort Leavenworth, Kans.: U.S. Army Command and General Staff College Press, 1994.

Gouillart, Francis J., and James N. Kelly. *Transforming the Organization*. New York: McGraw-Hill, 1995.

Grant and Sherman: Civil War Memoirs. New York: Literary Classics of the United States, 1990.

Greenleaf, Robert K. *Servant Leadership*. Mahwah, N.J.: Paulist Press, 1991.

Guertner, Gary L., ed. *The Search for Strategy*. Westport, Conn.: Greenwood, 1993.

Hamel, Gary, and C. K. Prahalad. *Competing for the Future*. Boston: Harvard Business School Press, 1994.

Hammer, Michael, and James Champy. *Reengineering the Corporation: A Manifesto for Business Revolution*. New York: HarperCollins, 1993.

Harrison, Bennett. *Lean and Mean*. New York: BasicBooks, 1994.

Heifetz, Ronald A. *Leadership Without Easy Answers*. Cambridge: Belknap Press, 1994.

Heller, Robert. *The Leadership Imperative*. New York: Truman Talley/Dutton, 1995.

Herbert, Paul. *Deciding What Has to Be Done: General William E. DuPuy and the 1976 Edition of FM 100-5, Operations*. Fort Leavenworth, Kans.: Combat Studies Institute, 1988.

Imparato, Nicholas, and Oren Harari. *Jumping the Curve*. San Francisco: Jossey-Bass, 1994.

Jablonsky, David. *The Owl of Minerva Flies at Twilight: Doctrinal Change and Continuity in the Military Technological Revolution*. Carlisle Barracks, Pa.: U.S. Army War College, 1994.

Katzenbach, Jon R. *Real Change Leaders*. New York: Times Business, 1995.

Kearns, David T., and David A. Nadler. *Prophets in the Dark: How Xerox Reinvented Itself and Beat Back the Japanese*. New York: HarperBusiness, 1992.

Kotter, John P. *The New Rules*. New York: Free Press, 1995.

Logsdon, Tom. *Breaking Through*. Reading, Mass.: Addison-Wesley, 1993.

Madden, Stephen. "So You Want to Be an Olympic Athlete?" *Sky* (September 1995): 126–132.

Michaelson, Gerald A. *Winning the Marketing War*, 2d ed. Knoxville, Tenn.: Pressmark International, 1993.

Mingo, Jack. *How the Cadillac Got Its Fins*. New York: HarperBusiness, 1994.

Montgomery, Cynthia A., and Michael E. Porter, eds. *Strategy*. Cambridge, Mass.: Harvard Business Review Press, 1991.

Moore, Lt. Gen. Harold G., and Joseph L. Galloway. *We Were Soldiers Once . . . and Young*. New York: Random House, 1992.

Morgan, Gareth. *Images of Organization*. Newbury Park, Calif.: Sage, 1986.

Morton, Michael S. Scott, ed. *The Corporation of the 1990s*. New York: Oxford University Press, 1991.

Negroponte, Nicholas. *Being Digital*. New York: Alfred A. Knopf, 1995.

Neustadt, Richard E., and Ernest R. May. *Thinking in Time*. New York: Free Press, 1986.

Pascale, Richard Tanner. *Managing on the Edge: How the Smartest Companies Use Conflict to Stay Ahead*. New York: Simon & Schuster, 1990.

Peters, Thomas J., and Robert H. Waterman, Jr. *In Search of Excellence*. New York: Harper & Row, 1982.

Petersen, John L. *The Road to 2015*. Corte Madera, Calif.: Waite Group Press, 1994.

Piore, Michael J., and Charles F. Sabel. *The Second Industrial Divide*. New York: Basic Books, 1984.

Ross, Gerald, and Michael Kay. *Toppling the Pyramids*. New York: Random House, 1994.

Scales, Robert H., Jr. *Certain Victory: The US Army in the Gulf War*. Washington, D.C.: Office of the Chief of Staff Army, 1993.

Schaaf, Dick. *Keeping the Edge*. New York: Dutton, 1995.

Scherman, Tony. "What Is Jazz? An Interview with Wynton Marsalis." *American Heritage* (October 1995): 67–85.

Schwartz, Peter. *The Art of the Long View*. New York: Doubleday, 1991.

Scurlock, James D. "A Cure for Corporate Depression." *Hemispheres* (October 1995): 35–39.

Senge, Peter M. *The Fifth Discipline: The Art and Practice of the Learning Organization*. New York: Doubleday, 1990.

Sentell, Gerald D. *Fast, Focused, and Flexible*. Knoxville, Tenn.: Pressmark International, 1994.

Sherman, Stratford. "How Tomorrow's Best Leaders Are Learning Their Stuff." *Fortune* (November 27, 1995): 90–102.

Simpkin, Richard E. *Race to the Swift: Thoughts on Twenty-first Century Warfare*, vol. 1, Future Warfare Series. London: Brassey's Defence, 1985.

Sorley, Lewis. *Thunderbolt*. New York: Simon & Schuster, 1992.

Spector, Robert, and Patrick D. McCarthy. *The Nordstrom Way*. New York: John Wiley and Sons, 1995.

Spitzer, Dean. *Super Motivation*. New York: AMACOM Books, 1995.

Starry, Donn. "To Change an Army." *Military Review* (March 1983): 20–27.

Stofft, William A., and Charles E. Heller, eds. *America's First Battles*. Lawrence: University Press of Kansas, 1986.

Sullivan, Gordon R. *America's Army into the Twenty-first Century*. Cambridge, Mass.: Institute for Foreign Policy Analysis, 1993.

———, and Anthony M. Coroalles. *The Army in the Information Age*. Carlisle Barracks, Pa.: Strategic Studies Institute, 1995.

———, and Anthony M. Coroalles. *Seeing the Elephant: Leading America's Army into the Twenty-First Century*. Cambridge, Mass.: Institute for Foreign Policy Analysis, 1995.

———, and James M. Dubik. *Land Warfare in the 21st Century*. Carlisle Barracks, Pa.: Strategic Studies Institute, 1993.

———, and James M. Dubik. *War in the Information Age*. Carlisle Barracks, Pa.: Strategic Studies Institute, 1994.

Taylor, Charles W. *A World 2010: A New Order of Nations*. Carlisle Barracks, Pa.: Strategic Studies Institute, 1992.

Tichy, Noel M., and Stratford Sherman. *Control Your Destiny or Someone Else Will*. New York: HarperCollins, 1994.

Toffler, Alvin, and Heidi Toffler. *War and Anti-War*. Boston: Little, Brown, 1993.

Treacy, Michael, and Fred Wiersema. *The Discipline of Market Leaders*. Reading, Mass.: Addison-Wesley, 1995.

Trout, Jack. *The New Positioning*. New York: McGraw-Hill, 1996.

Vuono, Carl. *Collected Works of the Thirty-first Chief of Staff, United States Army*. Douglas D. Brisson, ed. Washington, D.C.: Office of the Chief of Staff, United States Army, n.d.

Watson, Gregory H. *Business Systems Engineering*. New York: John Wiley and Sons, 1994.

Wheatley, Margaret J. *Leadership and the New Science*. San Francisco: Berrett-Koehler, 1992.

Wills, Garry. *Certain Trumpets*. New York: Simon & Schuster, 1994.

Womack, James P., Daniel T. Jones, and Daniel Roos. *The Machine That Changed the World*. New York: Macmillan, 1990; reprint, New York: HarperCollins, 1991.

INDEX

ABOUT THE AUTHORS

GORDON R. SULLIVAN was the thirty-second Chief of Staff of the United States Army (1991–95). As the Army's senior officer, he was directly responsible to the Secretary of the Army for its efficiency and military preparedness; he also served as a member of the Joint Chiefs of Staff. Born in Boston, Sullivan attended Norwich University and received an M.A. in political science from the University of New Hampshire. He commanded at platoon through division levels, including four tours in Europe, two in Vietnam, and one in Korea, and was commanding general of the 1st Infantry Division at Fort Riley, Kansas. Today, Gordon Sullivan is an adviser and consultant to a number of America's largest companies. He is co-chairman of Boston University's CEO Leadership Forum and serves on the board of several major corporations.

MICHAEL V. HARPER was director of the CSA Staff Group, the Army Chief's policy planning group. In this role, Harper helped develop the Army's strategic plan for the twenty-first century and played a key role in reengineering the Army's management processes. He has an M.A. from the Naval War College and an M.B.A. from the University of North Carolina, and he is a fellow of Boston University's CEO Leadership Forum. Harper left active military duty in 1995. Today, he is president of the Harper Group, a business consulting and executive development organization based in Springfield, Virginia.